MANHATTAN RAILWAY TERMINAL

CREATED AND OPERATED BY

THE SIBLEY SYSTEM

OVER THE WATER

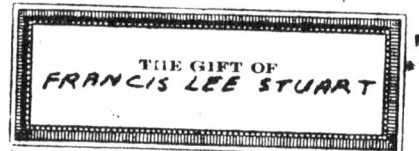

THE GIFT OF
FRANCIS LEE STUART

For
The President
Baltimore & Ohio
From Villard [?]

With Compliments of
the Author

15. April 30

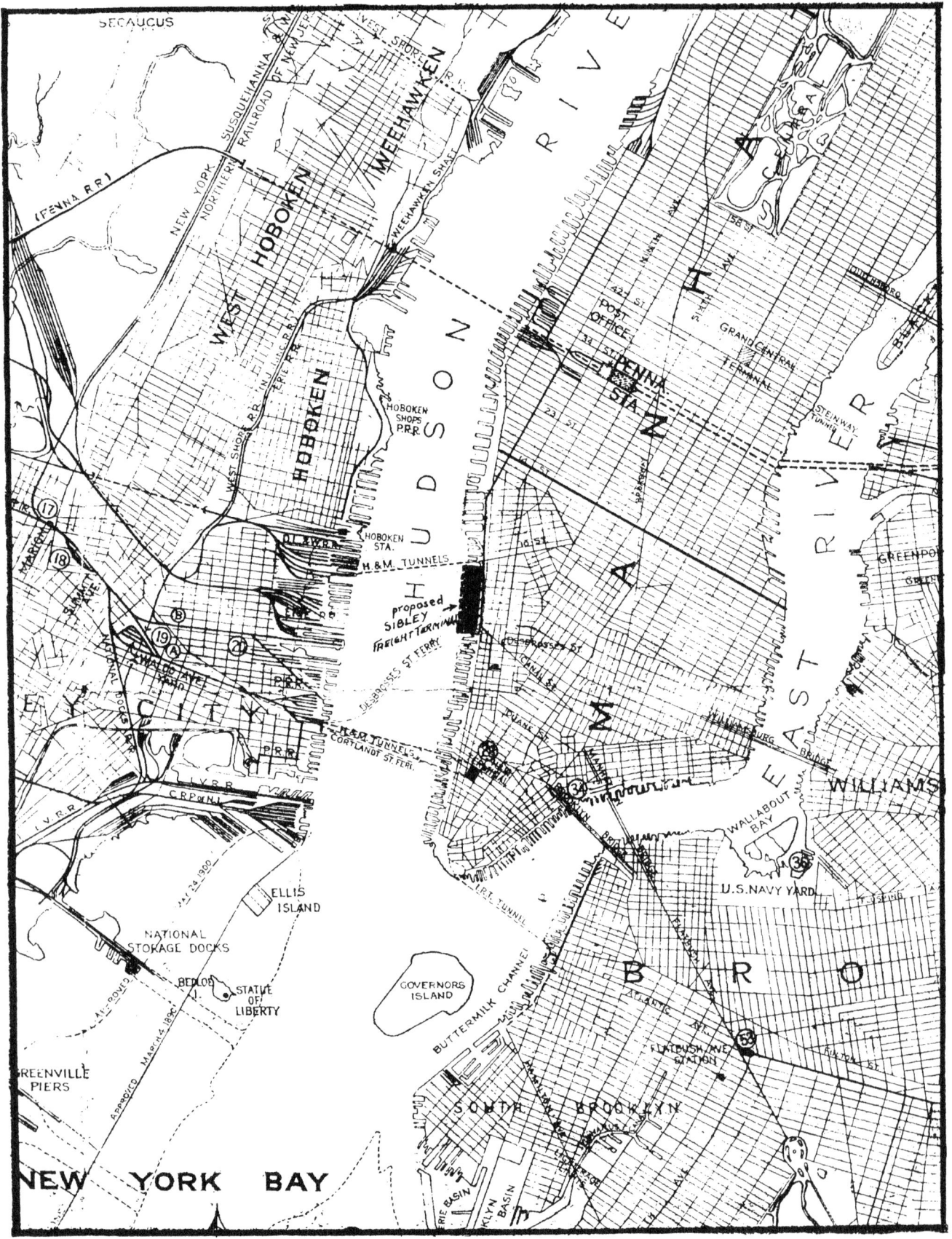

METROPOLITAN RAILWAY TRANSFER

CREATED AND OPERATED UNDER

THE SIBLEY SYSTEM

OVER THE WATER

THE LINK

BETWEEN RAIL AND STORE
FOR THE TRANSFER ACROSS THE HUDSON
OF THE TRUNK LINE FREIGHT TRAINS
BULK UNBROKEN
CHANGING THE DESTINATION OF A CENTURY
FROM NEW JERSEY TO NEW YORK CITY
THE FREIGHT TRAIN MOVING AS THE PASSENGER TRAIN
IN AND OUT—ON SCHEDULE—THE SAME DAY
FREIGHTS DELIVERED AND COLLECTED AT NIGHT

THE
SOLUTION
OF

THE GREAT DUAL PROBLEM AT THE CITY AND PORT OF NEW YORK
1. THE RAILROAD TRAFFIC PROBLEM OF CROSSING THE HUDSON
2. THE NEW YORK CENTRAL—WEST SIDE—PROBLEM

NEW YORK · PRIVATELY PRINTED · MCMXXIX

COPYRIGHT, 1928, 1929, BY RICHARD C. SIBLEY

THE TRUNK LINE RAILWAYS

1. PENNSYLVANIA
2. ERIE
3. DELAWARE—LACKAWANNA
4. CENTRAL OF NEW JERSEY
5. BALTIMORE & OHIO
6. LEHIGH VALLEY
7. WEST SHORE
8. NEW YORK CENTRAL

PRINTED IN NEW YORK, U. S. A.

CONTENTS

I: PRINCIPLE OF THE SYSTEM	7
II: OFFICIAL APPROVAL	15
III: MANHATTAN RAILWAY TERMINAL	19
IV: MOTOR TRUCK AND MOTOR FLOAT SERVICE	45
V: THE SYSTEM IN OPERATION	53
VI: MEMORANDA	71
VII: NEW YORK CENTRAL	87
VIII: CONSTRUCTION—ORGANIZATION—OPERATION	97
IX: ORGANIZATION	103
X: TABLES	105
XI: CAPACITY	115
XII. RAILROAD TONNAGE OF PORT OF NEW YORK	116
XIII. CHARACTER AND EFFECT OF THE SIBLEY SYSTEM — COMPLETE TRANSFORMATION OF RAILWAY TERMINAL OPERATION	116
XIV. FINANCIAL	120

THE SIBLEY SYSTEM: OVER THE WATER

The water that separates the port of New York into its several parts has been deemed a *misfortune*—it is on the contrary an *advantage* of the first importance. The location of the Railroad yards covering vast areas—with hundreds of acres of arriving—departing—switching—freight trains—on the shores of New Jersey—with the North River flowing between the Island and the mainland, offering at once the most facile and economical means of connection for the transfer of freight and freight cars to any point about the harbor, a switching system of unrivaled facility—without expense of construction or maintenance of way—creates an *ideal* traffic situation which constitutes a natural advantage to be ranked as *the most important* of the great commercial assets of the port of New York.

In the traffic distress which prevails at the water front of Manhattan and which has so long and seriously menaced the fortunes and even the supremacy of the port—it is *not the water* which is at fault but the Engineers and the Commissions who have been unable to provide a better method of using its supreme facility than that of the ineffective system of Car Float service with its equipment and structures that have come down out of a remote past.

For many years this great highway and methods for its use have been under study by the Engineering faculty—and men versed in transportation methods have coöperated in the search to find a way to avail of its natural advantages—and finally the recent New York and New Jersey Port and Harbor Commission with its great Engineering staff—Maj. Gen. Goethals its Chief Engineer—took up the study—reviewing and examining every plan and suggestion that time had produced. At the beginning of its appointed work—which extended through a period of more than three years—the Commission—in order to avail of the practical experience—thoughts and suggestions of those who were in daily touch with the traffic situation at the port of New York—familiar with the water and its methods—the defects of existing systems—and the necessities of the situation—sent out broadcast its general Questionnaire to all Shipping Railroad and Waterfront interests seeking information and soliciting suggestions—and one of its questions was this interesting one:

CAR FLOAT DELIVERIES

(a) Have you ever conceived of any plan by which the present method of Car Floats unloading at New York piers lying there during the day to be loaded in the later afternoon could be entirely superseded?

(b) If so would you outline such a conception in a general way.

Out of the silence no adequate suggestion ever came back to the Commission—*no one* had *ever conceived* of any such plan—and as the Commission's own studies had revealed no other or better methods for the use of the water than the inadequate ones now in service—it turned away to *the tunnel*—and *the great natural highway—the water*—was officially *abandoned*.

Precisely here—at this point in this abandoned field—*the Sibley System begins*.

Taking up the study where science had dropped it there have been discovered new methods capable of availing of this *great natural facility*—and these methods *supremely effective* constitute the *fundamental features* of the new Sibley System.

THE DEFECT OF THE OLD SYSTEM

Precedent to the application of a remedy for disease intelligent diagnosis of causative conditions is necessary and this is true as well with ills of the traffic system as with the physical.

The vital defect of the old system is the fact that the car *remains* on the Float moored at the side of the Manhattan pier and in that disadvantageous position is unloaded and reloaded over steep gang planks by hand trucks —a difficult operation requiring for its execution a large part of the day—while 2,000 cars on the decks of 160 Floats brought over by 50 to 60 tug boats occupy all day 30 to 40 docks, piers and bulkhead sheds—practically one-half the North River front of Manhattan—all waiting on this slow and tedious operation.

This is the cancer in the system, the cause of all the congestion, delay and distress at the Manhattan water front and the efforts of the Engineering faculty and the Commissions have been largely directed through many years to finding a way to *take the car off* the Float.

There was no room on the pier for it—none on the street—nor was there any way to take it off except to draw it up over the usual *transfer bridge*.

Struggling with this problem Engineers have elaborated many plans of method and of structure and while in some of these was displayed consummate skill in none was there introduced any feature of *radical novelty*—they all embodied only *obvious* methods. The Car was always drawn off the float over the *usual transfer bridge*—and none of the plans—therefore—reached the seat of the disease. The situation demanded a *vision* capable of seeing beyond the *obvious*—of reaching the *occult* in the field of *invention,* for in that domain and nowhere else, as events have shown, lay hidden *the solution* of the great traffic problem at the port of New York which has so long baffled the science of the Engineering faculty—the skill of the transportation expert.

THE INSET BASIN

THE NEW CONCEPTION—THE BASIC FEATURE OF THE SYSTEM—ITS MARVELOUS CONSEQUENCES

With the conception of the *inset basin* on the 22nd day of July, 1917—there was discovered what has proven—after all other known plans have failed—*the key* to the great traffic problem—a conception as simple yet as *radical* and *revolutionary* in its effect as that famous shifting of the eye of the needle that created the sewing machine with its wonderful train of consequence; or the internal combustion engine that created the automobile and the aëroplane.

The Inset Basin cut into the floor of the pier at the center of its sea line—(as shown in the blue print)—takes the float out of its disadvantageous position in the dock *alongside* the pier and permits it to glide into the warehouse—riding on the water under the pier—not the ordinary pier as shown in the blue print—(that only illustrates the principle)—but a specially constructed new wide pier adapted to the new facilities—340 ft. wide—1,000 ft. long—designed for the exclusive traffic of *one railroad*—and it actually enters the warehouse structure—built above with *four stories*—3 operating floors above one storage floor where *at the center* of the warehouse—500 feet from the pier head (including 150 ft. for a wide mouth bay of entrance)—it meets a series of *three elevators* made into a new kind of *landing stage* with railroad tracks for the freight car—(each Landing Stage having the capacity of one car)—which located within and at the head or inner end of the Basin and operating vertically—*descend into* the Basin through a *hole* or *well* cut through the warehouse floor—to the level of the *deck* of the Float—on the water under the pier structure—at any tide—to *take the car off* the float at *level* grade and *ascend* to deliver the car at *level* grade to tracks on any operating floor *above* to be switched and *spotted* for *loading—unloading* at any platform of the warehouse.

THE MAGICAL TRAFFIC EFFECT

The inset Basin which thus brings together in coöperation the Elevator and the Freight Car *afloat within—and under—the building* at once makes it possible to *take off* the car—and *release* the Float—and by *changing* the character of the Float from a *dead* to a *live—Motor Float—*and enlarging its capacity providing it with 3 instead of 2—and longer tracks—there is at once made possible *rapid—repeated—*trips between the *Basin* and the *Railroad yard*—the Float at each trip bringing over and *landing—*to be *unloaded* and *reloaded* on Manhattan Island—and *returned* to the yard a New Jersey *freight train* of 20 *standard cars.*

There is thus established a continuous *processional* movement of cars—always forward—on one line—as in a circle, from the Railroad Yard on the opposite shore *loaded* with Eastbound freight—to the *Basin*—*up* by the Landing stage—to the (3d or) Eastbound floor where unloaded they are sent *up*—*empty* by a *second elevator system*—(*for empty cars only*)—at the West front of the Terminal to the 4th or *Westbound* floor—where *reloaded* with Westbound freight they are sent *down* by the Landing stage to the Float and *back* to the yard—completing *one cycle of operation.*

SCHEDULE OF OPERATION

The schedule of operation governs these movements and all functions—at platform—on the elevators—across the river—are allotted their proper times with wide margins that insure easy operation within the schedule—and ample room for such variations of time—trains—or number of cars—whether empty or loaded—as the exigencies of traffic may require.

The system may be operated through a day of 8-10-12-16 or 24 hours as conditions may demand and it is so provided with facilities in reserve—areas—tracks—and capacity—that it is capable of meeting any traffic conditions that may arise—as the pages that follow will fully explain.

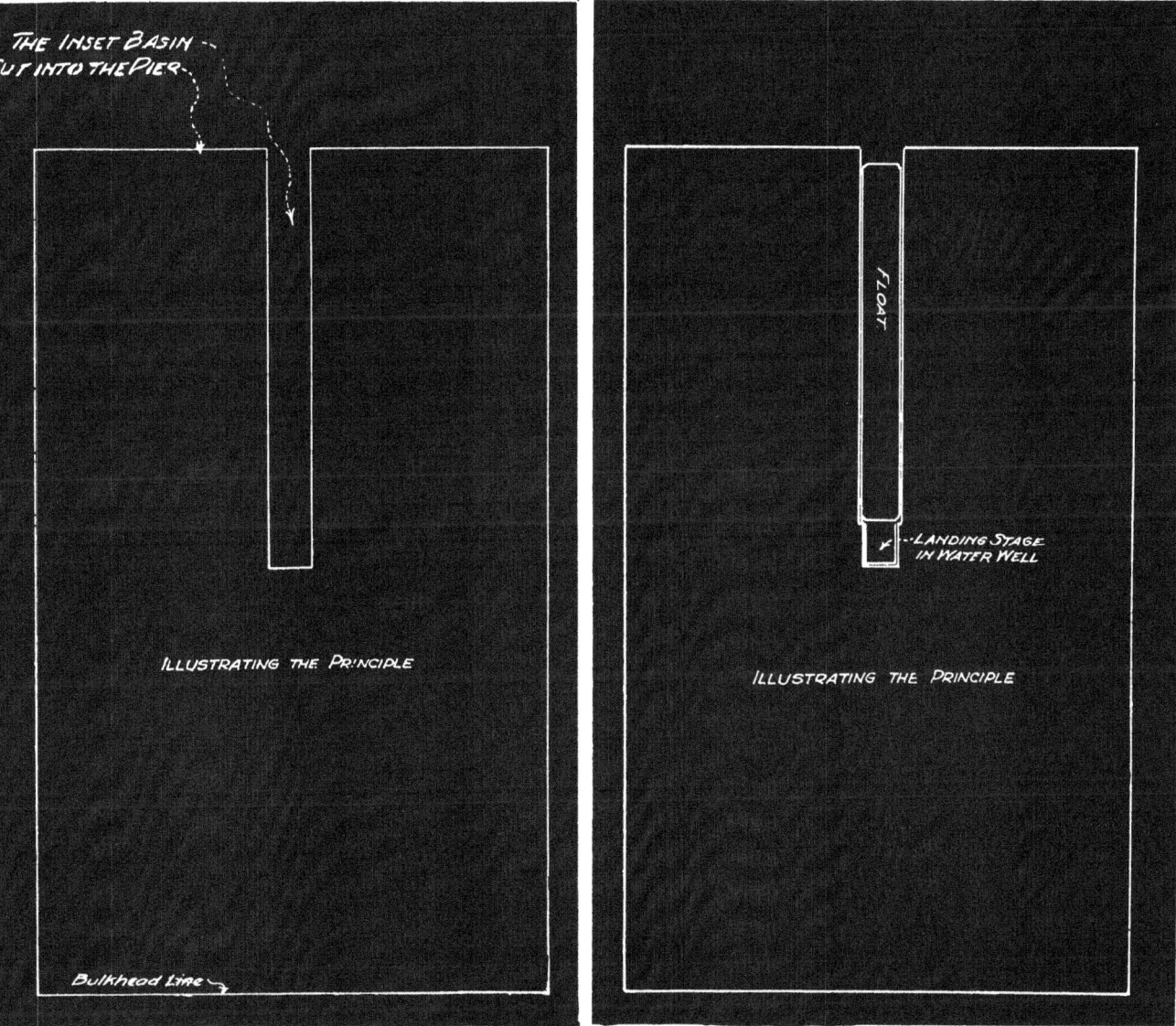

COMPARATIVE TRANSFER CAPACITY

With *sixteen* Motor Floats operating under schedule the *Sibley System* transfers across the Hudson *daily*—the same number of cars—1,920 over, 1,920 back—that now requires the services of 160 Floats and 50-60 Steam Tugs —and in those cars transfers *annually*—by reason of the superior loading facilities created by the new service— 28,800,000 tons of freight as compared with 8,500,000 tons, the present *annual tonnage*.

Otherwise stated, it transfers with *one-tenth* the fleet of Floats— in *one-third* the day—the tonnage that now requires for its transfer the *whole* period of the day.

EFFECTING THE IMPOSSIBLE

With these new facilities in coöperation at *structures of new design* and *purpose* it becomes instantly *possible* to do by the *Sibley System* what the New York and New Jersey Port and Harbor Commission—advised by *High Engineering Authority*—has officially declared—and its Engineering Faculty has *demonstrated* by drastic examination of all plans—that have ever been devised—*impossible* by *any known method*—namely, to *bring trains of standard freight cars* of the New Jersey Trunk lines to the Island of Manhattan—there to be unloaded—reloaded—and returned—or to otherwise transfer the freight of these trunk lines to Manhattan *without breaking bulk in New Jersey*.

THE SIBLEY SYSTEM SUPREME

By the dictum therefore of the most enlightened Engineering Commission that has ever undertaken the study of the Railroad traffic situation whose conclusions are final—the *Sibley System* stands out as *beyond* and *above* all other methods that have ever been conceived—since it is the *only* one capable of transferring the freight trains of the Trunk lines *without breaking bulk* in New Jersey—therefore the *only* and *perfect solution* of New York's great traffic problem.

THE STRUCTURES

Abolishing old methods the new System necessarily sweeps away the present Manhattan front Railroad pier structure and its complement the Bulkhead-shed—as well as the Water Railroad Yard—(the dock between railroad piers)—now occupied from daylight to dark with Floats and Cars—and with these structures the great fleet of Car Floats now in use and the Steam Tugs necessary to attend them—together with the confusion—congestion— dangers and delays—inseparable from them—and establishes at the water front—instead—the new *single pier* structure unlike both in design and purpose any transportation structures now in existence—capable of utilizing through the *basic features* of the New System the high natural efficiency of the *water surface*.

Eight such new *single pier* structures—one for each of the Trunk Line Roads—united as one—located at the North River front—Debrosses to Christopher St.—2,830 ft. long—1,080 ft. wide—form the new *Manhattan Railway Terminal*.

THE INSET BASIN

THE BASIC FEATURE—ITS EFFECTS—IN SEQUENCE
1. The Inset Basin makes the Elevator Landing Stage possible.
2. The Elevator Landing Stage:
    A. Releases the Float promptly—permitting it to make continuous rapid trips to and from the Yard.
    B. Makes the upper levels of the warehouse possible for the Freight Car.
    C. Multiplies operating levels—and areas—separating the current of traffic into *Eastbound* flowing *in* over one level—*Westbound* flowing out *over* another.
3. The multiplication of *areas* on *one base* permits the *concentration*—by bringing together the *eight new single piers*—of the freight activities—(including the offices of administration and accounting for the Metropolitan freight service) of *all* the *west side* Railroads—*the eight* great Trunk lines—*seven in New Jersey*—and one—the *New York Central*—in Manhattan now operated at many locations along the water front occupying in the aggregate 10,336,180 square feet of area—237 *acres*—to be operated with exceeding traffic advantage at *one structure*

built over the water as *one great pier*—with *three operating floors—one storage floor* constituting the *Manhattan Railway Terminal*—divided into *eight sections—one* for *each Railroad*—each of independent operation yet all operated under *one central control* as a *single machine*—a new *engine of commerce* which not only effects the solution of the traffic problem at the port of New York—but going on to its natural consequences proves *the key* and the *solution* of other commercial problems of great importance in related fields—hitherto resisting all efforts at solution.

At this new Terminal are provided more than *double* the freight areas at all the Manhattan Piers—and Bulkhead sheds—now in the service of the West Side Railroads the whole structure covering less than *one-third* the area now occupied by the Railroads and releasing from that service 34 Manhattan Piers with the docks and bulkhead sheds pertaining—27 on the North River front where the demands of Marine Commerce cannot now be met and an *aggregate area*—(including the City areas in West Side Railroad freight service)—of 7,279,780 square feet equal to *one hundred* and *sixty-seven acres* of Metropolitan Areas. A total area released—which—measured on the map of the City as one parcel would cover the area lying between 9th and 10th Avenues—800 feet wide—*one* and *three-quarter miles* long extending from 14th to 48th St.—representing in value the estimated sum of $40,000,000.

4. *The concentration* of the Roads at one location permits the handling of the Metropolitan traffic of *all* the West Side Roads as a whole by an Organized Motor Truck System centered at and radiating from a Terminal whose facilities are equal—for the first time in the history of transportation—to the high efficiency of the modern Motor Truck.

5. *The Organized Motor Truck Service*—in turn—makes it at once possible to establish a new continuous day and night service for store delivery and collection of freight based on a rate per 100 lbs.—creating an entirely new cartage situation destined to effect radically advantageous changes in the coöperating *land* service comparable with those on the *water*—the whole system operating but 420 Motor Trucks and trailers to handle what now demands the service of more than *three thousand trucks—four thousand five hundred horses*.

6. As the first effect of this service—the *taking out of the streets* the great physical bulk of *thousands of horses* and *trucks*—clears away the very physical objects that now litter and destroy the pavements and glut the highways, rendering them *impassable*.

7. *The enormous economies* effected in the expense of Collection and Deliveries shared with the Shipper save the New York Merchant in the aggregate—more than *five millions* of dollars *annually*.

8. And besides this great financial benefit the new system of *store delivery* and *collection* made possible by the Organized Motor Truck Service *radically* changes present methods—relieving the Merchant shipper not only of the expense but of the trouble, anxiety and worry attendant now upon making or receiving his shipments. When he moves the *outgoing* shipment into his new shipping rooms—(on the same floor)—and locks the door the shipment is made—the Terminal System takes it away during the night—the *incoming* shipment deposited in the Shipping Room by the Terminal System he finds in the morning—unlocks the door—and moves it into his store. (This system fully described in detail in later pages is shown diagrammatically on the blue prints.)

9. *New York Central.*—Since the New System supplies *New York Central* with facilities of traffic that are far superior to any it now operates and at an expense far less than that it is now under—the Manhattan freight system of that road would no longer be necessary for the handling of its traffic and the road would no longer object to its removal from the streets.

THE INSET BASIN

THE BASIC FEATURE—PHYSICALLY CONSIDERED

The Basin is a Slip or Dock—cut into the floor or deck of the new pier structure, extending at right angles from its outer water line inwardly—300 feet by 48 feet wide—(as shown typically on the blue print made to illustrate the principle)—cutting away and occupying the corresponding area of the floor of the Pier—to a point within and near the center of the pier structure—where it makes connection with the Landing Stage.

A WET DRY-DOCK

But the Basin is more than a *slip*—it is a new kind of *wall enclosed* dock which is in effect a *wet dry-dock*—its four walls of concrete structure are founded at the bottom of the water and extend—except the front wall—to the level of the pier. The front wall extends up from the bottom to a point 15 feet below low water mark and from that point up the Basin is left open for the entrance of the Float. After the Float enters the Basin is closed by a *water gate* which suspended on roller wheels located at the ceiling line of the second floor of the pier structure—moves across the front or outer end of the Basin at right angles to its longitudinal line—riding loosely in a groove made in the upper edge of the submerged front wall and shuts out *all motion* of the water—while through circular openings in the rear wall near the bottom—tidal water without motion other than that of the tide—has free access. The *closed Basin* therefore provides the same security and still water as that found in the closed *lock* of the canal—or that the vessel finds in the *Wet Dry-Dock* when she floats in and the gates are closed against the movement of the water outside. The Wet Dry-Dock of this System, however, possesses advantages over both the Canal Lock and the Dry-Dock. In both of these the walls must be of great structural strength to resist the pressure of the water from the outside when the Basins are partially or wholly empty—and the gateways are correspondingly heavy and operated by ponderous and powerful machinery—all entailing great expense. But in the new Wet Dry-Dock the tidal height of the water is the same within as without the Basin and the pressure being equalized amounts to nil. Therefore the walls of the Basin are of ordinary concrete structure. For the same reasons the Water Gate unaffected by the pressure which bears upon the canal lock gate or the dry-dock gate—slides easily into its grooved position separating the water and its motion without—from the quiet tidal water within.

THE ELEVATOR LANDING STAGE

The Landing Stages each 45 feet long—13 feet wide are located near the center of the warehouse at the head of the Basin—operating below the pier deck—within a Water Well.

The *Water Well* is a distinctive feature. It is a walled structure (of square dimension to admit the Elevators) located at the head of and within the walls of the Basin and extends from the level of the Pier dock down beneath the warehouse into the Basin—to and below the surface of the water at its lowest stage—and the head or inner end wall of the Basin and its two sides (brought by construction to a proper width) forming 3 of its sides or walls—while the 4th side that fronting the Basin Entrance—is open to the flow of the water in the Basin to permit connection between the rails on the Elevator Landing Stage and those on the deck of the Float. Within this well the

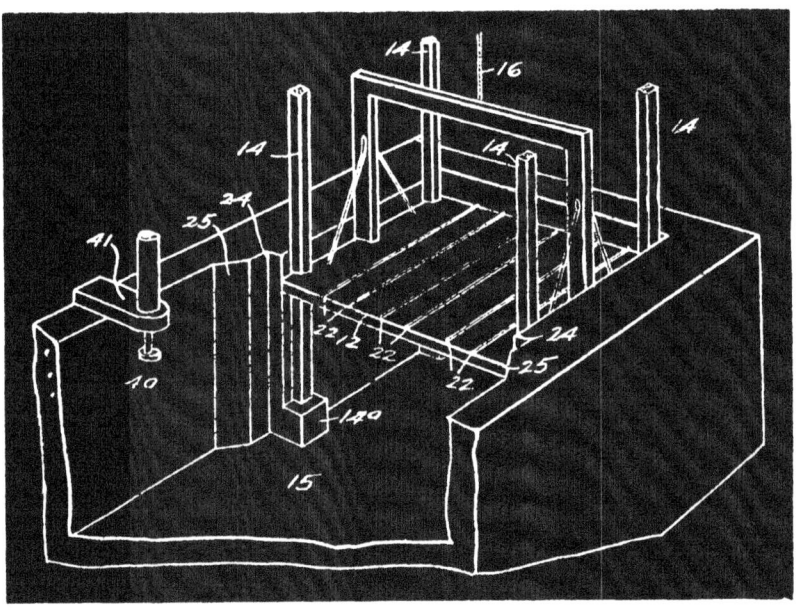

...anding Stage descends to the level of the deck of the Float in the Basin at any tide to take off cars—for delivery ...the floors above—as already described.

SUPPLEMENTARY CONCEPTION

To effect practical coöperation between Landing Stage and Float it is essential that level rail connections be ...aintained under all conditions. The Landing Stage is firmly held but the boat afloat is unstable—and in the move-...ent of heavy cars on and off its deck—even in still water—its level is changed violently. Rigidly maintained ...vel rail connection between Car Float and the shore has *never* been found possible—but it is now accomplished ...rough a conception of great advantage which renders the basic conception of the New System completely effective.

THE NEW METHOD—DEPRESSION

The Float in the Basin having on its deck—for example—dead weight cargo—cars and contents—of 1,000 tons ...subjected to mechanical pressure equal to 2,000 tons—and sinks in the water to corresponding depth—say one ...ot below normal load line—in which position it is held—on an even keel—immovably between the two forces ...the elastic buoyance of the water upward—mechanical pressure downward. It is obvious that as the boat is ...der 2,000 tons (mechanical) pressure no lesser weight can affect its fixed position in the water—the movement ...erefore of any part or the whole of its cargo of 1,000 tons—on—off or about the deck—is without effect—the ...vel remains undisturbed.

Electrically operated screw machinery for depressing the Float in the water is installed on the pier at the side of ...e Basin—contacting at proper points with the deck of the Float. The only movement of the hull of the Float ...ossible while so held under pressure is its gradual rise or fall with the tide and by electrically connecting a tidal ...uge with the motor of the depressing machinery—this movement is automatically followed up or down, and the ...tablished equilibrium maintained at all times.

To this firmly established level—in the quiet water of the Basin—the Landing Stage descends and the level ...nnection of the rails on the Stage with those on the deck of the Float thus made—is—whether the Float is loaded ...capacity—half empty—empty at one end and not at the other—or wholly empty—as rigidly maintained as that ...tween rails on land—and cars pass from one to the other with the same ease and security.

The depressing apparatus and its operation are described in engineering detail under Construction.

FURTHER FACILITY AND SECURITY

Devices are also provided (described under Construction) to effectively protect the Basin from floating ice, ...ifting débris—and the freezing effects of the winter. Briefly described they are two:

1. *The Propeller Wheel*

This is a submerged wheel installed at the center of the head wall of the basin—and its operation drives out of ...e basin all floating matter.

2. *The Steam Heating Pipes*

These are enclosed within the thickness of the walls of the Basin—located in the upper areas where surface ice ...ould form and become attached to the walls. In extreme weather a moderate heat in the pipes will serve to pre-...nt this formation—and the wheel will assist by keeping the water in gentle motion.

CONTINUOUS OPERATION

When the Float has entered the Basin and the water gate is in place—closing the Basin up to the level of the pier ...the sliding front doors of the pier structure may also be closed—closing the pier front from the floor up and thus ...e Float becomes actually housed within the warehouse—with doors closed against all weather conditions.

With this security of the closed basin—supplemented by the devices for the control of conditions within the ...sin—firm level connection between the float and the Landing Stage at *any tide* in *any weather*—is established ...d neither winds—boisterous waves—violent storms—floating ice nor the rigors of winter can intervene to prevent ...e operation of the Motor Float System—on schedule time and—*continuously*.

ENGINEERING FEATURES

There are no features either of construction or operation that are strange to Engineering science—none experimental. Floats have been crossing cars for half a century. The only one that seems to call for some elucidation is the operation of the Elevator Landing Stage down to the tide level under the warehouse in a well which is *open to the water*. This radical departure from known methods has been under examination by Elevator Construction Engineers and declared sound and practical, and the Otis Elevator Company stands ready to construct and guarantee the operation of the Elevator System.

The description of the structures—areas—capacities—equipments and operations of the Manhattan Railway Terminal and the scheduled coöperation of the Motor Float and organized Motor Truck Systems—follow under these captions on other pages.

OFFICIAL APPROVAL OF THE SIBLEY SYSTEM

THE SITUATION

The New York and New Jersey Port and Harbor Commission, having completed its three years' traffic studies, exhausted the field of research and determined that the tunnel for the freight train was impossible; that bulk must be broken in New Jersey (a transaction alone entailing a loss of $10,000,000 to $15,000,000 annually); and the freights reloaded into special carrier cars sent electro-automatically through the tunnel—had reported to the legislatures at January, 1921, the Automatic Electric Tunnel Plan—embodying this principle—as the basis of its Comprehensive Plan for the Port and as the only possible solution of the railroad traffic problem.

The legislature of January, 1921, had accepted the report of the Commission—created the compact between the states of New York and New Jersey and under it the Port Authority to carry out its purpose—which—in the main was the relief of the railroad traffic distress at the Port of New York. The Port Authority—however—was to exercise none of its granted powers of administration until it had during the year 1921 proven the worth of the Automatic plan—prepared and submitted to the legislature at January, 1922, for its consideration a practical method of carrying out the Automatic plan—therefore the Comprehensive plan.

During the spring and summer of that year—(1921)—under public examination—the Automatic plan had been rejected universally by engineering science as fundamentally unsound—impracticable—incapable of the service—and so officially by all the railroads. There was no single voice of approval—the verdict of condemnation was unanimous.

At September, 1921, the Port Authority had proven—not the worth—but the worthless character of the only visible plan it had—the Automatic Electric. It therefore had no practical plan to report to the legislature at January, 1922, as required by legislation—as the basis for further contemplated legislation approving the Comprehensive Plan—continuing the Port Authority—and investing it with the withheld powers of administration.

THE SIBLEY SYSTEM APPEARS

This was the hopeless situation when the *Sibley System* appeared November 3rd, 1921. It had been in elaboration through a period of three years about coincidental with the similar period occupied by the New York and New Jersey Port and Harbor Commission in its own studies—in seeking the solution of the great railroad traffic problem—the work of neither being known to the other—and was ready in November, 1921. Immediately upon completion it was submitted November 3, 1921, to the Port Authority at No. 11 Broadway as the solution of the dual traffic problem at New York—that of the transfer of the freights of the New Jersey trunk lines—and that of the elimination of the New York Central—west side rail system—to undergo any examination desired.

The plans so submitted were illustrated on 27 engineering tracing sheets and described in principle construction and operation in 86 typo-pages in five parts:

    I—The System
    II—The Structure   IV—The System in Operation
    III—Motor Float and Motor Truck Service   V—General Memoranda

THE EXAMINATION

The Engineering Staff of the Port Authority with Maj. Gen. Geo. W. Goethals, Chief of Staff, was the same that had served the New York and New Jersey Port and Harbor Commission for 3 years—the same that had examined and rejected every other known plan and it had now become through much experience and complete familiarity with every requirement of the traffic situation a staff of experts quick to detect the slightest defect or fault.

It was also naturally a prejudiced arbiter since its certain conclusions were already unalterably fixed in printed book form made and delivered to the Legislature. In these printed pages it had been declared:

1. There is no solution if the Automatic Electric Tunnel Plan shall fail. (Yet after the Automatic had failed this new water plan presented the solution.)

2. The water surface offers no hope of the solution. (Yet this new plan found the solution on that "hopeless water surface.")

3. The freight train can *not* be brought to Manhattan Island. (Yet this new plan *brought it* to Manhattan Island, and not only the New Jersey Freight Train but the New York Central Train taken on at Weehawken.)

Here were three reasons for expecting an adverse judgment. Moreover it was a tragically severe staff of examiners—it had already condemned all other known plans—22 in number. None had escaped—alive.

THE REMARKABLE VERDICT

On November 30th, after 27 days exhaustive examination—during which 35 sets of blue prints and reproductions of the typo-descriptive sheets prepared by the Port Authority in its own laboratory were placed—one set in the hands of each member of the Commission—the staff and its Advisory Board—for analytic study—at a formal conference at No. 11 Broadway with the Port Authority and the assembled Staff—Maj. Gen. Geo. W. Goethals, Chief of Staff, arose—the only formal speaker—and officially announced the verdict in *one word:*

"THE SIBLEY SYSTEM IS PERFECT."

Perfection is a goal seldom reached in human affairs and to win such an award from such a high Engineering Authority which is the official High Court at the Port of New York and in spite of naturally adverse influences, may modestly enough be called—remarkable.

The Author went over, shook hands with the General, and remarked: "General, that is very high praise." He replied: "You deserve it!"

THE SYSTEM NOT ACCEPTED

Notwithstanding this unique stamp of its own approval the *Sibley System* offered unconditionally for the relief of the distress at the port was not accepted by the Port Authority. It could not be because at that very moment the Port Authority was—under previous unanimous action of the Board—committed to another course—which the intimate inter-relation of the Compact—the Comprehensive Plan—the Automatic Plan and the Port Authority —demanded. The failure of either of these seemed the failure of all. The Automatic Plan had been adopted.

THE PORT AUTHORITY AND THE TRUTH

Had the Port Authority reported to the legislature of 1922—*the truth*—there would have been no legislation confirming the Comprehensive Plan—hence no Port Authority with powers to prevent the relief of the distress at the Port of New York—and the Compact—without methods to carry out its purpose—namely, mainly the relief of the distress at the port—would have been without meaning—a gainful consummation for the state.

THE RESULT

In such an event the *Sibley System* no longer fettered by inimical official port control would have been constructed within two years—in operation by 1924—and it is demonstrable that in the 4 years that have followed (to 1928) the economies of the System resulting to the railroad and the shipping merchant would have aggregated the vast and incredible sum of far beyond *one hundred million dollars.* (Thus, briefly shown here, demonstrated in detail on other pages):

	Annual Tons	Cost of Present Service Per Ton	Cost of Sibley System Per Ton	Economies
Pier Station Freights	7,500,000	2.86	1.24	12,000,000
Lighterage Mdse. Freights	12,000,000	3.00	1.24	21,000,000
Merchant and Other Deliveries	11,000,000	2.17	1.00	12,000,000
One Year				45,000,000
Four Years				180,000,000

THE PORT AUTHORITY AND ITS REPORT

Suppressing *the truth* and *all mention of the Sibley System* as though it had never been seen the Port Authority—Eugenius H. Outerbridge, its chairman, the active agent—reported to the legislature of 1922 that:

"The Automatic Electric Tunnel plan is the only plan that has stood the economic test."

It had stood no test of any kind—physical or financial.

On this unsound basis legislation was procured through the active leadership of the Chairman—establishing the present legal structure—and the flow of interstate commerce has been seriously hindered ever since—the port of New York tied up. The Governor of New York in his recent veto of the effort of the Port Authority to take up other service unrelated to the purposes for which it was appointed said, April 6, 1928, that it had been a great disappointment to him to find that nothing of the main purposes for which it was created had been accomplished.

This public declaration by the Chief Officer of the State—an early and consistent advocate of the Port Authority as an institution—is official warrant for the statement that it is a distinct failure in that it has failed to accomplish the purpose of the state.

To those who understand—and they are few—the administration of the Port Authority—erected on this unsound basis—has seemed to be a continuous effort by misleading methods in the press and otherwise to divert public attention from the true situation—as Governor Smith sees it—that nothing of its main purpose has been accomplished.

The latest manifestation of that effort to divert public attention from the true situation is the proposition to cart the freights over the ferries to an inland station that is part of an entirely different and defunct system. A proposition not only rejected by all the railroads, but derided.

THE SIBLEY SYSTEM—THE SOLUTION OF THE GREAT RAILROAD TRAFFIC PROBLEM
FUNDAMENTAL PRINCIPLES

The principles that underlie the System are in character radical and of exceeding advantage. Methods and structures of a century are abandoned. There is effected an entire transformation of Railway Terminal Operation.

1. ONE DELIVERY POINT

The carrier's service—by his contract—ends at the shore line of New York City.—The nearest point—and *one single point*—directly opposite the end of the rail—one mile across the Hudson—meets the obligation. For lack of facilities at such point and through competition between the roads freights are now sent to *one hundred points*, 5, 10, 15 miles away.

At the nearest point—one single point—one structure—directly opposite the end of the rail—one mile across the Hudson—is located the new Manhattan Railway Terminal of the *Sibley System*—with all necessary facilities for all freights of all the trunk lines. *One* delivery point and that the *nearest*—takes the place of scattered and distant—*one hundred*—a revolution!

2. LIGHTERAGE LIMIT DELIVERIES

The custom of deliveries to many and distant harbor points is an ancient one established through competition. When all roads are at one terminal competition ceases and the *lighterage limit* passes. The millions of wasteful expense gathered up by the new system are paid into the treasuries of the roads—a revolution!

3. THE FREIGHT TRAIN

The New Jersey freight train has never been seen on Manhattan Island. This system brings it over. The destination of a century is changed from New Jersey to New York City—a revolution!

4. THE FREIGHT CAR

The freight car that now lingers in the yards 10, 20, 30 days or more and is switched about as a dray to move freight from point to point within the terminal—or stands on side tracks as a storage warehouse—arrives under the new system at the Jersey Shore—crosses—is unloaded—reloaded—recrosses—and is on the rail again ready to go west—in 9 hours 45 minutes. It has made no stop at New York. Result—250,000 cars do the work of 820,000—more than 500,000 cars are released from service—a revolution!

5. THE SIDING

All cars are unloaded at once. Goods—at order of consignee—are either dropped down to the storage floor beneath the train or to trucks for delivery. The siding is abolished. The merchant who has heretofore had to seek a location for his warehouse convenient to some one road—locations valuable and expensive because of that convenience—released from that necessity will be in touch with all roads through the organized Motor Truck System of the terminal where his goods may be stored to wait his convenience—a revolution!

6. THE SHIP

Deliveries by lighterage to ship-side is at the expense of the road—competition compels such deliveries.

With all roads at one New York City terminal deliveries by lighter cease. The ship receives its freight by truck—in lots and character—as and when needed for cargo—ideal—and though at its own expense—this is reduced to nothing by the economy of shorter stay in port—a revolution!

7. THE BELT LINE

In other days when roads were muddy and hilly and rutty and horses struggled with heavily loaded drays—and distances so reached were short—the rail and the loaded car for terminal delivery was not only a convenience but a necessity. Hence the belt line. It was better than the dray.

In these modern times when roads are broad and smooth and the swift motor truck with noiseless rubber wheels glides over them with the speed of a swallow—carrying a car load of freight to Philadelphia 100 miles—to any point within metropolitan terminal areas of no greater spread than 25 miles with ease and celerity and at half the cost of freight car service—the era of the belt line is closed—a revolution!

8. MOTOR SERVICE

Organized—centered at—RADIATING from—the Railway Terminal—and operating under schedule covering zones of traffic—a facility now unknown—a revolution!

METROPOLITAN RAILWAY TRANSFER, INC.—
THE LINK—THE NEW DEPARTURE

Railroad freights are now handled in the City streets in haphazard fashion by *two* separate interests—*one* the *railroad* from the yard to the Manhattan pier—*the other* the *Trucking interest*—(more than 3,000 trucks) from pier to store. The railroad operating independently knows nothing of the truckman's plans. The hundreds of trucks that drift through the streets operate independently of each other and of the railroads—result chaos. In the great war the Allied armies separately controlled faced defeat—under one control Armistice Day quickly followed.

The Metropolitan Railway Transfer is the *single control*—the *link* between the railroad and the shipper. It takes charge of *the train* at the end of the rail—crosses and unloads it on the platform of the Railway Terminal in New York City—where the service of the railroad ends (and begins); takes charge of the unloaded freight on the terminal platform and delivers it on the floor of the consignee; and the reverse.

COMPARATIVE CONSTRUCTION—OPERATION—TONNAGE

	Construction	Tonnage	Operation Per Ton
Automatic Electric			
Initial Development	256,000,000	10,000,000	$3.76
Complete Development	631,000,000	10,000,000	7.18
Present System			
Pier Station Freights		10,000,000	2.86
Lighterage Freights		10,000,000	3.05
Sibley System	85,000,000		
Pier Station Freights		10,000,000	1.24
Lighterage Freights		10,000,000	
Pier and Lighterage		20,000,000	.98

SOME RESULTS OF THE SYSTEM

Thousands of horses and trucks taken out of the streets—confusion and congestion relieved.

Thousands of railroad vessels taken out of the stream—confusion and congestion relieved.

Two miles of the Hudson River front of Manhattan released from railroad occupation and opened for ocean steamship service—where now not a pier can be had.

Refrigerated food system—with new *market areas*.

Expense reduced below *one half*.

New York Central—West Side rail system eliminated.

Riverside Park delivered from its iron bondage.

The streets cleared of rails.

IN BRIEF—*The Solution* of the great Railroad traffic problem at New York that has for more than 30 years *defied solution*.

MANHATTAN RAILWAY TERMINAL

Located on the Hudson River water front of Manhattan—centered at Canal Street—the New Terminal is designed for the freight service of *all the West Side* Trunk Line Railroads—which includes—with those having their rail terminals on the New Jersey mainland—also the freight service of the *New York Central* at Weehawken.

It serves—therefore—*eight* Railroad systems as follows—(in the order of their location on the water front—from South to North):—

1.	Baltimore & Ohio	Staten Island
2.	Lehigh Valley	Communipaw
3.	Central of New Jersey—(Phil. & Reading)	Communipaw
4.	Pennsylvania	Jersey City
5.	Erie	Jersey City
6.	Delaware-Lackawanna	Hoboken
7.	West Shore—(Ontario & Western)	Weehawken
8.	New York Central	Weehawken

CONNECTIONS ON THE WATER

The Terminal is connected over the water with the Railroad yards by a *double service* of rapid—*motor driven—schedule operated—car floats*—2 for each Railroad—each of capacity to transfer a *freight train of 20 cars*.

CONNECTIONS ON LAND

An organized *motor truck service*—centered at the Terminal provides *night* and *day* service—Delivering and Collecting freight through a New System of direct connection with warehouse areas of shippers under Terminal key—the business districts mapped into zones.

CONSTRUCTION AND OPERATING COMPANY

It is designed that the Construction of the Terminal and its operation shall be undertaken as a whole by an independent industrial company in which related interests will hold capital shares—the *Metropolitan Railway Transfer Inc.*—performing the *two*—now separate services—*one* the railroad from the New Jersey shore to the Manhattan water line—the *other* the Merchant shipper from the water front to the warehouse—THE LINK—therefore—between the *yard* and the *store*.

THE SITE

There is *one* site for the Manhattan Railway Terminal on the Hudson River water front that is adapted to all the requirements of the new service—and its total area (save one pier)—is the property of the City of New York.

It includes the areas of the Piers, Docks and Bulkhead platforms between Desbrosses and Christopher St. ferries—piers 31 to 43. At this location is found the width and length of area the construction requires. Suitable in this essential it is also well adapted in other respects:

1. It is directly opposite the center of the line of Railroad yards on the Jersey shore—only one mile away—to and from which the great bulk of Manhattan freights are to be transferred;

2. Opposite the center of the densest business areas of the city where within a circle of one mile radius originates and is received the greater part of all the Manhattan freights of the Trunk line roads;

3. At the center of the market areas—for the delivery of the Metropolitan *food supply*;

4. And—of great importance—opposite small blocks of buildings on West St. now of comparatively low commercial value—whose areas both in conformation and location are well suited for the construction of the series of eight new *entrance* and *exit* buildings—for Trucks—(a feature of the system)—on the upper levels of which—(above the driveways)—are to be created for Merchant Shippers—(as explained under another heading)—new business areas of great convenience.

The Vehicular Tunnel issues at Varick and Vestry Sts. 2 blocks South—4 blocks East of the nearest point of the Terminal site—and as nearly the whole of the site area lies above Canal St. neither the Tunnel structure nor its traffic offers serious obstacle to the traffic operations of the Terminal during the day while at night—when the greater part of Terminal traffic will be moved—vehicular traffic is largely suspended.

Thirteen cross streets (including Canal) intersect the line of West St. in front of the site—providing special avenues of approach, making short direct connection with the wide north and south thoroughfares—Hudson and Varick Sts. and West Broadway—over which all business areas are readily reached.

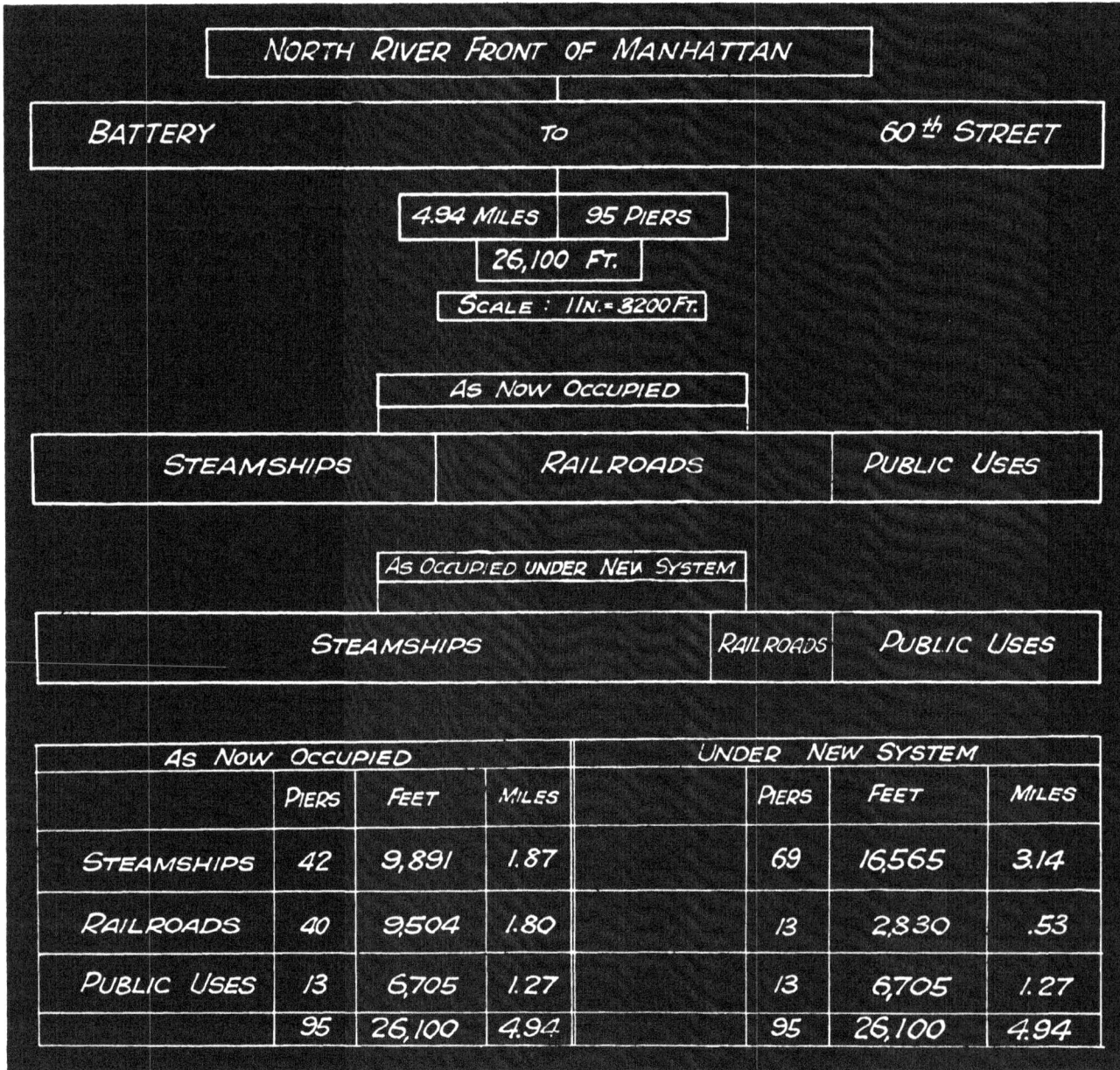

THE BUILDING

The structure 2,830 ft. long (N—S)—1,080 ft. wide (E—W) 72 ft. High—with 4 floors—which covers the area of the site—its East line coinciding with the East line of the Bulkhead platform—its West with the pierhead line—is built over the water as one great pier—of concrete and steel construction—floors finished with asphalt surface—founded on pile and concrete substructure—the first floor at street level.

The height of the 1st story is 14 ft.—2nd—20—3rd—20—4th—18—of the building 72 ft.

(An *apron*—(or exterior marginal platform)—projecting from the bases of the walls of the building at the level of the first floor—extends along the 3 water fronts—5 ft. at the ends—10 at the West front.

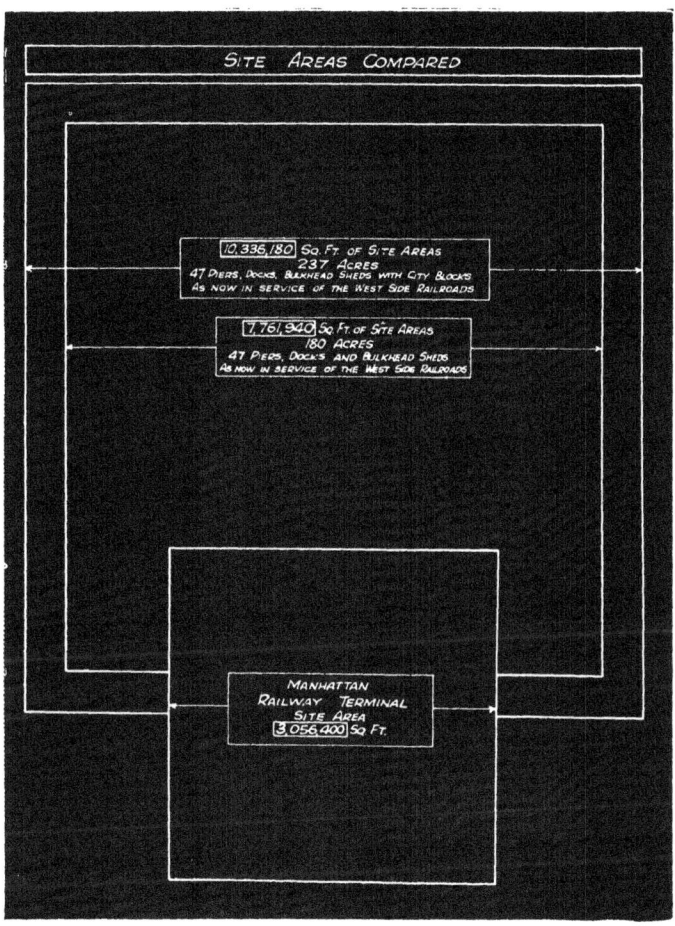

RAILROAD OFFICE SECTION

At the front of the building—on the 3rd and 4th levels, part of the structure 50 ft. in depth from the East line and extending the length of the building—set apart for the uses of the Railroad—is divided into Offices with plate glass frontage on the Marginal Way. Over a wide corridor at rear of this section extending the length of the Terminal structure the offices open on the operating areas of all Railroads on both levels.

THE CENTRAL DIVISION

For the establishment of the *garage* and the uses of the general Terminal *administration* there is interposed at the center of the structure a Central Division 100 ft. wide (N—S) and in length the width of the Terminal—corresponding in height and floor levels with those of the Terminal and this interposed structure separates the Terminal into *two wings*.

THE WINGS

Each wing, 1,360 ft. long, is a composite of 4 sections.

THE SECTION

THE STRUCTURAL UNIT

The section 340 ft. wide (N—S)—1,070 ft. long (E—W)—the structural *unit*—represents the *single pier* for the service of a *single railroad*. There are *eight sections*—one for each of the *eight* Trunk Line railroads.

ELASTICITY OF THE SYSTEM

The areas and facilities of the Terminal are far beyond the demands of to-day—and if at a time far in the future a Railroad outgrow its section—or a place be required for a new—a section may be added at either end —without disturbing the poise and organization of the system as a whole as it is permanently centered at the interposed Central Division.

This *structural elasticity* is supplemented—(as shown on later pages)—by that excess of capacity and equipment in every department of service which ensures equally *operative* elasticity—the combination of these enabling the system to meet the traffic situation not only for the present but for the distant future.

USES OF THE CENTRAL DIVISION

1. ADMINISTRATION.—The General Offices of managment and operation of the Terminal system.
2. GARAGE.—The Motor Truck service—with floor capacity of 600—800 motor trucks. The floors are connected with each other by passenger Elevators and stairways and for motor truck service by Ascending-Descending Ramps—with the Railroad offices and operating areas by corridors at the *east* front—and for motor truck service with the freight platforms of all sections (on all levels—and with the street level)—by Transverse Driveways at the *west* front.
3. ELECTRIC LIGHT—HEAT AND POWER PLANT.—The power plant is located on the 1st level at the west end (100 ft. square)—above it on the 2nd level are located the Coal Pockets and Oil Tanks—which are connected by the Transverse Railway (on 2nd level at front) with all Railroad sections—for the receipt of fuel supply. Coal falls from 2nd to 1st as needed and on the water beneath ride barges into which the waste falls —one is on duty while another moves away to discharge its cargo. Pipes from the Oil Tanks are on tap at every Basin of the system—for the Motor Float fuel supply.

RAILROAD OPERATING OFFICES

Offices for Railroad operatives are provided in the office areas at the front on the 3rd and 4th levels and six Elevators—and double Stairways in each Railroad section at the front of the building connect all levels.

On the 3rd (Eastbound) level at front are located *receiving* and *delivering* freight offices for East- and Westbound freight and *weighing scales* embedded in the Driveways at the *entrances* and *exits* register within the freight offices—and a pedestrian entrance and exit corridor at center of section connects with the Gallery (of the same width) which spans the Marginal Way to the 3rd level of the Entrance—Exit Building on West St.

On the 2nd level Railroad offices are provided on the East end of the freight (or Food) platform itself— (The Transverse Railway occupying the office section area on that level).

There are on the 3 operating floors 608 Railroad offices (16x13) besides 16 Receiving (77x18) and Delivering (106x18) offices—76 for each Railroad. These offices overlooking and in touch with the activities of the Roads will render unnecessary the many West Side freight offices now in use—they will be concentrated here.

GENERAL RAILROAD OFFICES

Besides these Railroad offices *within* the Terminal the whole 3rd floor area of the entrance—exit building— on West St. opposite each Railroad section—200 ft. square—fronting on 4 streets with light on all sides—on a level and in immediate touch with the freight offices and platforms of the Terminal—over the elevated gallery spanning the marginal way—are reserved in each building for the Administration and General offices of that Road as far as may be needed—to be laid out as desired.

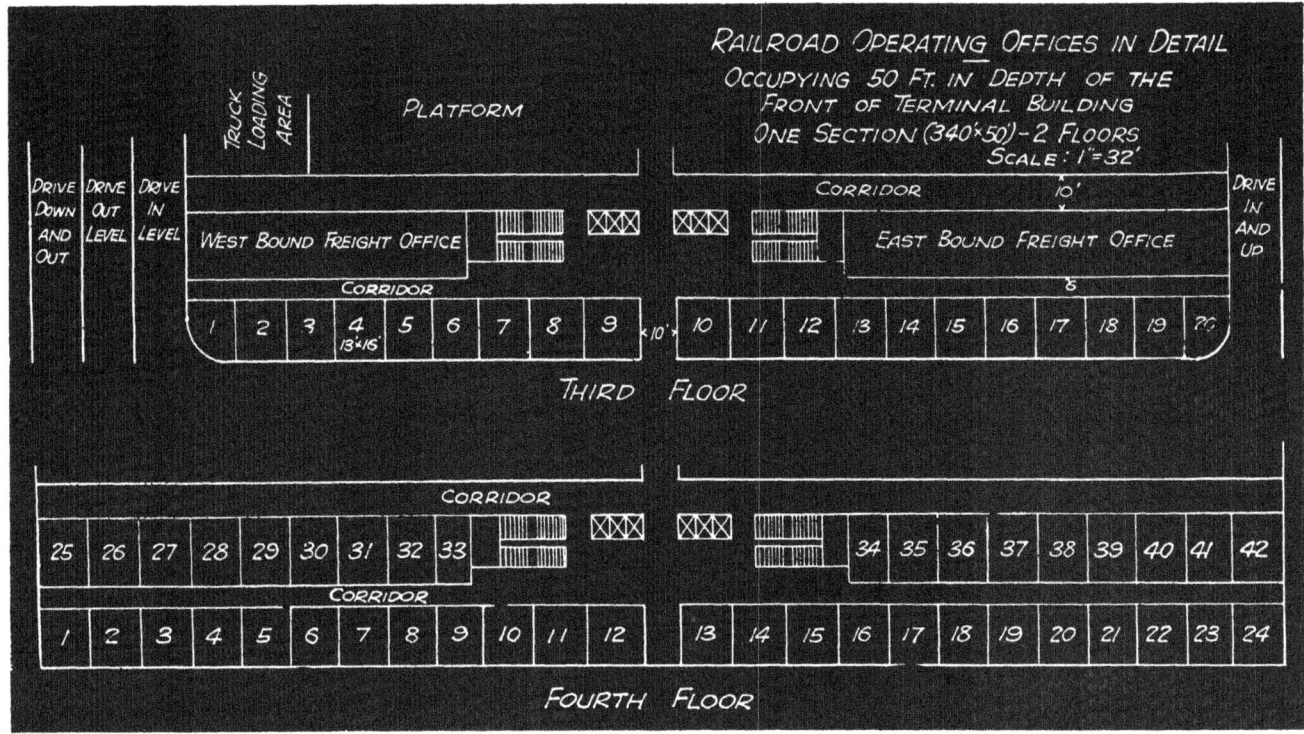

GENERAL BUSINESS OFFICES

It is a part of the plan to add—later—a *fifth floor* for general offices. The situation is exceptionally attractive—at the center of the great city's water front activities—at the heart of the market area—opposite the center of its busiest areas—convenient to ferries, in touch with the Metropolitan Passenger System—easy of access by bridges of approach spanning the current of West Side traffic—and overlooking a panorama of water life and movement not surpassed in interest elsewhere.

GENERAL ARRANGEMENT OF FLOORS—TRAFFIC RESULTS THAT FOLLOW

FIRST FLOOR—AT STREET LEVEL
    THE BASIN
    COLD STORAGE AND DRY STORAGE AREAS
    ENTRANCES AND EXITS FOR TRUCKS UP TO FOOD PLATFORM ON SECOND LEVEL
    THE SUBWAY DRIVE—FOR HEAVY FREIGHTS
SECOND FLOOR—EAST BOUND
    METROPOLITAN FOOD SUPPLY
THIRD FLOOR—EAST BOUND
    MERCHANDISE FREIGHTS
    ENTRANCES AND EXITS FOR EAST AND WESTBOUND GENERAL FREIGHTS
FOURTH FLOOR—WEST BOUND
    MERCHANDISE FREIGHTS

CONNECTIONS

The four levels are connected by
DRIVEWAYS—ascending—descending—of *2.6 avg. grade* for *trucks*
ELEVATORS—and *stairways*—(at front) for *passengers*
ELEVATORS—from the water *under* the Warehouse for (*loaded*) *Railroad cars*

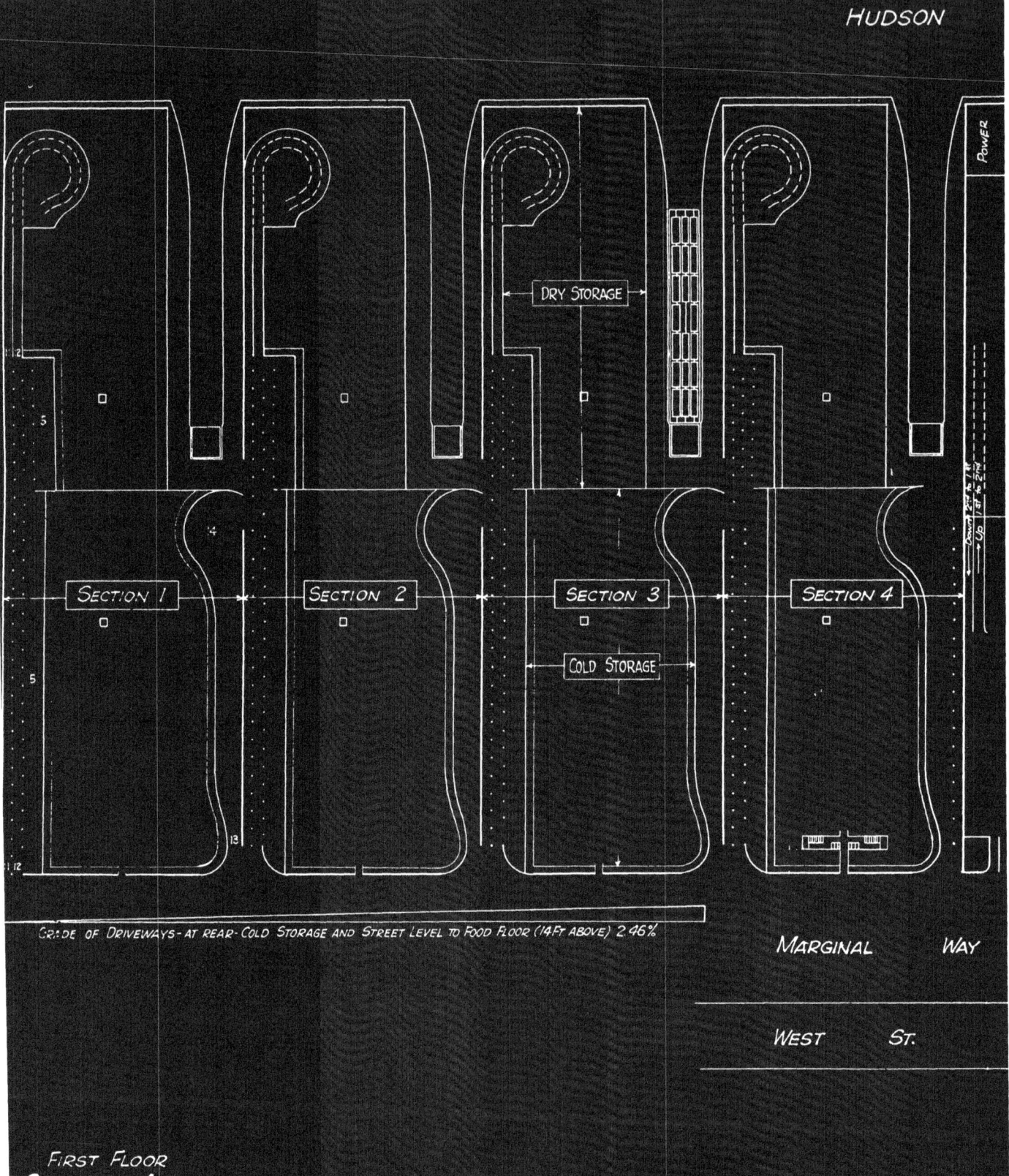

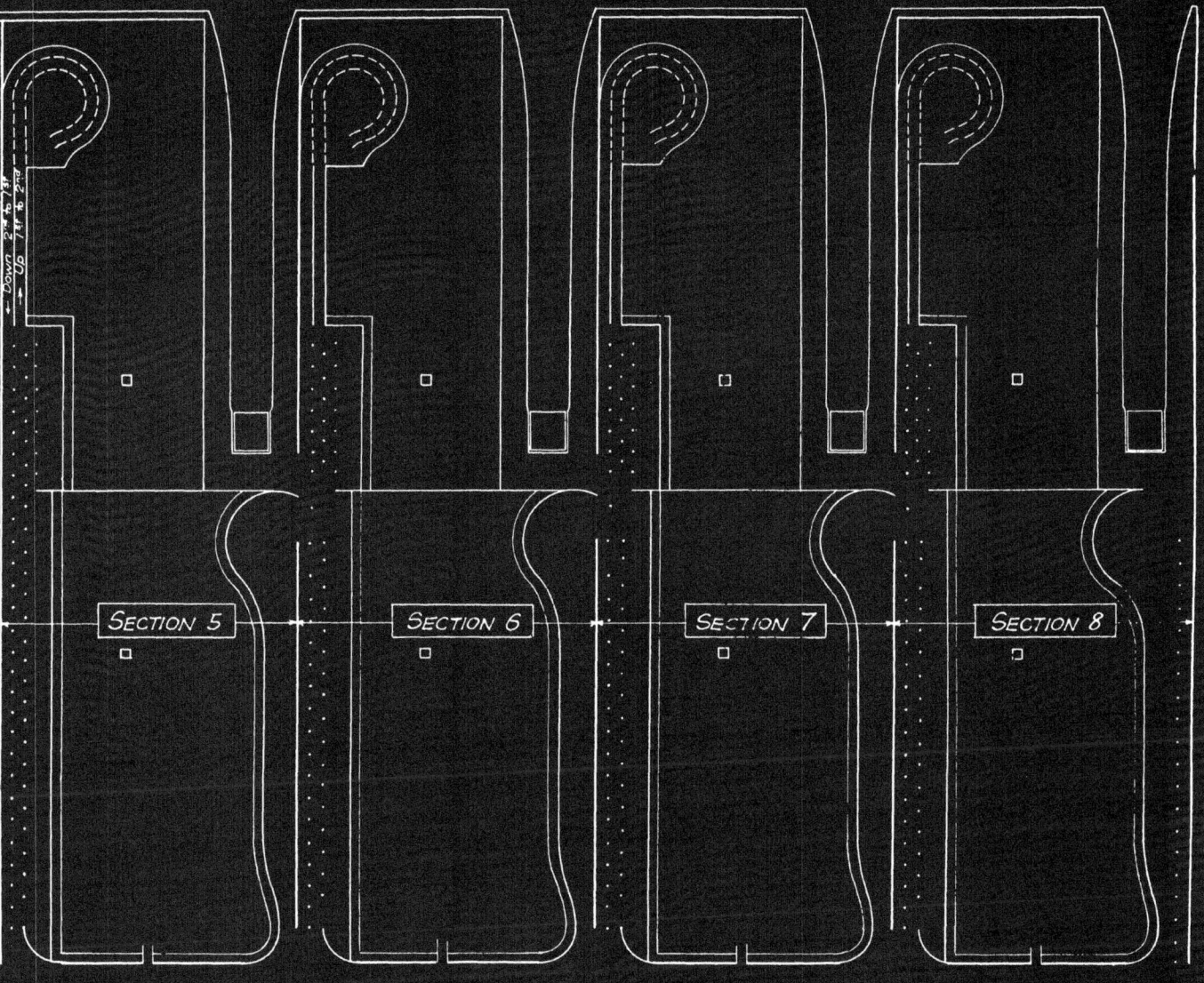

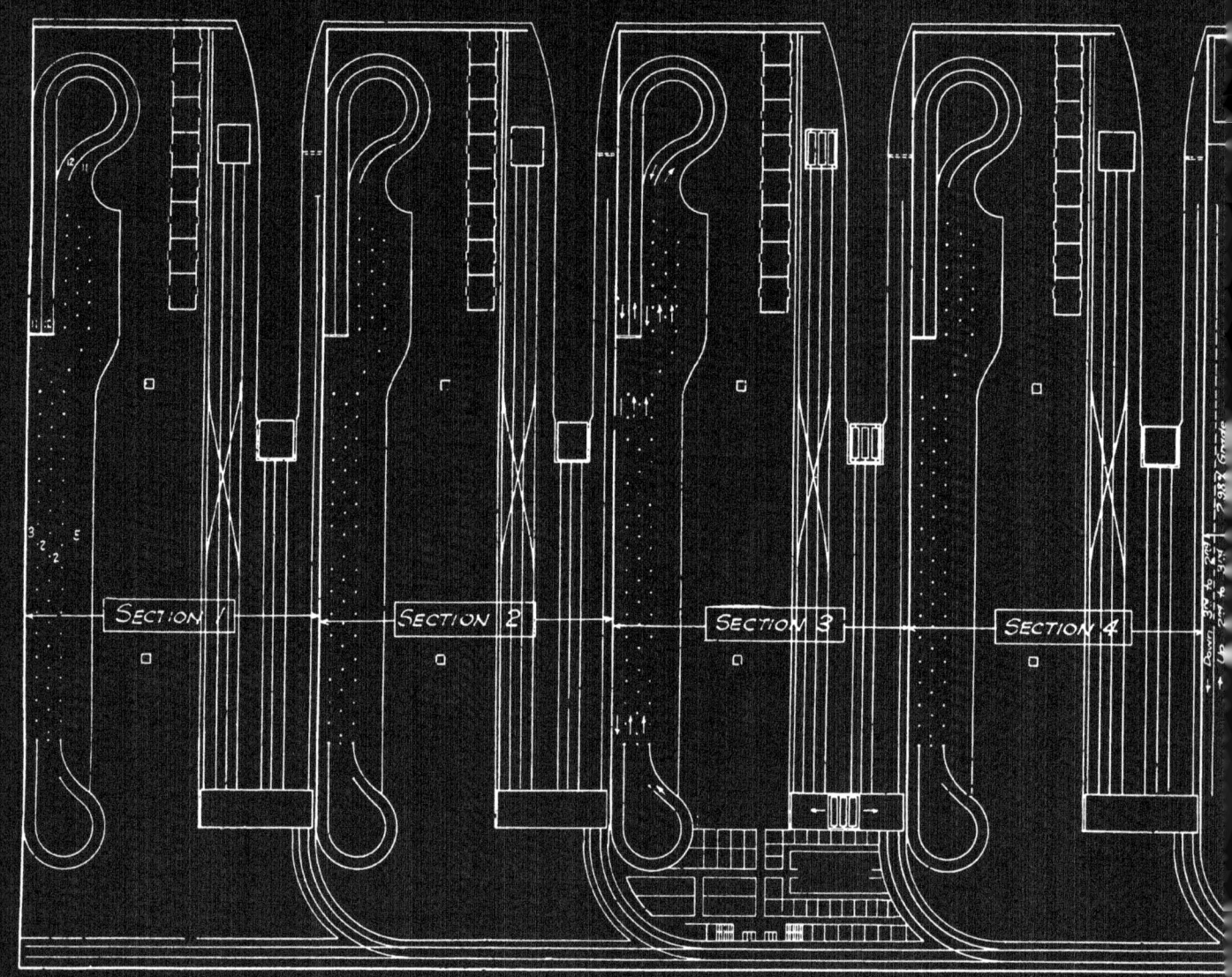

HUDSO[N]

GRADE OF DRIVEWAYS- AT PEAR-COLD STORAGE AND STREET LEVEL TO FOOD FLOOR (14 FT. BELOW) 2.46%

METROPOLITAN FOOD SUPPLY

SECOND FLOOR
EAST BOUND

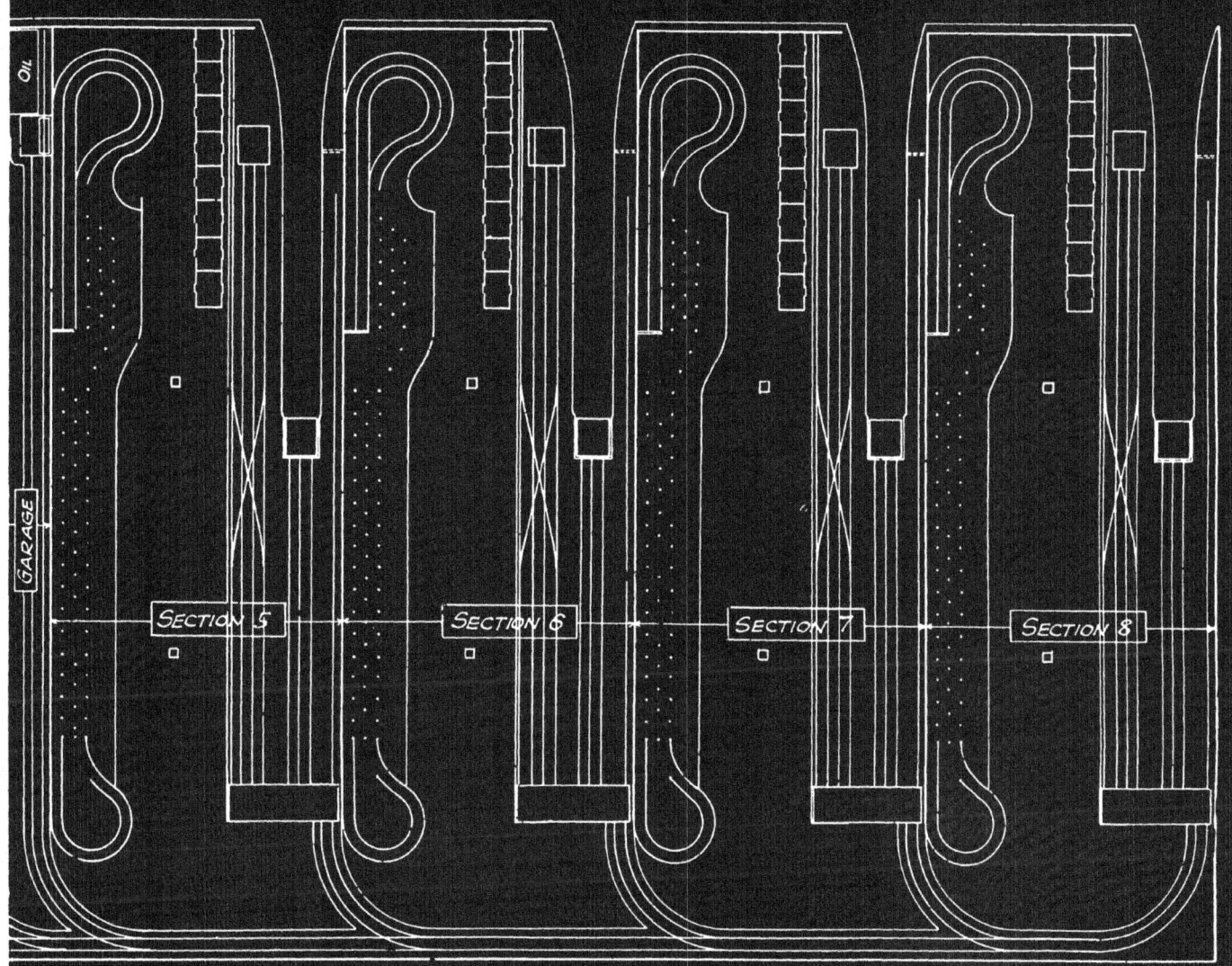

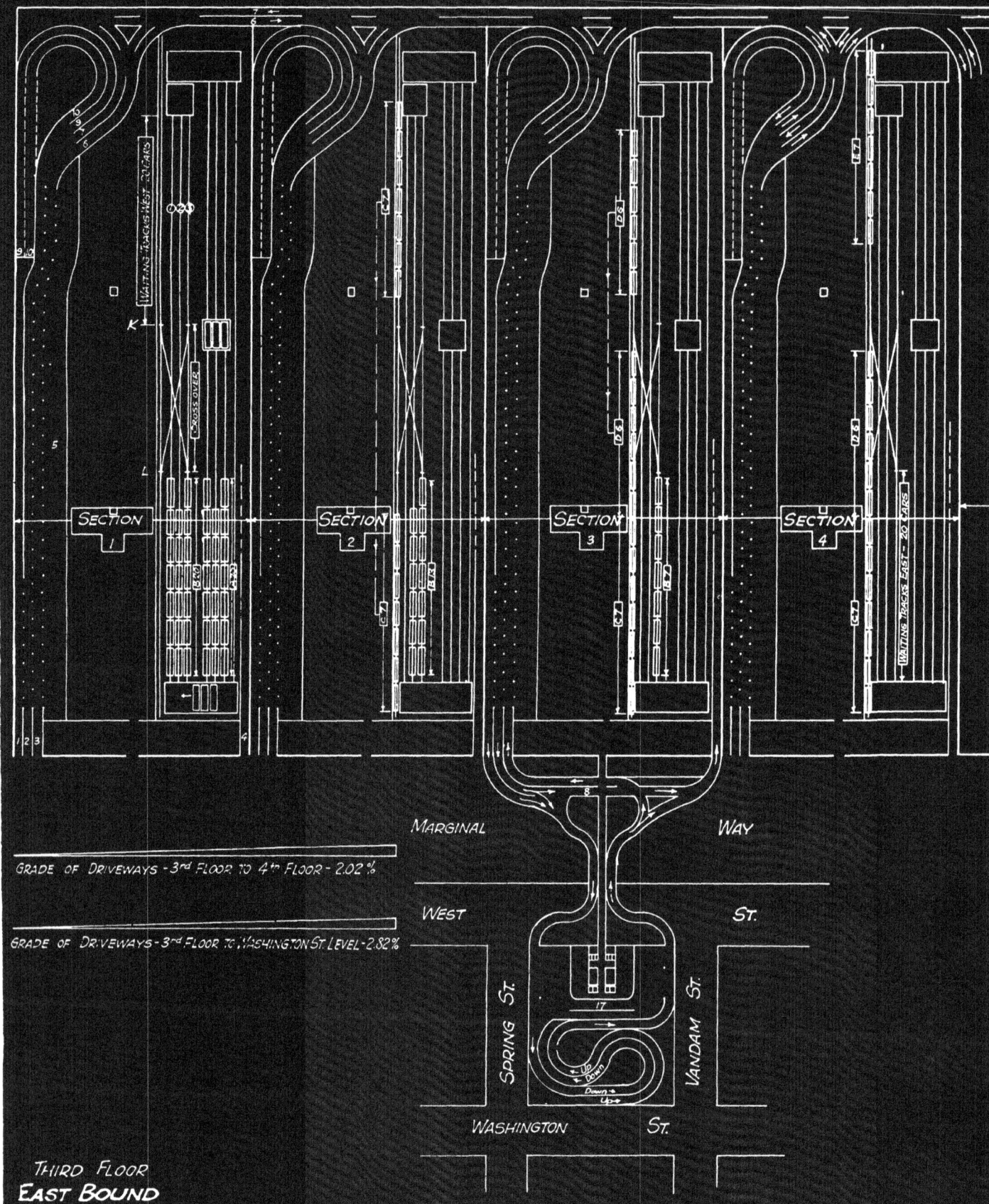

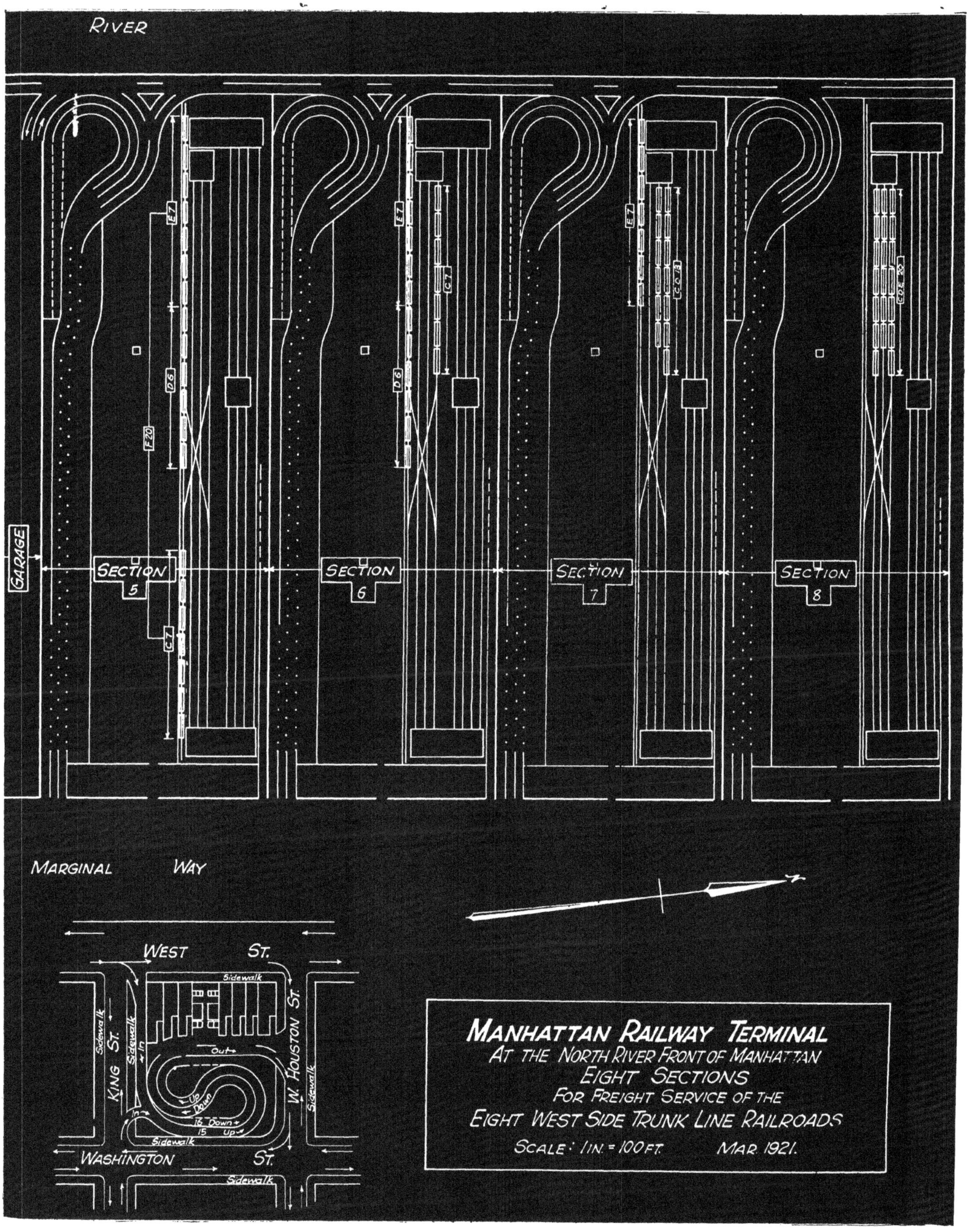

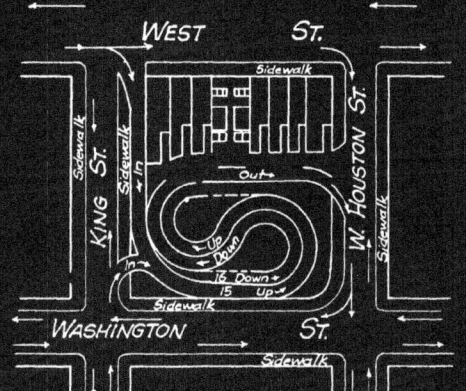

RIVER
E7
D6
F20
C7
E7
C7
D6
E7
C.O.18
C.D.E. 20
GARAGE
SECTION 5
SECTION 6
SECTION 7
SECTION 8
MARGINAL WAY
WEST ST.
Sidewalk
Sidewalk
KING ST.
Sidewalk
In
Out
Up
Down
In
15 Down
15 Up
Sidewalk
W. HOUSTON ST.
Sidewalk
WASHINGTON ST.
Sidewalk
MANHATTAN RAILWAY TERMINAL
AT THE NORTH RIVER FRONT OF MANHATTAN
EIGHT SECTIONS
FOR FREIGHT SERVICE OF THE
EIGHT WEST SIDE TRUNK LINE RAILROADS
SCALE: 1 IN. = 100 FT. MAR. 1921.

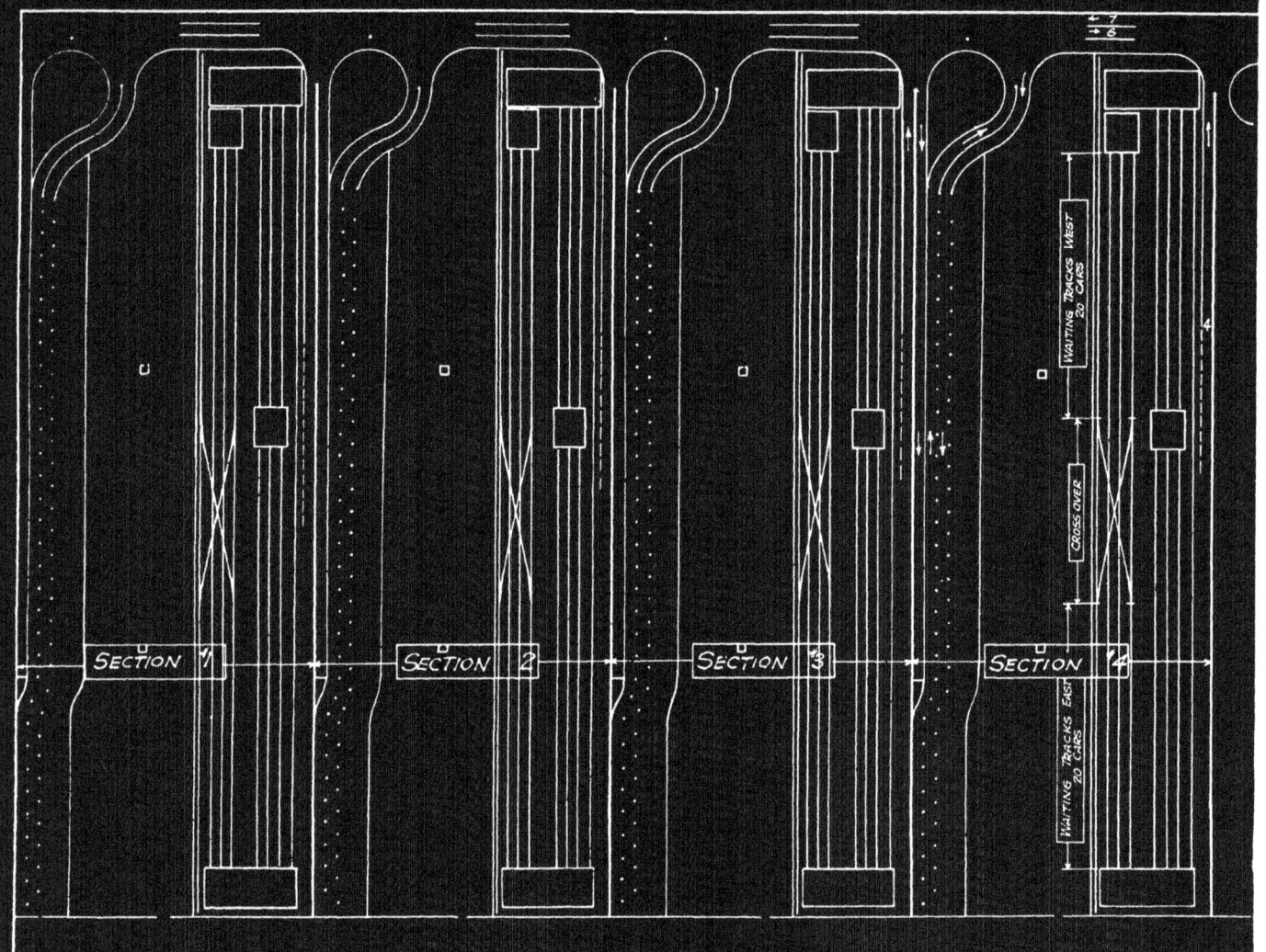

GRADE OF DRIVEWAYS 3RD FLOOR TO 4TH FLOOR 2.02%

FOURTH FLOOR
WEST BOUND

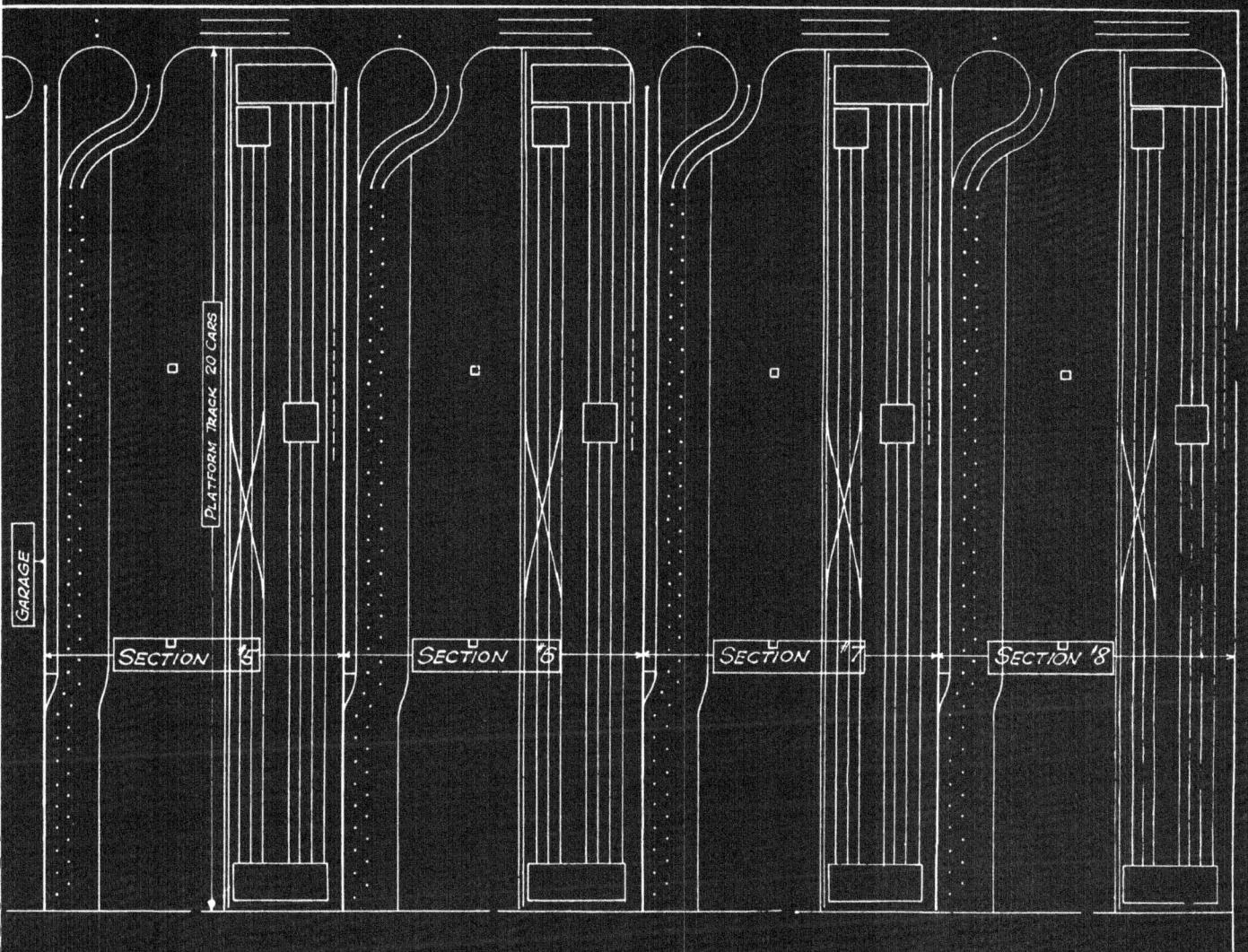

ELEVATORS—between floors—*within* the Warehouse for (*empty*) *Railroad cars*
ELEVATORS—rising through all *freight* areas for *freights*
ESCALATORS—connecting 1st and 2nd levels—at front for *foodstuffs*

NEW LOCATION FOR THE ENTRANCES AND EXITS—THE DOMINANT FEATURE OF THE WAREHOUSE ARRANGEMENT

The Terminal Entrances and Exits for *trucks* are *lifted from the usual* location at the level of the street *up to the third floor level*—34 ft. above grade—and there connected with *elevated driveways* that—*spanning* the marginal way and West St. ride *over the head* of the current of traffic on West St.—pass through a specially constructed entrance building occupying the block—200 ft. square—between West and Washington Sts.—one for each Railroad—and reach the street level near Washington St. in the adjoining *one way—cross street*—500 ft. from the Terminal front—where the exit issuing into one cross street at one side of the building—the entrance coming in from another cross street at the opposite side of the building—the streams of traffic are separated—and trucks entering or leaving move always with the current in that street. These one way cross streets in which no congestion can occur—connect at distances of but a few hundred feet away with the broad longitudinal thoroughfares *Hudson* and *Varick* streets and *West Broadway*—giving free access to all business areas of the city.

THE CONSEQUENCES

1. WEST STREET.—Not only is the Railroad traffic lifted out from the obstructive congestion with which it now struggles in West St. and set down in quiet currents far beyond the troubled areas but since this congestion in West St. is densest in—if not almost entirely confined to—the lower half of the Hudson River water front and on that front the Railroads occupy about 60%—or 26 out of the 45 piers from the Battery to Pier 47 at Perry St.—the *Railroad traffic itself* constitutes the greater part of all congestion that now prevails in that street and the removal of that traffic—with its long lines of trucks waiting at pier stations will at once render the remaining stream—*liquid*—and *congestion* will *disappear* all along the line from the Battery to 60th St..

2. STORAGE AREAS.—The Storage Areas which in storage warehouses of usual basic dimensions are necessarily located on all levels from the street to the 5th or 10th story reached only by Freight Elevator service—are in this system all on *one level*—and by the arrangement of floors noted—this floor is brought down from its usual place at the top—to the *bottom*—at *street level*—where trucks having easy access from the street may drive *in* and *out* from West St. made *free of congestion* and over a marginal way made *clear* of general railroad traffic—to reach the *cold storage* areas—the *dry storage* areas—and the *food platform* on the floor above *street level*.

3. METROPOLITAN FOOD SUPPLY.—As the West bound freight constitutes the smaller part of the entire volume of railroad traffic—it is placed at the top on the 4th floor—and the Eastbound—the larger part—is given two floors—the 3rd and 2nd. The East bound current is thus separated into *two* currents—*one* the general *merchandise* freight which is assigned to the *third level*—and *the other—food stuffs*—to the *second*.

The location of the *food supply* is therefore directly over the storage areas where Food-stuffs may drop by freight elevators from the platform to either *cold* or *dry*—storage areas—(14 ft. below) at street level—or trucks may drive *in* from and *out* to the marginal way—and where by Escalator market food-stuffs may slide down to the market areas at front on the marginal way.

THE ENTRANCE AND EXIT BUILDING

The block between West and Washington Sts. opposite each of the 8 Railroad sections of the Terminal—(approximately 200 ft. sq.—8 Blocks in all)—is taken as the exclusive *entrance* and *exit* of the Driveways of that one railroad to and from the 3rd (Eastbound) level—34 ft. above the street—to and from the street level in the cross street near Washington St.—(grade 2.82%). The new structure on this area is of 10 stories—the 1st 18 and 2nd 14 and 8 upper floors 12 ft. each, total 128 ft. high, 220 ft. square. The first and second stories are used primarily as driveways—the upper floors as merchants' and manufacturers' business areas—(as explained in other descriptive memoranda).

1. ON THE STREET LEVEL—(as shown typically by the blue print).—On the West St. front at the center is

an entrance (40 ft. square) with stairways and six Passenger Elevators that rise to all floors—for Railway Officers—employees—occupants and others.

At the rear of the Hall are 4 freight elevators which rise to all the merchant floors above. At either side of the entrance Hall are stores for Merchants—(7 in all—20-25x75-90) fronting on West St. with trucking driveways at rear. The East half of the block area is occupied by the circular ascending-descending driveways.

THE ENTRANCE AND EXIT DRIVEWAYS (OF THE RAILWAY SECTION)

1. There are—on the *first level*—two *entrances*—one at the N. E. corner of West St.—the other at the N. W. corner of Washington and the cross street—both coming *in* out of the street current moving in the same direction; one *exit* at the opposite side of the block—at its center—on the cross street—issuing into the street current moving

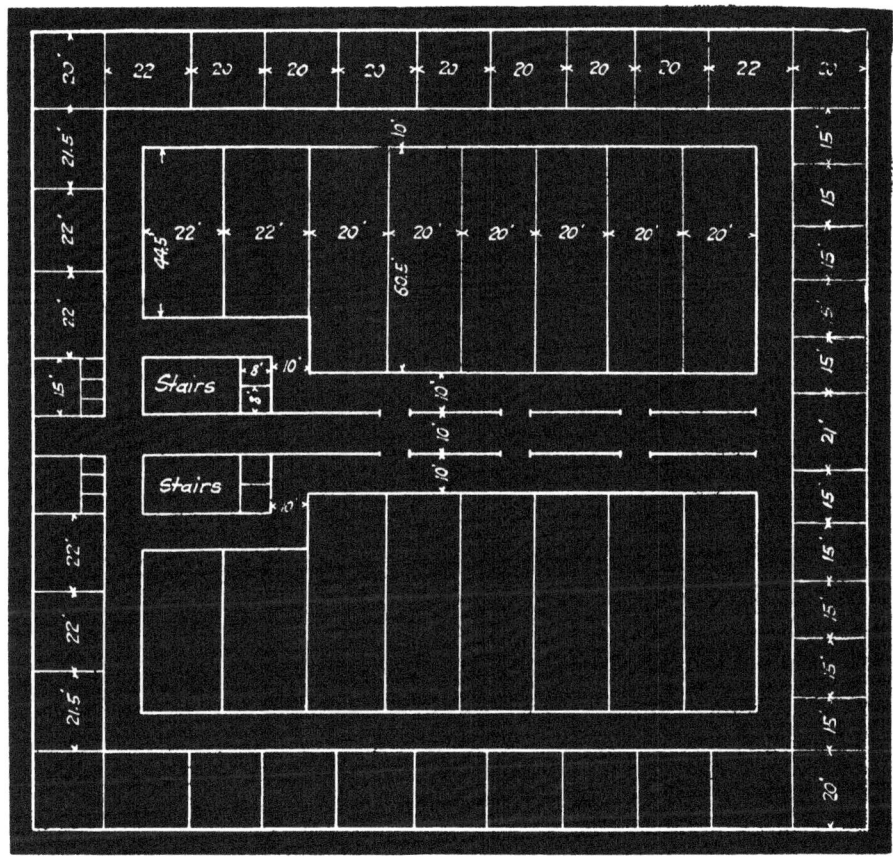

TYPICAL PLAN OF UPPER FLOOR—ENTRANCE AND
EXIT BUILDING

in the same direction. These are shown on the blue print Typical First Floor Entrances and Exit as at Spring and Vandam Streets respectively—and on the blue print of the 3rd Terminal floor—as at King and West Houston.

The Entrance and Exit of each Railroad are separated therefore—by one block—and these from corresponding Entrances and Exits of the next Railroad by one block.

2. ON THE SECOND LEVEL.—On the second level—(shown on the Typical and also the 3rd Terminal—blue prints)—the East half of the area is occupied—(as on the 1st)—by the circular driveways.

At the front of the West half is the Entrance Hall with stairs and Elevators corresponding with those in the similar area on the floor below. At the sides of this area are freight platforms, each 25x75, connected at rear by platform with 4 Freight Elevators that reach all levels. The platform at one side is for the *in*—at the other the *out*—traffic of the merchants and manufacturers on the floors above and the stores on the floor below. Both

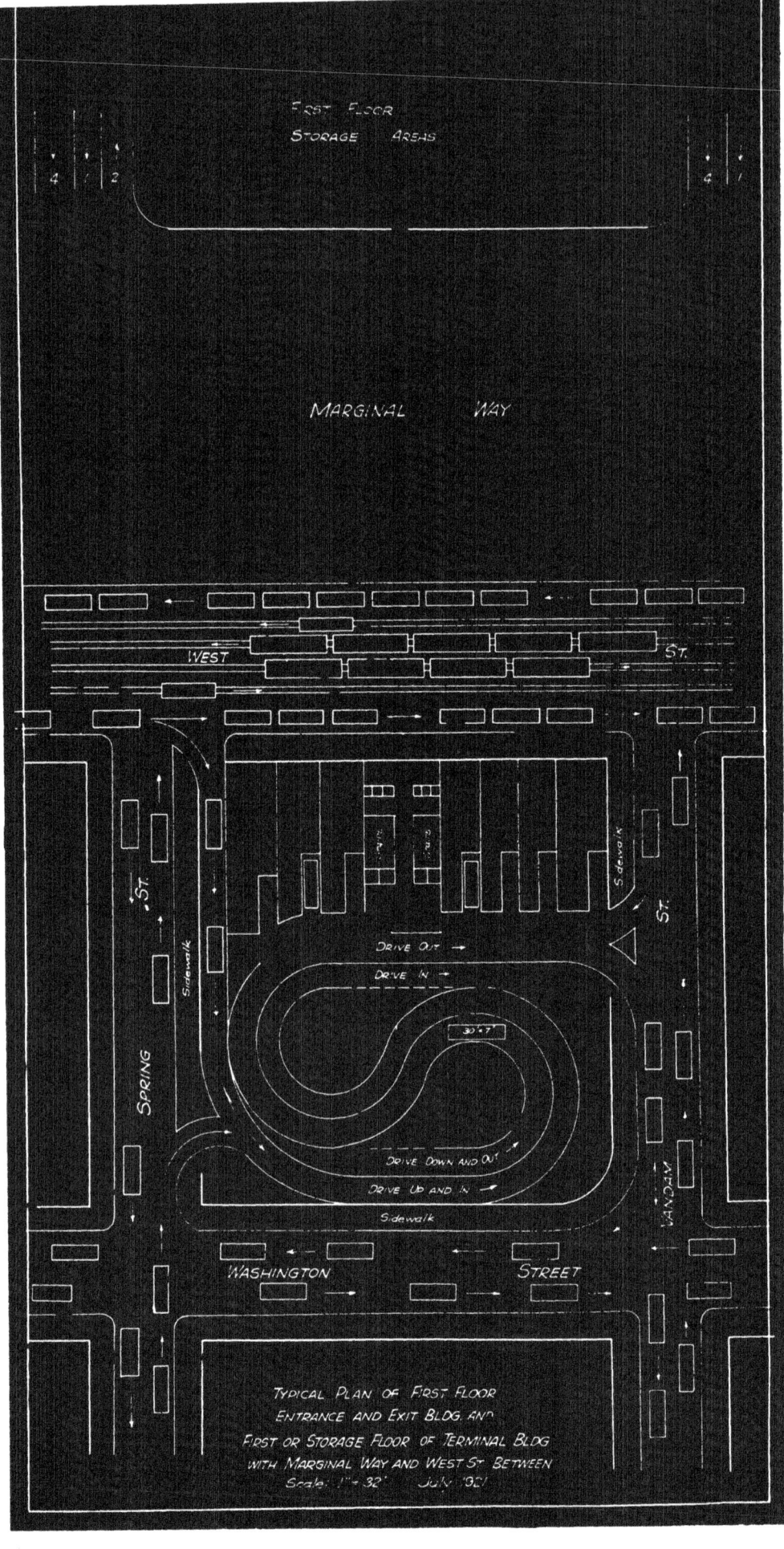

THIRD FLOOR
EASTBOUND FREIGHT

MARGINAL WAY

WEST ST.

Freight Platform   Stairs   Stairs   Freight Platform

SPRING ST.

DRIVE UP AND IN
DRIVE DOWN AND OUT

DRIVE DOWN AND OUT
DRIVE UP AND IN

LANDAM ST.

WASHINGTON ST.

TYPICAL PLAN OF SECOND FLOOR
ENTRANCE AND EXIT BLDG. THE
ELEVATED DRIVEWAYS ACROSS THE MARGINAL WAY
UP TO LEVEL OF THIRD OR EASTBOUND FLOOR OF TERMINAL
Scale 1" = 32'   July 1901

platforms are in connection for trucks with the exit and entrance Driveways of the Railroad section and therefore with the Freight platforms of all Railroads on all floors of the Terminal.

3. ON THE THIRD LEVEL.—At the front—at the center—is the Entrance Hall area with Stairs and Elevators corresponding with those on the floor below and from this Hall issues a practically level corridor—(10 ft.)—for foot passengers—(shown typically (for convenience) on 2nd level plan) which located between the Driveways spans West St. and the Marginal Way connecting with the corridors of the Office Section of the Terminal, and there with Stairs and Elevators for the Exchange and Sales Rooms on the Food Floor—and all other levels.

4. ON THE UPPER LEVELS.—The area of the *manufacturer* or *merchant's* floor—(3rd to 10th levels as shown by typical blue print) is divided into offices (15x20) at the four sides—each having the unique advantage of being at the front. Corridors skirt these at their rear. The space at the center within the surrounding corridors is divided into large long areas (25x80) for the uses of manufacture—or for the keeping or display of merchandise or of samples—these are in connection at rear with freight corridors—by rubber wheel warehouse wagons and these with the freight Elevators which rise from the lower levels.

With his office at the front of the floor—his sample room or store at center—and the facilities provided—the Merchant without descending to the street level is in touch with his goods in the Cold Storage and Dry Storage areas of the Terminal—with the platforms of all the great Trunk Line Railroads—and therefore with the Continental Railroad system for the receipt of goods coming in—the care of goods while held—the shipment of goods going out—*ideal facilities* that cannot be found elsewhere.

The Butter and Cheese merchant for example—now located in Murray St. occupies a store house at a round rental—and the several floors except for a portion of the first used as a counting room are occupied simply for storage. Moreover the very goods he has first carted from the Railroad station have often after sale to be carted back to the Railroad station for shipment out.

Located in the new areas of these Terminal Buildings—he may send his goods on arrival by rail from the freight platform down to the Terminal Cold storage areas where they will be kept in better condition than would be possible in the Murray St. store—and at less than half the expense—display only samples on his areas in the new building—and dismissing his carmen—closing his garage or stable—ending this burden of expense—make deliveries by the Terminal Motor Truck service—at a fraction of his present cartage expense—to any point in the City or within the Terminal to any Railroad for reshipment and without—to any steamship.

Similarly the goods of the Manufacturer may on arrival by rail go down to the storage floor and be withdrawn for manufacture as needed.

It needs no vision to foresee that such areas are a *new facility* which will be in great demand—they will be taken up long before the structures are completed for they cannot be duplicated elsewhere.

THE TERMINAL—WITHIN

NOTE: The Terminal being a composite structure of 2 wings connected by an interposed Central Division—each wing of 4 sections—the descriptive detail of *the section*—and *the Central Division*—with explanation of their relation to the general plan—is a description of the Terminal.

THE SECTION

The section 1,070 ft. long 340 ft. wide for *one railroad* is divided in its width—generally—and on all operating floors alike into 3 longitudinal—(E-W)—strips or areas. The middle strip 126 ft. wide is the Freight platform—having at one side parallel Railroad tracks—(and at the 1st and 2nd levels the Basin and its upper areas)—in a strip 138 ft. wide—at the other—parallel Driveways—occupying a strip 76 ft. wide.

THE BASIN AND ITS BAY

NOTE: As the structure of the Basin in its simplest form—as illustrating the principle—its conformation and use—is described on other pages it remains to describe here only its adaptation to Terminal structures.

At the outer—(or Pier head)—end of the Railroad track strip the first and second floors of the pier structure are cut away from the pier head line inward creating for the admission of the Motor Float to position *within* and *under* the warehouse to connection with the Car Elevator Landing Stages—a *basin* 355 ft. long 48 ft. wide—

and—(by the extension of the side walls of the Basin in outward curves to the pier head line—also a *bay* of *entrance*—100 ft. wide at its mouth—150 ft. deep to the outer end of the Basin walls—a total depth of Bay and Basin from the pier head line to the location of the Landing Stages (near the center of the structure) of 505 ft.

The Bay provides a safe harbor of entrance and exit for the Float in all weathers and for its further facility and security the *apron* 10 ft. wide extending along the sea front at the 1st level is elevated at the Bay to span its mouth at the level of the 3rd floor—and from these vantage points operatives with proper equipment may aid in controlling the movement and direction of the incoming—outgoing boat in severe weather.

THE WATER GATE—(in two sections of 24 ft. each)—Suspended from the 3rd floor level moves transversely across the outer end of the Basin riding loosely in the grooved upper edge of the submerged front wall of the Basin, closing it from that depth up to the level of the first floor against the motion of the water without.

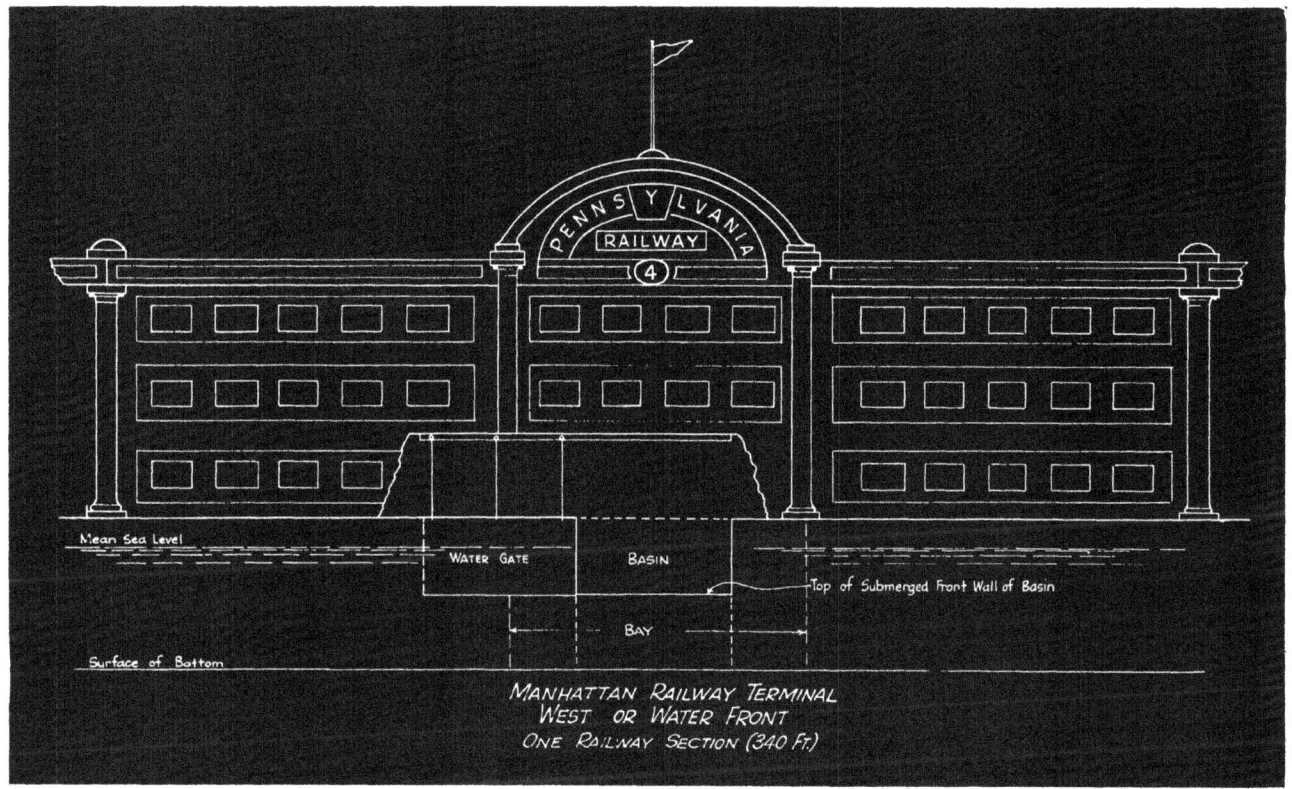

THE WATER FRONT CLOSED—THE WAREHOUSE DOOR

The operating areas of the 1st and 2nd levels are closed at the water front by an *outer wall* that extending inward from the mouth of the Basin at one side—in a line parallel to and 10 ft. from the line of the Bay and Basin (leaving a 10 ft. operating border at the Basin side) crosses at right angles at the head of the Basin and continues at the opposite side—(leaving a similar operating Basin border)—out to the mouth of the Basin at the water front. Extending at right angles from this wall at a point opposite the outer end of the Basin—a *transverse* partition wall—similarly rising to the 3rd level and provided with doorway)—reaches to the edge of the Basin.

In position adjacent to the Water Gate—similarly suspended and operated—the *warehouse door* (in two sections of 27 ft. each) moves at right angles across the outer end of the Basin closing the warehouse from the pier level to the 3rd floor—enclosing the Basin and its areas.

THE FLOAT ENTERS THE WAREHOUSE—THE GATES AND DOORS ARE CLOSED

The Motor Float—therefore—actually *enters the warehouse* floating in along the levels of the 1st and 2nd floors—*under* the 3rd floor which extends above it as a roof—and the water gate and the warehouse door being closed—the Float delivers its cars at the *center of the warehouse* resting on the water under the warehouse which regardless of weather conditions outside is *without motion*—and between the rails of the Float and those of the Landing Stage—firm level connection is established.

THE ELEVATORS

There are *two sets* of Railroad Car Elevators one (the Landing Stages) for the use of *loaded*—the other for *empty*—cars.

1. THE LANDING STAGES.—At the inner end of the Basin—its side walls are thickened on the inner side—reducing the width of the Basin—for 45 ft. in length—from 48 to 40 ft.—and these with the rear wall from 3 sides of the *water well* into which—as already explained—the Landing Stages descend to the level of the water (or to the deck of the Float) at any tide—the fourth side being left open to the water—to permit the floor of the Elevators and the deck of the Float to meet.

The Landing Stages—three—each 13 ft. wide—45 ft. long—operating simultaneously—are equipped with tracks each to take one car at a time and are used for cars *loaded* with Eastbound freight going *up* for delivery at the 2nd or 3rd Eastbound floors—and cars *loaded* with Westbound freight going *down* from the 4th or Westbound floor to the Float—going *out*.

2. THE EMPTY CAR ELEVATORS.—At the outer or West end of the platform Tracks—located across the 3 waiting Tracks West are 3 empty car Elevators of the same dimensions—capacity—and equipment as the Landing Stage Elevators. These operate only between the levels of the 2nd and 4th floors—and are used only for *empty* cars which if they are to be reloaded are sent up from the Eastbound to the Westbound floor; if to be returned to the yard empty—down to the Float;—if to be delivered to the rails of another Railroad—to the Transverse Railway on the 2nd level.

NOTE: The Landing Stage Elevators—operating down to the water are called for convenience the *wet elevators*—the empty car Elevators operating between the floors *dry*. Their operation in the processional scheduled movement of traffic through the warehouse is explained in detail under the caption—*The System in Operation*.

THE DRIVEWAYS—IN ALL SECTIONS ALIKE

1. Descending Drive *out* .... from 4th to 3rd level (and next).
2. Level Drive *out* .... parallel to the Level Drive *in* (on 2nd-3rd-4th level.)
3. Level Drive *in* .... parallel to and next the Loading Area (on 2nd-3rd-4th level).
4. Ascending Drive *in* .... from 3rd to 4th level.
5. Loading—Unloading—Area .... parallel to and next the platform (on 2nd-3rd-4th level).
6. Level Transverse Drive *in* .... at West Front on 3rd and 4th levels—extending N-S.
7. Level Transverse Drive *out* .... length of the Terminal—connecting all sections.
8. Level Transverse Drive *across* .... East Front of section on 3rd level to connect level Drive *out* 2—with Ascending Drive *in* 4.
9. Descending Drive 3rd to 2nd level .... connecting 3rd with Food Floor.
10. Ascending Drive 2nd to 3rd level .... connecting 3rd with Food Floor.
11. Descending Drive 2nd to 1st level .... connecting Food Floor with 1st level.
(11). Level Drive *out* .... from storage areas and *down* from Food Floor.
12. Ascending Drive 1st to 2nd level .... connecting Food Floor with 1st level.
(12). Level Drive *in* .... to storage areas and *up* to Food Floor, and in to Heavy Freight Circle.
13. Level Drive *out* .... from Heavy Freight Circle.
14. *Heavy freight subway circle* .... under opening between tracks on floor above.
15. *Ascending entrance* Driveway .... from street level at Washington St. across marginal way *up*
16. *Descending exit* Driveway .... to 3rd level 34 ft. above grade.
17. *Driveways* .... connecting freight platforms on 2nd floor of Entrance Exit building with all Railroads.

GRADES

Entrance and Exit Drives *up to* 3rd *Level*	2.82%
1st to 2nd *Level*	2.46
2nd to 3rd *Level*	3.14
3rd to 4th *Level*	2.02

THE SYSTEM OF DRIVEWAYS

All operating areas of every section of the Terminal on all floors—are in connection with each other and with the garage and easy of access over separate exclusive Driveways *in—out*—in which trucks move always in one direction. Trucks, both Horse and Motor, reach all operating levels from the street level up or from level to level over light grades with the same ease that they move along the streets. Trucks having goods for or receiving goods from several Railroads may pass from one platform in any section on any level to any other platform of the Terminal.

All single Driveways are 14 ft. wide—double 28—turning circle radius—40 ft.

The *highways* of traffic provided within and without the terminal while affording extreme facility are made more effective through *three new conceptions* of important traffic advantage.

1. *The new Post Line Driveway.*
2. *The Enclosed Loading Area.*
3. *The Heavy Freight Subway.*

1. THE NEW POST LINE DRIVEWAY.—Instead of the usual structural border timber strips forming the boundary lines of driveways—a line of short metal—cylindrical—round top posts 6 inches diameter—rising but 12 inches from the floor—set down 26 ft. apart and located diagonally opposite on alternate lines—are used to define the Drives (the posts are indicated on the blue prints by dots).

Trucks driving *in*—pass without disturbing trucks at platform within the loading area—and when they reach the desired platform location maneuver through the post line to position at the platform. Leaving the platform they go through the post lines into the Drive *out* at any point along the line joining the line of vehicles in that Drive all moving in the same directions. The necessity as with other driveways—of going to the circle at the end of the drive in order to turn around and go out—is eliminated. The new post line in addition to affording these new facilities of movement in and out—also in effect—widens the driveway so that trucks may use the areas of two driveways in maneuvering through the post line to position at the platform.

2. THE ENCLOSED LOADING AREA.—At existing Terminals there is always more or less confusion caused by the collision of trucks passing trucks backed up to the platform loading or unloading. In this new Terminal system a separate area 34 ft. wide next to the platform extending its whole length is set apart as the *loading* (or *unloading*) *area*. It is closed by structure at either end and defined at its outer edge by a line of posts which separates it distinctly from the passing drive. Within that area no trucks enter except at the point where they back up to position at the platform and trucks loading at the platform are unmolested by trucks passing in the parallel driveways.

3. THE HEAVY FREIGHT SUBWAY.—There is a class of freight brought in by Railroad Cars in large quantities that is too heavy or too bulky or in shape too awkward or in length too long—to be handled over the platform or through the regular driveways like ordinary merchandise freights—which requires to be delivered from the car, as at a siding or switch track, by crane directly to the truck. Such delivery or receipt is now necessarily made at the Railroad yard or on Railroad siding. For freights of this class a new facility has been provided in the Subway Drive.

This drive—(see blue print Heavy Freight Subway)—enters (as shown) at drive 12—turns in at the circle 14—(on the street level)—112 ft. diameter—directly under a long opening between the tracks on the floor above where cranes and other handling facilities—deliver such freights as structural steel—railroad iron—building materials, etc., directly to the truck beneath. The wide circle affords ample room for handling the material and the drive out 40 ft. wide—narrowing to 20 at the exit (13) meets the difficulties of handling these freights now unloaded in New Jersey and carted across the ferries.

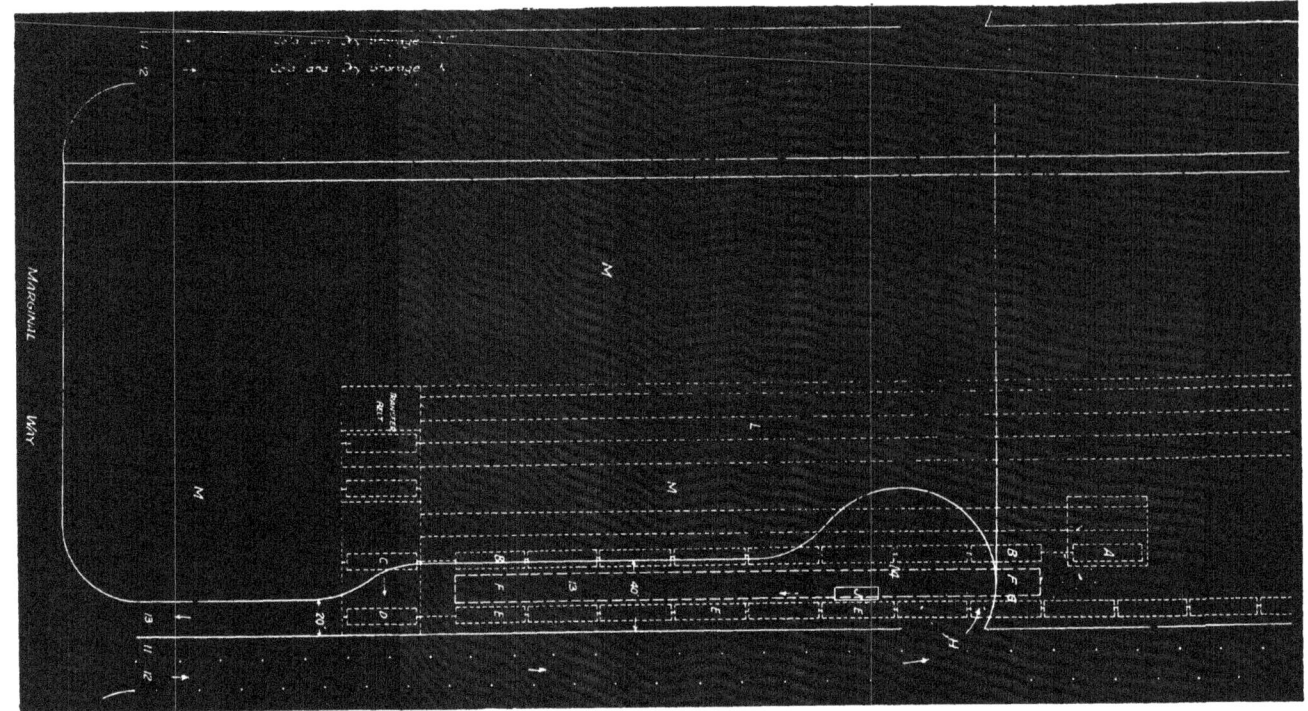

HEAVY FREIGHT SUBWAY

THE PLAN: Dotted lines show on second level 4 parallel platform tracks L—landing stage—A-3 landing stage tracks—B—and sidetrack E with cars—a longitudinal opening in the floor—F—between the tracks B and E—13 ft. wide, 336 ft. long—with a floor margin—G—(for operatives) of 10 ft. (from rail to opening) on both sides. Overhead are traveling cranes and mechanisms for lifting and lowering the pieces to the truck below.

Full lines show on street level below—storage areas M—the Subway Circle—14—(diameter 154 ft.) the Drive-in—12—(defined by posts—represented by dots)—the Drive-out—13-40 ft. wide, narrowing to 20 at exit.

IN OPERATION: Cars with heavy freights are delivered by the landing stage A—over the Receiving Tracks—B—to the Transfer Belt at—C—transferred laterally to D—then to position on the sidetrack—E. The truck drives in at 12, turns into the circle at H, takes position under any car—J—the freight is lowered down into it—and the truck drives out at 13.

EXTENT OF THE DRIVEWAYS

There are within the Terminal 136 separate Driveways with 40 Truck Loading Areas—(at platforms)—which aggregate in length—(at 14 ft. average width) *thirty-seven miles*—and without the Terminal 16 separate drives aggregating 4.1 *miles*—a total of—41.1 *miles* of *driveways*.

THE DRIVEWAYS IN OPERATION

1. Trucks passing *in* over the Elevated bridgeway from Washington St. destined for any level—enter the Terminal at Drive 3—if for the Eastbound floors or the storage floor—or 4 if for the Westbound floor—and reaching the proper platform location maneuver through the post lines to position within the Loading Area 5.

2. Leaving the platform they pass through the post lines to the parallel Drive *out* (2) and on the 3rd level—to *exit* over the Elevated Driveway—on the 2nd to the Drive *up* 10 to 3rd—and to Elevated Exit—or to the Drive *down* 11—to 1st and *out* over the Marginal way—on the 4th to the Drive *down*—1 and to Elevated Exit.

3. If the truck at Eastbound platform of any section is to go to any other platform on that level—it takes the Drive *in* 3—to the Transverse Drive 6—(or 7) from that Drive turns into the Drive *out*—2—of the desired section—and reaching the proper platform location—manoeuvers through the post lines—to position.

4. To go from its position at Eastbound platform to Westbound platform on 4th floor—it takes the Drive *out* 2—to the Transverse Drive 8—at front—crosses the width of the section to the Drive *in* 4—and on the 4th

the Transverse Drive 6 (or 7)—turning into the Drive *in* of the desired section and reaching the proper location maneuvers to position at platform.

5. To go from any Westbound platform (on 4th) to any Eastbound platform—(on 3rd or 2nd)—the truck —takes the Transverse Drive 6 (or 7)—turns at the proper section into the Drive *down*—1 and on the 3rd— level maneuvers through the post lines—enters to position at the platform or takes the Drive *in*—to the Descending Drive 9—to 2nd—and along—the parallel Drive *in* 3 on that level—and through the post lines to platform position.

THE RAILWAY SYSTEM—THE TRAFFIC UNIT—A TRAIN OF TWENTY FREIGHT CARS

The width of the Terminal site from the bulkhead line out to the pier head line—1,080 feet (of which a part is taken up for transverse construction)—determines the length of the car load line track at the platform— and the capacity of this line—(with proper margin at either end)—establishes the *traffic unit*—to be a *train of twenty freight cars* and this *unit* becomes the controlling measure of the coöperating parts and movements of the system. Accordingly the Motor Float is constructed to be 300 ft. long with capacity of 20 cars on 3 parallel tracks 7 at the sides 6 at the center (one car space reserved).

Similarly the switch tracks parallel to the platform tracks and the landing stage tracks—East—and West— are arranged in sets of 3—each set with capacity to take 20 cars in 3 lines and the elevators are in series of 3 —each with 1 track—with 3 operating as one to take up 3 cars at a time from the 3 tracks of the Float for delivery to the 3 Landing Stage Tracks on the floors above (or the reverse). So that all measures and movements in the warehouse—on the water—are interrelated as parts of one coördinate system.

THE TRACKS

NOTE: On the blue prints (except that showing special Track work)—a car track of two rails is represented by a single line.

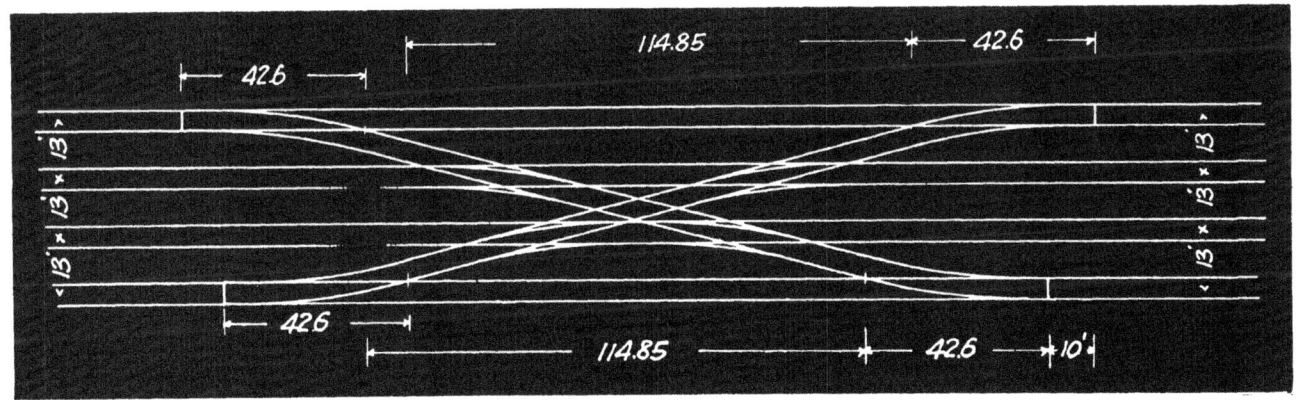

SPECIAL TRACKWORK

A. PLATFORM TRACKS.—There are on each of the 3 operating floors alike 4 parallel tracks at the side of the platform—that next the platform the *car load line* extending the length of the platform—capacity 24 cars. The other 3 lines—the switch tracks—are divided—(in their length)—into 3 sections.

1. THE WAITING TRACKS EAST (W.T.E.).—Extending 300 ft. to the crossover rails—for the location of 20 Cars (one motor Float cargo) in 3 lines (7.6.7) while waiting to be switched to the platform or to the Landing Stage Elevators.

2. THE WAITING TRACKS WEST (W.T.W.).—Extending 300 ft. to the crossover rails—for the location of 20 cars—in 3 lines—while waiting to be switched to the platform—or delivered to the Empty Car Elevators.

3. THE CROSS OVER TRACKS (K.L.).—Extending 210 ft. between the waiting Tracks East and West.

B. RECEIVING AND DELIVERY TRACKS.—The 3 Tracks connecting the Landing Stage Elevators with the

Transfer Belt are—on the 2nd and 3rd levels—the *receiving*—and on the 4th the *delivery—tracks* (cars come *in* over the 2nd and 3rd levels go *out* from the 4th).

    C. SIDE TRACKS.—The Tracks at the wall parallel to the Receiving—Delivery tracks are *side tracks* for the temporary location of cars—empty or loaded—from the deck of the Float—the operating tracks—or from other Railroad Sections over the Transverse Railway.

    D. TRANSVERSE RAILWAY.—The *double* trackway located on the 2nd level at the East front extending N-S the length of the Terminal connects *all* Railroads with each other—for the *exchange of cars* empty or loaded—and with the power plant (at center) for the delivery of Fuel—Oil and Coal.

    E. RAILROAD OPERATING OFFICES.—Located in the section of the building at the front extending (N-S) on the 3rd and 4th levels—the length of the Terminal and also at the East end of the Food platform on 2nd level.

    F. TRANSFER BELTS.—Transfer Belts extend—at the East and at the West across the heads of all tracks to deliver cars by Transfer Table (moving laterally)—from rail to rail.

THE RAILWAYS IN OPERATION

The operation of the Railway system reduced to schedule is explained in detail on the Cycle Table in later pages under the Caption—*The System in Operation*.

EXTENT OF THE RAILWAYS

There are 244 separate Railroad Tracks within the Terminal—in length from 338 ft. (the Landing Stage Tracks) to 2,820—(the Transverse Railway)— aggregating 29.23 *miles* of *railways*—with the capacity of *three thousand seven hundred and sixty cars*.

THE SYSTEM OF FREIGHT AREAS—PLATFORMS

    1. CONSTRUCTION—OPERATION.—Freight platforms are raised by construction to meet at one side the floor of the car—at the other that of the truck. On the 2nd and 3rd floors the level of the rails is that of the floor—the floor of the car is therefore about 4 ft. above the floor of the Warehouse and at the other side the level of the floor of the truck is 2 ft. above the warehouse floor.

Similarly—but in reverse order—on the 4th floor—the Car tracks are slightly depressed—the driveway slightly raised. By this construction a descending grade of about 1.5% is created—across the platform from car to truck on the Eastbound floors and from Truck to Car on the Westbound floor. Freight flowing always—on each of these floors—in but one direction.

These gravity grades controlled electrically are utilized in the operation of moving freight carrying belts to facilitate rapid freight movement—and with other electrically operated mechanisms reaching across and along the platform with adaptable extensions into the car at one side on to the truck at the other—will largely eliminate hand trucking methods, their expense and delay.

    2. AREAS—CAPACITIES.—*All platforms*—are 126 ft. wide—varying in length—on the 4th Westbound floor 987 ft. on the 2nd and 3rd Eastbound floors—912—and 992 ft. respectively.

		Sq. Ft.	*Sq. Ft.*
East Bound			
SECOND LEVEL—PLATFORM		136,857	
THIRD LEVEL—PLATFORM		126,802	
	ONE SECTION	263,659	
TERMINAL	EAST BOUND		2,109,272
West Bound			
FOURTH LEVEL—PLATFORM	ONE SECTION	126,946	
TERMINAL	WEST BOUND		1,015,568
ONE SECTION—TOTAL OPERATING AREAS		390,605	
TERMINAL—TOTAL OPERATING AREAS			3,124,840

NOTE: The U. S. Government standard ton of measurement is 100 cubic ft. The compressed Cotton bale measures—3 ft. wide—2 thick—5 high and occupies standing 6 square—30 cubic ft.—weighs—500 lbs. 4 bales—120 cubic ft. 2,000 lbs. *one ton*.

Applying these measures to the operating freight areas of the New Terminal the result is as follows:

One Section—One Railroad—One Day		Net Sq. Ft.	Cubic Ft.	Cubic Tons
Freight Platform areas	327,166			
Less Cons'n and Gangways—30%	98,120	229,046		
5 high			1,145,230	9,543
Estimated—(Present *annual volume*—8,500,000)—*daily*				2,833
Excess—239%				6,710

COMPARATIVE FREIGHT AREAS—OLD AND NEW SYSTEMS

	Old	New
East Bound—sq. ft.	1,163,178	2,109,272
West Bound—sq. ft.	388,780	1,015,568
Totals	1,551,958	3,124,840

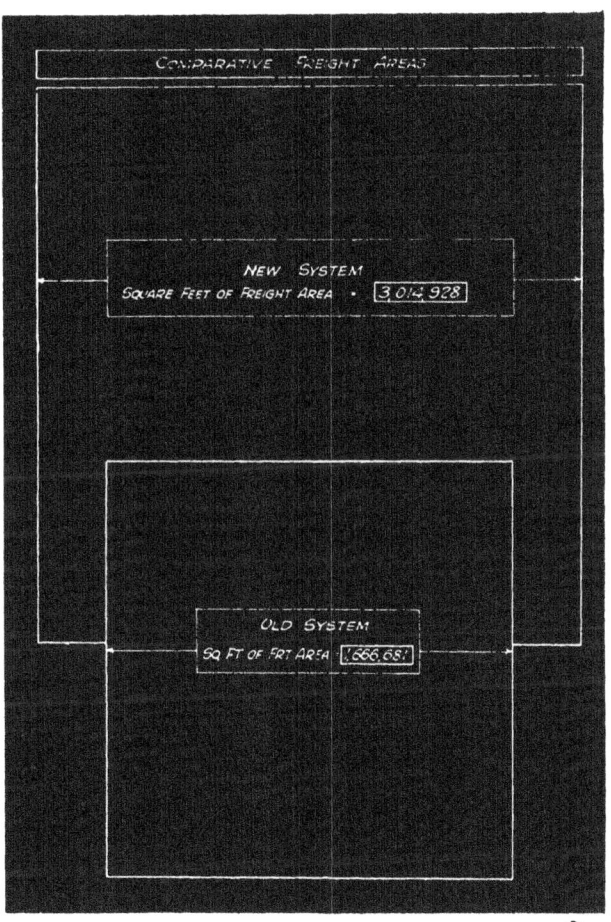

EXCESS OF AREAS

The net operating areas of *one* Railroad section for Eastbound freight—are equal to the corresponding net areas of *eight* average Manhattan North River Railroad piers—and for West bound freight—to the corresponding net areas of *thirteen* Bulkhead sheds. This excess of areas is graphically shown by the accompanying diagram.

While the excess of the New system is very marked as shown—it is much greater in effect by reason of its superior facility of freight movement. By the methods of the old system it is impossible to use its areas more than *once* in 24 hours. In fact they are so congested with freight which lingers and occupies them for the greater part of the day—and part of it for days—that spaces *insufficient* at most for the traffic of the day—are so *reduced* still further.

The areas of the New system—on the contrary *more* than sufficient—at least—are cleared and re-used *many times* in 24 hours—and so—in effect—are prodigiously *multiplied*.

It is this *facility* and *celerity* of freight movement by schedule—the *distinctive* operative feature of the New system that marks its *radical* nature and establishes its great capacity.

This will be better understood by the following illustration:

The area of the 3rd Floor (Eastbound) platform is capable of taking on (as shown above) 4,575 cubic tons —yet but 20 cars (of 30 tons) 600 tons—less than *one-seventh* the platform capacity—are to be unloaded on it in the schedule period—of one cycle—(2 hours)—and during that same period the platform may be cleared by delivery to the Motor Truck system which is moving in correspondence—or to the storage floors below—so that if it were possible to use the area to its capacity—all departments of operation brought into effective coöperation —12 times during the 24 hours—54,900 tons could pass over this single platform in one day—while the load of 20 Cars—(600 tons) repeated 12 times in the 12 Cycles of operation would be only 7,200 tons.

The utmost capacity of the platform is therefore *seven times* as great as the volume of freight to be handled under the rapid schedule of Terminal operation and that volume is itself much greater than the estimated present volume of the daily traffic.

PLATFORM FACILITIES FOR TRUCKS

The accompanying diagram shows a part of the platform Truck line—the operation of the Truck system and the facilities of entry—location at the platform and exit.

At the platform line trucks are located 13 ft. between centers providing the ample operating area of 6 ft. between Trucks. A line of motor and double horse teams are shown so located.

Trucks are also shown coming *in* at 3 maneuvering through the post lines to F and backing into position at the platform at G and H—other trucks J K—leaving the platform driving obliquely through the two post lines into the outer Drive *out* at L on their way to the exit.

The length of the Eastbound platform Loading areas—on 3rd floor—992 ft. affords location for 76 trucks at one time. If for illustration each truck takes on its load in 20 minutes—and but 2 tons (the organized motor Truck service is estimated to handle 8 to 10 and to load in that time) it would be possible to load 5,472 trucks at the platform in 24 hours—with 10,944 tons of freight—an aggregate 560% greater than the estimated flow of Eastbound freight for the day.

The truck facilities at the platforms on the 2nd and 4th floors are similarly excessive—and it is evident therefore that there is no chance for confusion or delay in the Motor Truck service.

MOTOR TRUCK AND MOTOR FLOAT SERVICE

MOTOR TRUCK SERVICE

Congestion at the water front and in the West Side streets of New York is due to the *horse-cartage* service—and that service in turn—though the time for the disappearance of *the horse* from the streets arrived long ago—is continued as a necessary adjunct of the present Terminal system.

If trucks are to wait in line for lack of facilities *within* the terminal—it is obviously cheaper to employ the horse-truck at $1.80 per hour—than the Motor Truck at $3.32.

The Motor Truck—the great modern aid to transportation with an efficiency capable—in coöperation with Terminal facilities of equal efficiency—of clearing the streets of New York of all semblance of congestion—is itself reduced to the capacity of a one-horse truck when it takes its place in the *standing line*. The Terminal creates the standing line—the standing line demands the service of the horse-truck—and the consequent congestion paralyzes traffic—the vicious circle is complete.

The New Terminal meets and masters this situation by providing for the Motor Truck—and for the first time—facilities *within* the warehouse equal to the highest efficiency of which it is capable—and at once the whole situation is changed—the *standing line* is *eliminated*—and *congestion disappears*.

The rapid methods on the water are in coöperation with equally rapid methods in the warehouse—and supplemented by an organized Motor Truck Service—as here described—the New Water System will represent efficiency of *one hundred per cent*.

It is realized that it might be impracticable to establish a new method of cartage that would *at once* supplant an old system—the development of time—entrenched by custom—rooted by reason of investment—nor is that the purpose. All trucks of any kind—horse or motor—will have equal access to the New Terminal. But in view of the greater facility of the New Truck System—its enormous economies—shared with the merchant shipper through material reductions in his present expense—and the lifting from his shoulders of all the burdens and cares of present methods—he will not long consent to the continuance of the old cartage system. These new conditions are mandatory in nature and the withdrawal of the old system—a relic of other times—even if not immediate—is nevertheless inevitable.

The financial plan would hasten this consummation by an equitable exchange of interest in the Terminal for vested cartage interests and the transfer to the new service of the employers as well as employees of the old—fitted by experience and capacity for the new duties—as far as practicable.

OPERATION OF THE SERVICE

Railroad and Traffic Experts will determine by experience the most advantageous periods of the 24 hours for the collection of freight and for its delivery—and freight movement across the water and through the Warehouse will be brought into coördination. The excess of capacity of both the Float System and the Warehouse equipment will render such coöperation easy and effective. It may be determined that *deliveries* will be made in the *day*—*collections* in the *night*—or *deliveries* and *collections*—both—in the *night hours*—from 6 P.M. to 6 A.M.—when the old cartage system is still in the stable. That is the *ideal system*.

NIGHT SERVICE

From 6 P.M. to 6 A.M. the streets are practically clear of operating trucks and this is the advantageous period for the movement of freight. With the coöperation of shippers it will be both practicable and profitable to begin with the establishment of an efficient *night service* for the collection of the westbound traffic of the 24 hours.

THE METHOD FOR COLLECTIONS

The Merchant Shipper sets apart by a partition (which may be of slats)—an area of his store—on the main floor—as a *shipping room*—say 10x15ft. for the average shipper—(varied to suit conditions). The area may be at the front—(1 on the diagram)—or at a side door opening on the lane (2) or in any part of the main floor reached by a walled-off passageway from the street front (3)—or in a shed extension in the yard fronting on a back street or lane (4)—with one door entering from the store—one from the street. The inner door has two locks—the key to one is held by the merchant—(that secures the privacy of his warehouse)—the Terminal holds the key to the other—and also the key to the single lock on the street door—(of the enclosed area).

During the day the merchant advises the Terminal over the wire of the shipment of the day—and deposits the goods within the shipping room—with Bills-of-Lading and shipping instructions—(via Penn. R. R. or B. & O. or Merchants Dispatch).

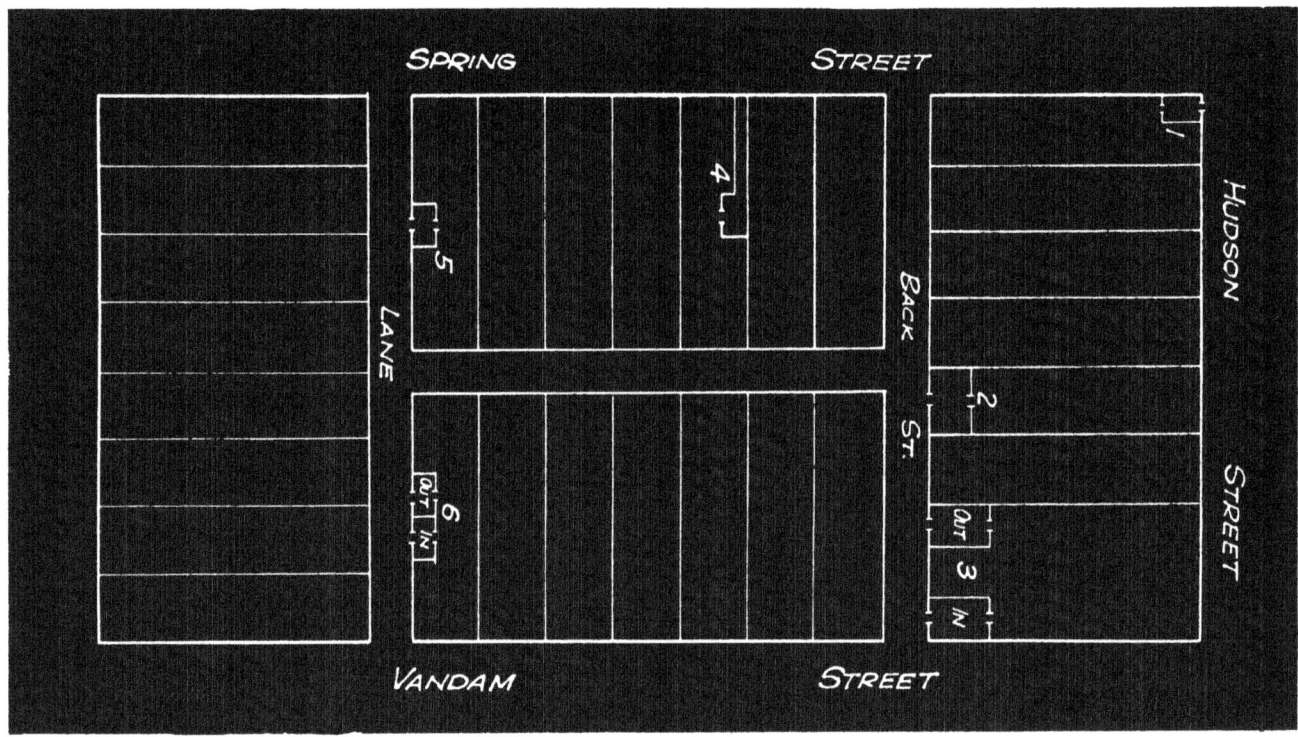

TYPICAL CITY BLOCK SHOWING THE NEW SHIPPING ROOM VARIOUSLY ARRANGED

1. At Front—average capacity.
2. At Rear—double capacity.
3. At Rear—separate room—large capacity.
4. Mid-store—with corridor to front.
5. On Rear Lane.
6. On Rear Lane—double.

The Terminal having during the day located and charted *all* the shipments to be collected by the night service—is able to proceed intelligently. It sends out its shipping clerks in auto-runabouts who make the rounds reaching all shippers before their closing hour—(6 P.M.)—verify the details of shipment—and sign and deliver to the merchant his Bills-of-Lading. The inner door is then locked by both the merchant and the Terminal. The merchant has shipped his goods—they are now in the hands of the Terminal and the outer or street door is then locked by the Terminal agent. During the night the Terminal Truck Driver opens with his key the street door of the Shipping Room—turns on the light—takes on the goods.

NIGHT DELIVERIES

Similar methods will be followed in making *night deliveries*. The inner door of the Shipping Room is locked by the merchant at the close of the day—his premises are secure. During the night—the Terminal Truck Driver opens the street door—deposits the goods and locks with Terminal locks both the inner door and the street door. The goods are still in the hands of the Terminal.

At the opening of business in the morning the Terminal Clerk appears, unlocks the Terminal lock on the inner door of the Shipping Room—takes proper receipt—and the merchant takes the goods into his store. The transaction is complete. (NOTE: Reduced to its simplest form—under suitable regulation—the merchant may close and open the shipping room without the intervention of the terminal official.)

DOUBLE NIGHT SERVICE

For the *double* night service—Collections and Deliveries—the shipping room is divided into two sections—one for incoming—one for outgoing—goods.

DAY SERVICE

With suitable variations similar methods may be used in the Collection and Delivery of freight during the day, and for special or unusual freights special arrangements may be made.

ZONE SERVICE

The business areas of the city will be divided into zones—bounded by arcs of 1 mile—2 miles—3 miles radius—the Terminal at the center. An arc of 2½ miles radius encloses the whole area of Manhattan Island—North River to East River—from the Battery to Central Park—and (over the bridges)—the business areas of Brooklyn from the East River out to City Hall, and also the areas of Williamsburg and Long Island City. The upper parts of the City and the Bronx constitute special service zones. The zones will be sub-divided into districts according to character—such as wholesale and retail areas—heavy and light goods—the market districts—etc.—(as may develop through experience.)

The bulk of the traffic lies within the 1 mile arc—while the 2½ mile arc covers it nearly all—and such a radial distance is a run for the motor truck—even at low speed—of no more than 15 minutes. (Details of Districts—Streets and Avenues are given on other sheets.)

OPERATION

The great power of the Motor Truck demands that it be loaded rapidly and to its full capacity. Trucks will be specially constructed for the service—of large capacity—with chassis adaptable to a variety of demountable bodies suitable for the carriage of all kinds of freights from construction girders—Railroad iron and lumber to boxes of tea—and new and rapid methods of loading and unloading will be developed by the organized system—impracticable heretofore.

The districts and routes—night and day—will be reduced to scientific method—managed from the Chart Room—the runs shortened—the loads increased by the supplemental use of *trailers*—delays eliminated—the average time out and back reduced—the flow of freight facilitated.

The detail analysis of the service—(on other pages)—shows that—420—8-10 ton Motor Trucks and Trailers in continuous service—operating in three shifts will be required to move the Railroad tonnage of the day *in* and *out*—and that the expense over an average radial distance of 2.05 miles—covering 38.8 miles per day—will average .3952 cents per ton or about 2 cents per 100 lbs.

THE NEW CARTAGE CHARGE—A RATE PER 100 POUNDS

Based on this low average expense of operation—in handling the whole tonnage by the organized methods of the New System—it becomes at once possible to establish as the distinctive feature of the new service—a new and attractive charge based on the *actual weight* of the shipment.

A charge per 100 lbs. for cartage is no new thing but its application to *all* freights and all quantities is distinctly new—(except as it is in practice with the express companies). The new rates may be graduated into classes of freight—according to tonnage of the shipment and its zonal location.

The analysis of present cartage methods and rates as made by the recent Commission shows that for the horse-drawn truck the average expense is $1.80 per hour—the average charge $2.07 per ton—for the Motor Truck

$3.32 per hour—$2.40 per ton—the average for both services $2.17 per ton. These comparative figures and facts establish beyond controversy that the present cartage system—both by team and by motor car—is an extravagantly expensive one for the merchant from the burdens of which he will be glad to escape—an equally unsatisfactory one for the cartage man who does not profit by the waste.

APPLICATION OF THE NEW SYSTEM OF FIXED RATE

If the merchant has a small shipment to make—say 500 lbs.—and it is taken at the carman's lowest possible charge for the shortest undelayed round trip—say 1½ hours—($1.80 per hour)—$2.70—the rate *per ton* is $10.80. The New Service takes this shipment for 25 *cents*—(500x5c). If the shipment is 2,000—1,500 or 1,000 lbs.—the cartage remains the same ($2.70)—and the rate amounts respectively to $2.70—$3.60 $5.40 *per ton*. The New Service may take these shipments at 75c—.5625 and .375—saving to the merchant shipper—in the first instance 90% of the whole charge—and in the other three instances—respectively—72-79- and 86% of the whole present expense.

METHODS COMPARED—THE OLD WAY

The Merchant in making shipment which he purposes to catch the Westbound trains of that night—must have it loaded on the truck and started through the streets by the noon hour—or shortly after—in order to secure—favorable position in the Westbound waiting line—accumulating at the Bulkhead shed—for the later the truck gets position in the line—the greater the chance of its being shut out before reaching the shed.

But besides the great expense the merchant is under with his truck waiting in line at the Pier at $1.80 per hour there is the far more serious fact that the necessity for the early shipment not alone hurries him unduly during the morning hours—but—limits his shipping day to a *half day*—and if he have orders for other shipments later—they must lie over to the next day.

THE NEW WAY

The merchant has nothing to do with the carman—hurrying to get him loaded—worrying over the chance of his being shut out—nor with the trouble time labor and the heavy cartage expense. His shipping day is *doubled*. He has before him the whole day down to his closing hour in which he may accept orders for shipment out *that day*. He accumulates his outgoing goods by simply moving them into his *shipping room*—and when the door is locked at the close of the day—*the shipment is made*—and the goods go out *that night*—on the same Westbound trains that his carman now stands in line for hours—to catch—while the expense is *less than one half* that of the *old way*.

THE MERCHANT'S PROFIT

It is estimated the merchant's saving on the annual tonnage of the Railroad traffic—aggregates $5,880,000.

OCCUPANCY OF THE HIGHWAYS

The great physical difference between the cartage systems of the old and the new service is very striking.

The inefficiency, wasteful expense and particularly the disastrous street blockading character of the present method of trucking freight through the streets of New York are only vaguely understood. There have been available heretofore no statistics or records to afford a measure of the service—to indicate the number of trucks employed—horses operated—the expense of time and money—and above all the extent of their occupancy and ruinous use of the highways.

Assuming—as the figures show—that there are 3,232 trucks—viz:—970 Motor Trucks—2,262 double teams drawn by 4,524 horses—now engaged in the railroad service—this number of trucks standing in four lines would fill up West St. *solid* from curb to curb for *four* and a *quarter miles*. That is to say they would occupy the street along the North River front from the Battery up to 47th St. and if they were all teams—for *five miles*—the entire front line from the Battery to New York Central 60th St. Yard.

These figures enable one to visualize the great physical bulk of the trucks and horses now necessary to the movement of the Railroad tonnage and to appreciate the measure of relief that is demanded.

While it is true that the trucks of the present service are not *all* and *always* in West St.—they are *all* and *always* (during the day)—*in the streets*—principally in the *West Side* streets and the *larger part* of them for the *greater part* of the day *in West St.*—standing or drifting—and principally *standing*.

ON THE OTHER HAND

The 10 Ton Motor Truck of the New Service measures 28 ft. and if all the 420 Trucks of the system were similarly lined up in 4 lines—they would cover a little more than *half a mile*—(2,940 feet).

The New Terminal Service will take out of the streets the great congestive and destructive bulk of about *three thousand trucks—four thousand horses*.

MOTOR FLOAT SERVICE

With the establishment of this new *water facility* obstacles physical and financial which together have made it difficult to operate the old car float system with success—*disappear* and the *water route* becomes the natural easy and advantageous means of connection between the Railroad yard and Manhattan Island. It is not too much to say that the phrase—*"schedule of operation"*—is the expression in words of *the key* to the *traffic problem at New York*. The effect of this rapid scheduled service is to bring the rails over from New Jersey to terminate on the Island of Manhattan—and in the *only way* that that is physically *practicable*.

THE FLOAT

The Float is of Catamaran construction—double pointed steel cylinders—combining the maximum of stability and buoyance with the minimum of frictional resistance—fitted with proper surface guards against floating ice and débris,—300 ft. long—44 ft. beam over all—5 ft. draft—3.5 ft. free board (with cargo)—operated by the Diesel fuel oil marine engine—speed 14 knots with cargo against the usual harbor currents—elevated pilot bridge and wheelhouse athwart either end—crossing above the level of the car-tops, connected by fore and aft 3 ft. galleries at the same level—at either side. It is equipped with three parallel tracks on its deck to take 7, 6, 7 cars respectively—capacity a *train of 20 cars*—(space of the center car reserved).

For the complete control of the Float in its passage across—as at moments of impending collision—and especially when entering or leaving the Basin—propeller wheels—(properly housed to avoid friction)—are installed at opposite sides of the boat at either end—operating separately—and at right angles to its axial line—electrically controlled by the Pilot on the bridge—by the use of which as auxiliaries to the rudder—the Float moving in the stream is made to change direction promptly to avoid collision—or at entering or leaving the Basin—its outer end is so held up against cross tidal and storm forces—enabling the boat to enter and leave her dock—not like the Ferry Boat—in oblique lines—its exposed ends swept helplessly up or down stream by the winds and tides while under insufficient headway to be controlled by the rudder—but with precision in a direct line at right angles to the pier head line. The side propeller wheels operating with the same effect as the steam tug pushing against the nose of the steamship when docking.

The facilities at the Basin are described—under the captions—*the system* and *Manhattan Railway Terminal* and the schedules of operation explained—under—*The System in Operation*.

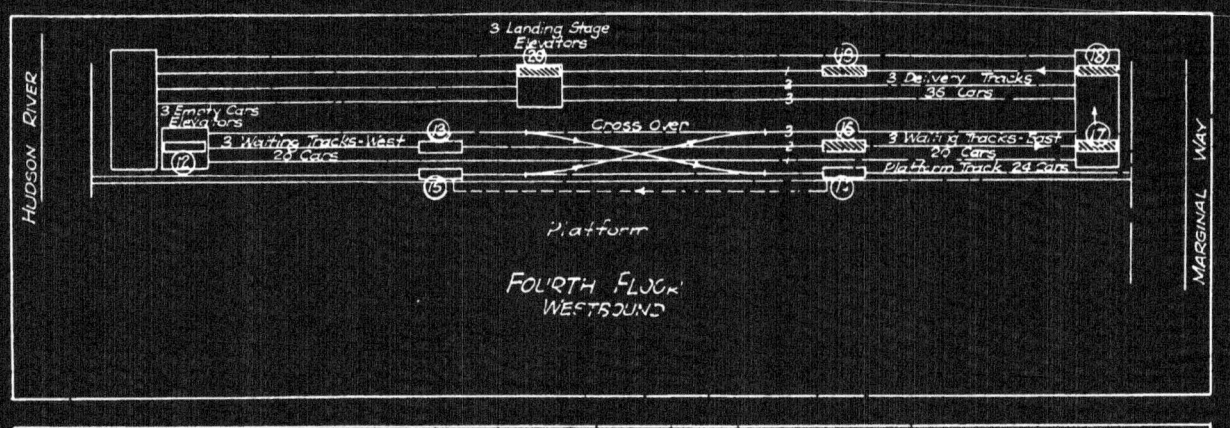

FOURTH FLOOR
WESTBOUND

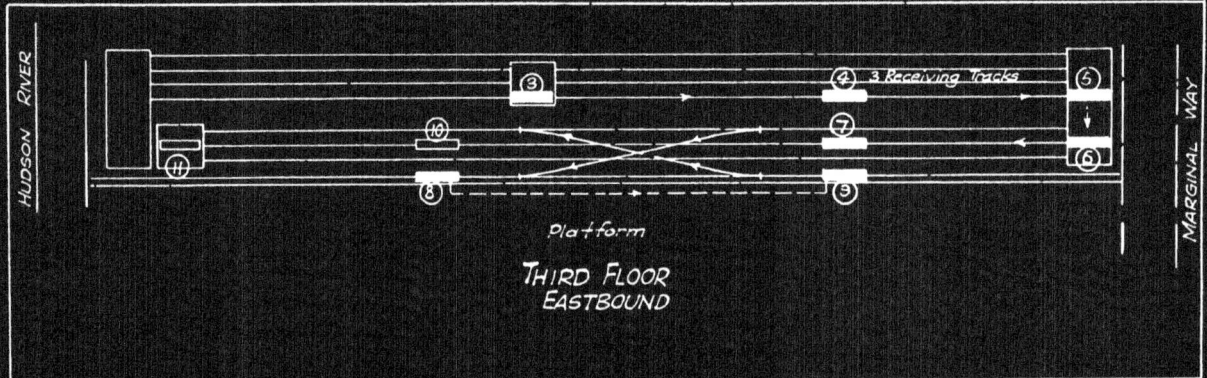

THIRD FLOOR
EASTBOUND

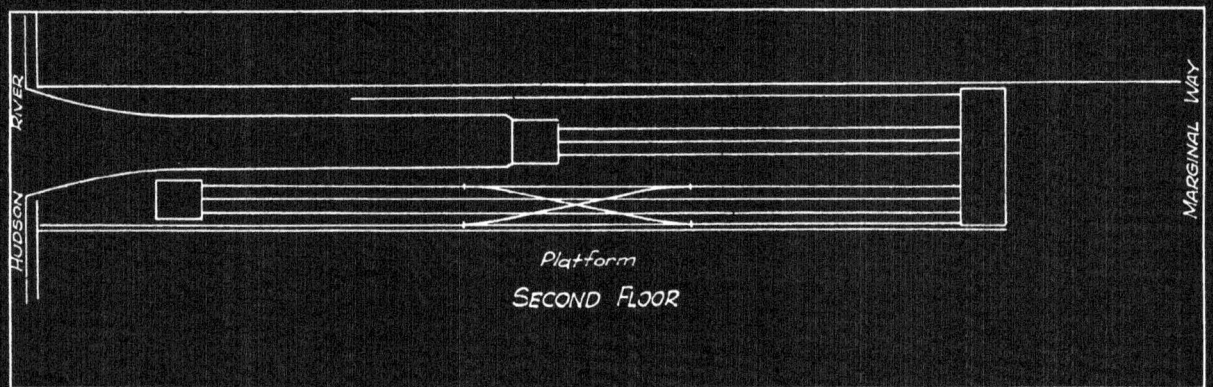

SECOND FLOOR

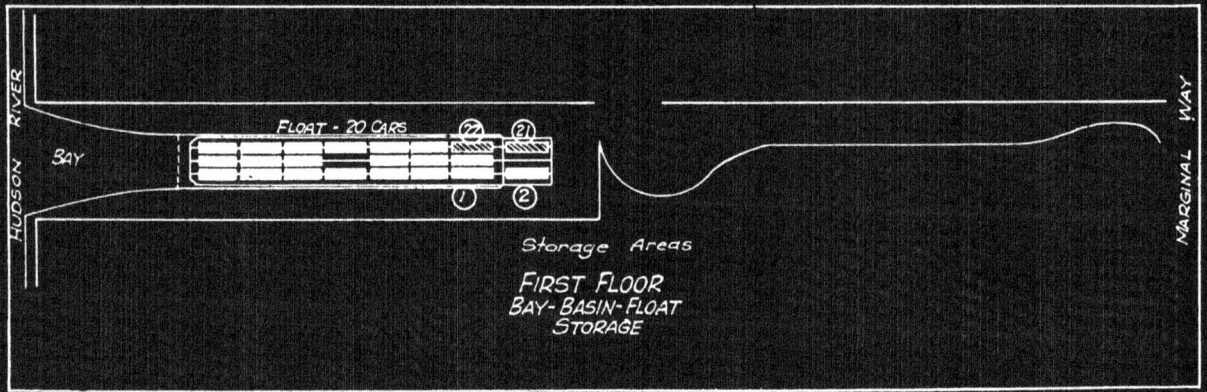

FIRST FLOOR
BAY-BASIN-FLOAT
STORAGE

THE PROCESSIONAL MOVEMENT OF THE SIBLEY SYSTEM OVER THE WATER

The Operative Feature of the Sibley System is the Processional Movement of cars from the New Jersey and New York Central Yards—across the water by rapid float service (the operation of Motor Floats—two for each Railroad Section—leaving opposite sides of the river simultaneously at intervals of two hours—each of capacity to transfer a freight train of Twenty Cars—the Traffic Unit of the System)—to the Basin of the Manhattan Railway Terminal—up by the Elevators to the Eastbound floor and their continuous passage through the Terminal during which—unloaded on the Eastbound floor they are reloaded on the Westbound floor—sent down by the Elevators to the Float in the Basin—and back again to the Yard.

The procession as a whole is governed by a Schedule of Operation which assigns to its various movements and stages ample time for the necessary functions—with a proper margin for emergencies—coördinates movements within the yards—with operation on the tracks of the Terminal—and these with the connecting operations of the Motor Float System on the water—the Motor Truck System on the land—and with all its parts thus brought into harmonious relation—the Terminal as a whole operates as a Single Machine—and the flow of traffic is rapid easy continuous—without confusion—congestion—or serious interruption.

THROUGH THE WAREHOUSE

The movement—always forward in a single line—as in a circle—is here illustrated diagrammatically by the movement of a single car—typical of the movements of Groups of 3 Cars (by the Elevators and Transfer Belts) of Strings of Cars —7—6—7 over the tracks (as illustrated on sheet 3 of the Floor plans and explained in detail on the Schedule of Operation).

NOTE: The Single Car of the diagram if loaded with East bound freight is shown thus ▬▬; with Westbound ▨▨; empty thus ▭; and its successive positions are indicated by numbers from (1) the arrival of the Float in the Basin (at 1st Floor level) with 20 loaded Eastbound Cars (usually—but for this illustrative occasion one space (22) is left vacant) progressively through the warehouse to (22) when it is returned to the Float reloaded on its way back to the yard.

AT THE BASIN

The Float from the Yard arrives with 20 loaded East bound Cars—on 3 tracks—7—8—7 (one car space at the center left vacant). They are sent up in groups of 3 by the 3 Elevator Landing Stages—which descend to the level of the deck of the Float—here typified by the movement of one car (1) to its position on the Elevator (2).

ON THE 3RD OR EAST BOUND FLOOR

The Elevator rises with the (illustrative) Car (in practice 3 elevators rise with 3 Cars) to the level of the 3rd or Eastbound floor (3); it moves East to the Receiving Tracks (4) in the Transfer Belt (5) laterally to (6) to the Waiting Tracks East (7) is switched In by the by the Cross over to the unloading track at platform (8) reversed and run back to final unloading position (8) switched Out—Empty—to Waiting Tracks—West—(10) sent up by the (3) Elevators for Empty Cars (11) to the 4th or West Bound floor to be reloaded (12).

ON THE 4TH OR WEST BOUND FLOOR

The Empty Car from the Eastbound floor below arrives at (12) is run out to the Waiting Tracks West (13)—switched In by the Crossover to the loading track at platform (14) reversed and run back to final loading position (15)—switched Out loaded—to the Waiting Tracks East (16) to the Transfer Belt (17) moved laterally to (18) to the Delivery Tracks (19) to the Landing Stage Elevator (20) sent down to the level of the Float in the Basin (21) and delivered to the Float (22) for transfer to the Yard.

NOTE: For the purpose of this illustration only one car is taken off the Float—and one returned—but in practice—of course—all are similarly taken off and returned—*also* for the purposes of this illustration—Eastbound freight is handled over the 3rd Eastbound floor—while in practice it is handled in part and similarly—on the 2nd (Eastbound) or Food Floor.

THE SCHEDULE OF OPERATION

For each of these movements cars have not only their exclusive times and therefore "right of way" but exclusive tracks—and these on separate floors—over which they move always in one direction—as on a single line.

Similarly Loaded cars have the exclusive use of the 3 Landing Stage Elevators (at the center), Empty cars—the 3 Empty Car Elevators (at the West end).

Cars enter the floor at one end—leave it at the other—on the East Bound floors they enter at the East leave at the West end—on the West bound floor they enter at the West and leave at the East end.

In their progress through the warehouse—therefore for cars to meet—collide, cross or interfere with the movements of others—is not physically possible.

ACCIDENT—THE ELEVATORS—THE FLOATS

The Elevators are in sets of 3—so that for each section—or Railroad—there are 3 Landing Stages—3 Empty Car Elevators and if accident happen to any one of these there are 2 others in the same set with excess capacity sufficient for the work of 3.

Any such disability—however would at most affect only the railroad section in which it occurred—curtailing its capacity temporarily by $\frac{1}{3}$ and that of the Terminal by 1/24th.

But (as will be seen) the facilities of the Terminal are so far in excess of those necessary for the transfer of the present annual volume of traffic that their curtailment by such a fraction or even in much larger proportion could not diminish the current of traffic—the Terminal would still be capable of handling the volume to be transferred.

Other possible happenings are such as might ordinarily occur in any large industrial plant—and may be promptly met.

In a word the Margin of Excess Capacity of the Terminal is an Insurance against the effect of accident—and an Assurance of Uninterrupted Operation and the Continuous Flow of Traffic.

THE PROCESSION

One Hundred Cars are in progress through the warehouse in any given cycle and the time of passage of a Single Car—or the Unit of Traffic of 20 Cars—Loaded—from the time of sailing of the Float from the Yard—to the time of re-arrival of the Float at the Yard with the same car or cars reloaded—is 8 Hours—25 Minutes. The time required from break-up yard—to break-up yard again by the present system (as reported by the Harbor Commission) is $3\frac{1}{2}$ days.

MOTOR FLOATS

The number of Motor Floats employed is 2 for each Railroad—16 for the Manhattan Railway Terminal substituting a system which now uses in the Railroad Pier Station Service—165 Floats—65 Tug Boats.

CAPACITY

The transfer capacity of the System for the day of 24 hours on one-twelfth schedule is 3,840 Cars if loaded with but 10 tons In—667 tons Out—9,600,000 annual tons—with 30 tons In—20 tons Out—28,800,000 Annual Tons—the present volume to be transferred is estimated by the Commission at 8,500,000 Tons.

THE EFFECT OF THE SYSTEM

In practical effect The Sibley System extends the rails of the West Side Trunk Line Railroads Across the Water—to terminate on Manhattan Island—each in its Own Exclusive Terminal—a consummation Otherwise Impossible.

THE SYSTEM IN OPERATION

The distinctive operative feature of the System—(illustrated graphically by—blueprint—*the processional movement*)—is the establishment of a *continuous current* of Cars—which flowing from the yard—crosses the Hudson—passes through the Terminal—and recrosses the water—back again to the yard.

The current enters the Manhattan Terminal at the Basin—rises from the Float by the first set of Elevators —(at the center of the warehouse)—to the East end of the 3rd or Eastbound floor—then turns and flows over that floor from East to West—first *in* to the platform where cars are *unloaded*—then *out*—(cars *empty*)—to the West end of the floor. Thence it rises by the second set of Elevators—(for *empty* cars)—to the West end of the 4th or Westbound floor directly overhead—and flows over that floor in the reverse direction—(from West to East)—first *in* to the platform where Cars are *reloaded*—then *out*—to the East end of the floor—down by the first set of Elevators—(at center)—to the Float and back again to the Yard.

In this *procession* movements *within* the warehouse are in accord with movements *across* the water—and all its separate *functions* in every department are so correlated with ample time assigned to each—that the flow is orderly—constant—rapid—without haste yet without delay—and the current of movement being along a single line—always forward—as along the line of a circle—cars never meet—never overtake or cross each other—and therefore collision, congestion and confusion are eliminated.

The movement of the current—and the periods of its several functions—are governed by a definite *schedule of operation*—which controlling as well at the yards—and on the water—as within the warehouse—the *system as a whole* operates as a *single machine*.

THE OPERATING KEY

In regulating the movement of this current and determining the periods of its separate functions *two units* are developed as *standards*—one of *traffic*—the other of *time*—and these together form the *operating* basis or *key* of the system and determine its Schedule of Operation.

The *traffic unit* is a *train of twenty standard cars*—the *time unit* is the time allowed for the *loading*—(or unloading)—of *one* car—(or simultaneously a train of 20 cars—the traffic unit)—at the platform—(including the time of switching in and out)—with a proper margin of time and trackway for the necessary related movements.

The *time unit* is fixed by Schedule at—(various periods—adapted to the traffic—that used here for the purposes of illustration is the period of)—*two hours*—a multiple part—(*one-twelfth*)—of the day—and all other related movements are effected within that definite period—called the *Cycle of Operation*.

THE SWITCH SYSTEM

To effect rapid and easy movement of cars within the Warehouse from rail to rail *two* electrically controlled and operated switching methods are used:—

1. *The cross over* for connection of the Waiting Tracks with the parallel *load line* track at the platform.
2. *The transfer belt* extending across the heads of all tracks at East and West end of platform—(except the platform line)—over which the Transfer Table moves laterally to transfer cars between Waiting and parallel Receiving—Delivering Tracks.

NOTE: The Crossover rails—Waiting Tracks East and West—Platform Track—Receiving Tracks—Delivering Tracks and Transfer Belts—are shown on the *main floor plans*—and the Crossover rails in working detail on the blue print *special track work*.

SCHEDULE MOVEMENTS WITHIN THE WAREHOUSE

The movement of the car or a *string* of *seven* cars over a straight track—or the crossover rails—or of one car—or groups of 3 cars abreast—on 3 tracks—either on the tracks of the warehouse or into and out of the Elevators—to and from and over the Transfer Belt—to and from and on the Float—is effected by electrically operated cables laid along the lines of track with adaptable attaching—detaching—mechanisms—the operator starting the car or a string of cars promptly and stopping it with precision.

PRACTICAL DEMONSTRATION

These methods need no other *demonstration* of practicability than that afforded by their adoption and use by the Engineering Staff of the recent Commission in the preparation of its Automatic Electric plan—and the fact that they are all well within the practice of Electrical Engineering—already established and in use.

THE ELEVATORS

The Elevators are in sets of 3—each of capacity to take one car—and though constructed and operated independently—(as a guard against accident)—are nevertheless practically operated as a unit of 3 cars capacity.

NOTE—ON PRACTICAL OPERATION

The movement of cars on and off the Float and their elevation to upper levels are governed with precision by micro-leveling and interlocking devices which bring the elevator to a stop promptly at the exact level of the floor or the float and hold it there. Similarly their movement on the floors of the warehouse and over the switches are effected with celerity and certainty—cars stopping at a line without chock or brake.

These methods of movement within the terminal devised three years prior to the publication of the Automatic Electric plan proved to be essentially the same as those used for that plan by the Engineering staff of the Commission and therefore need no demonstration.

But while the movements in the two systems are somewhat similar—the margins of time allowed by the water system are greater than those which the Engineers of the Commission deemed ample for the Automatic plan—for example:

In describing the elevator movement of the Automatic system the report of the Commission says:

Making due allowances for the time required for opening and closing gates—moving cars on and off the elevators—and accelerating and decelerating the elevators—the cycle of the main elevator will be approximately 230 seconds under the most unfavorable conditions—namely when the elevator (takes on the inbound car (1) at the track level in the tunnel)—goes the 91 ft. to the top floor to discharge its inbound car (2) descends 34 ft. to the bottom floor to receive an outbound car (3) and then descends the remaining 57 ft. (to track level to discharge its outbound car (4)).

Analysis of these movements shows that the corresponding cycle of the main elevator of the Water System—(moving up in its longest flight 61.5 ft. to the Westbound floor and down again to the Float deck—total 123 ft.)—with 2 gate movements (in and out) as against 4 by Automatic—the time allowed by the Automatic scale is 131.2 seconds—while the time allowed by the scale of the Water System is 167 seconds—a marginal excess of 27% beyond that considered ample by the Commission's staff.

Other schedule periods for movements of cars—at the cross over—at the Transfer Belt and by the Empty Car Elevators—of the Water System—are similarly excessive.

SPEED—DISTANCE—TIME

The speed of the transfer facilities—the distances traversed and the estimated time required for all such movements—as reckoned from position on one level to position on another—or from one set of tracks to another on same level—are as follows:

Speed	Miles Hour	Feet Min.
Elevators	1.13	100
Transfer Belt	2.00	176
Crossover Rails	4.00	352
Average Speed of Switching in Yards	5.00	440

		Feet	*Required Time*	
			Min.	*Sec.*
DISTANCE				
Elevators—longest flight *up* or *down* 61.5 (x2)		123	1	17
Transfer Belt—longest movement *over* or *back* (91)		182	1	3
Crossover Rails—(as below)				

TIME
  At the Elevators

	Min.	Sec.
Putting cars on and off	1	30
Up and *down* (123 ft.)	1	17
Total	2	47
Schedule Time	5	00
Margin 80 per cent	2	13

  At the Transfer Belt

	Min.	Sec.
Putting cars on and off	1	30
Over and *back* (182 ft.)	1	3
Total	2	33
Schedule Time	5	00
Margin 96%	2	27

At the Cross-over Rails	*Distance Ft.*				*Full Speed Dist.*	*M.*	*S.*	*Required Time Min.*	*Sec.*
STRING 1—OVER	(210	280	40)	530	440	1	15	1	45
REVERSE	(280	280	40)	600	510	1	27	1	57
2—OVER	(	240	40)	280	190	0	33	1	03
REVERSE	(40	240	40)	320	230	0	40	1	10
3—OVER	(	280	70)	350	260	0	45	1	15
FINAL REVERSE of No. 2	(	70	40)	110	20	0	03	0	33
Total				2190				7	43
Schedule Time								15	00
Margin 94%								7	17

NOTE: In the above table—(at the Cross-over Rails)—30 seconds are added in the column of required time of each string movement for stopping and starting.

In estimating time at Cross-over 45 ft.—(a car length)—at each end (for starting and stopping)—is reckoned at half speed rate—remainder at full.

In estimating distances—strings 2 and 3 are reckoned from the *in* switch—as both take positions there—in order)—during the time used for other movements.

Similarly—cars are moved to or from position at the Elevator gate—at the Float—or on the floors—and to or from position at the Transfer Belt on the floors—during the movement of either the Elevator or the Transfer platform and the required time for each such movement therefore includes but the time necessary to move the car (its length) on or off Elevator or Belt—plus the round trip movement in either case.

MOTOR FLOAT OPERATION—AT THE FLOAT

Two floats are operated in each Railroad section—leaving opposite sides of the River at the same schedule time—passing in midstream.

To take on or put off its complement of 20 cars at either side of the water—in *seven* movements—operating under the *2 hour cycle:*—

	Min.	*Sec.*
SCHEDULE TIME	35	00
ESTIMATED REQUIRED TIME (2 M. 47 S. x 7)	19	29
MARGIN—80%	15	31

TO CROSS THE HUDSON

SPEED.—The capacity speed of the Motor Float is 14 Knots with cargo against the normal Harbor currents. The average speed of the North River Ferry Boat is about 12 Knots and the regularity of their trips is a daily demonstration of the practical operation of the Motor Float Schedule.

DISTANCES.—The Railroads are located in the Manhattan Railway Terminal (tentatively) in the order shown—section 1 at the South—section 8 at the north end—which corresponds with the order of their location on the shore line—by which arrangement the Float fairway—across the water—of no section is crossed by that of any other.

The distances from the Manhattan Railway Terminal to the several Railroad yards—and the time required for the Motor Float—to cross—at *full*—at *three-quarter* and at *half speed*—and (for comparison) the time required by the North River Ferry Boat to cover the same distances—at average speed—are as follows:

| | | | Motor Float | | | Ferry | Terminal |
| | | Dist. | Full | ¾ | Half | Avg. | Schedule |
Railroads	Location	Miles	Min.	Min.	Min.	Min.	Min.
SECTION 1 Balto. & Ohio	Staten Island	6.40	24.6	32.8	49.2	33.2	33
2 Lehigh Valley	Communipaw	1.80	7.5		15.0	10.1	25
3 Central of N. J.	Communipaw	1.80	7.5		15.0	10.1	25
4 Pennsylvania	Jersey City	1.40	6.0		12.0	8.1	25
5 Erie	Jersey City	1.00	4.6		9.2	6.2	25
6 D. L. W.	Hoboken	.86	4.0		8.0	5.0	25
7 West Sh. (Ont.-W.)	Weehawken	2.90	12.5	15.5	25.0	15.7	25
8 N. Y. Central	60th St., Man.	3.60	14.2	18.9	28.4	19.3	25
	Manhattanville	7.10	27.2	35.3	54.4	36.7	36
	Spuyten Duyvil	11.70	44.4	59.1	88.8	59.7	60

NOTE: In computing the crossing time for the Motor Float at all speeds as well as the time for the Ferry Boat—1,200 ft.—viz.—600 at the beginning of the trip in getting under full headway—600 at the end—for slowing down and coming to a stop—are reckoned at one-half the speed of the remainder.

The time required for the Crossing of the Railroads is as follows:

| | *Required Time* | | | | | |
| | Full Speed | ¾ Speed | Half Speed | Schedule Time | Margin | Per |
Railroads	Min.	Min.	Min.	Min.	Min.	Cent
1. Balto.-Ohio	24.6	...	...	33.0	8.4	34
Balto.-Ohio	...	32.8	...	33.0	.2	0
2. Lehigh Valley ⎫						
3. Central of New Jersey ⎬ Avg.	5.9	...	...	25.0	19.1	323
4. Pennsylvania ⎭						
5. Erie ⎫ Avg.	...	...	11.8	25.0	13.2	112
6. Del.-Lackawanna ⎭						
7. West Shore	12.5	...	...	25.0	12.5	100
		15.5	...	25.0	9.5	60
8. N. Y. Central			25.0	25.0	.0	0
At 60th Street	14.2	...	...	25.0	10.8	76
At 60th Street	...	18.9	...	25.0	6.1	32
At Manhattanville	27.2	...	...	36.0	8.8	32
At Manhattanville	...	35.3	...	36.0	.7	0
At Spuyten Duyvil	44.4	...	...	60.0	15.6	35
At Spuyten Duyvil	...	59.1	...	60.0	.9	0

FLOAT SCHEDULE COORDINATION

While the Schedules for the several sections of the Terminal are arranged with the same intervals for and between functions and the Cycle of Operation is the same in every section—nevertheless—the time of *beginning* the Cycle in the several sections may be varied—as traffic advantage may require without affecting the Cycle itself—for illustration:

The Floats of Sec. 1—leaving opposite sides of the water at 12.45 reach their respective docks at 1.10. They do not leave again until 2.45—therefore between 1.10 and 2.45—1 hour and 35 minutes—the stream is clear of Motor Floats. Availing of this period of 95 minutes of free fairway—the following schedule arranged with 5 intervals of 19 minutes each—(95 min.)—between the operations of the first 6 sections will be of traffic advantage:

FIRST CYCLE—FLOAT

	Begins to Load at Either Side	*Sails*	*In Opposite Dock*
Sec. 1	12.00	12.45	1.10
Sec. 2	12.19	1.04	1.29
Sec. 3	12.38	1.23	1.48
Sec. 4	12.57	1.42	2.07
Sec. 5	1.16	2.01	2.26
Sec. 6	1.35	2.20	2.45

SECOND CYCLE

Sec. 1	2.00	2.45	3.10
Sec. 2	2.19	3.04	3.29
Sec. 3	2.38	3.23	3.48
Sec. 4	2.57	3.42	4.07
Sec. 5	3.16	4.01	4.26
Sec. 6	3.35	4.20	4.45

The Float fairway of Section 1 is *down* the stream—2, 3, 4, 5 and 6—*across* the River—and—7 and 8—*up* the stream—therefore the last two 7 and 8 may without interfering with operations of other sections—operate at the same schedule time respectively as sections 1 and 2.

CLEARING THE STREAM OF CONGESTION

By this advantageous arrangement of schedule there need *never* be more than 8 Floats in the stream—at *any time*—but 4 for more than *two-thirds* the time—and only *two*—for the *major part* of the time—and this substitution of at most *sixteen*—at least—only *eight*—four or two Motor Floats—for the more than *two hundred*—Car Floats and steam Tugs now used in the Manhattan Railroad traffic—must greatly relieve the stream of its present crowded conditions.

THE SCHEDULE PERIOD CONSIDERED

The time of loading the freight car under existing conditions—varying from 2 to 3 hours—affords no proper measure of the time necessary at the new Terminal where the distinctive features are *facility* and *celerity*.

Electric mechanisms for the movement of the freight car the continuous operation of moving freight belts for the rapid transfer of freight across the platform from truck to car—from car to truck and modern electrical appliances—are accessories that together with the relative location of the car and its particular freight exactly opposite each other will wholly eliminate the Terminal delays of to-day. The 8-10-ton truck will be loaded or unloaded at one side of the platform—rapidly—the function reduced to the least possible period by the anticipatory classification and location of freight by zones—routes—consignees—*inward*,—by cars—routes—destinations—consignees *outward*,—all made *practical* now by the new facilities but *never before possible*. *Truck* movements and truck loading so expedited will be further reduced to a lesser fraction of time by the use of demountable bodies ready loaded—while cars with these new facilities of segregated—classified and routed freight—definitely located—*in* and *out*, will be *loaded*—or *unloaded*—within *one hour*.

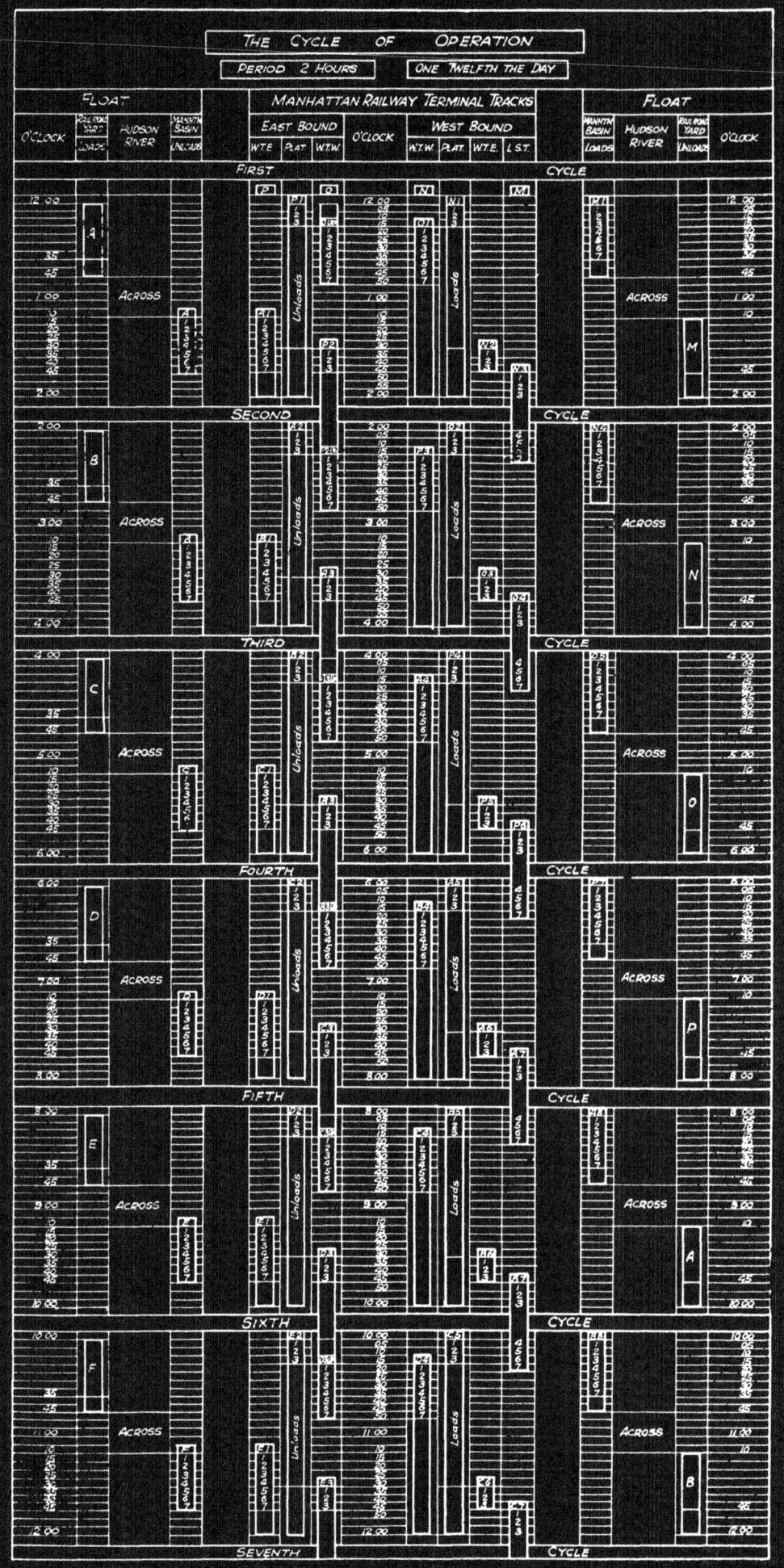

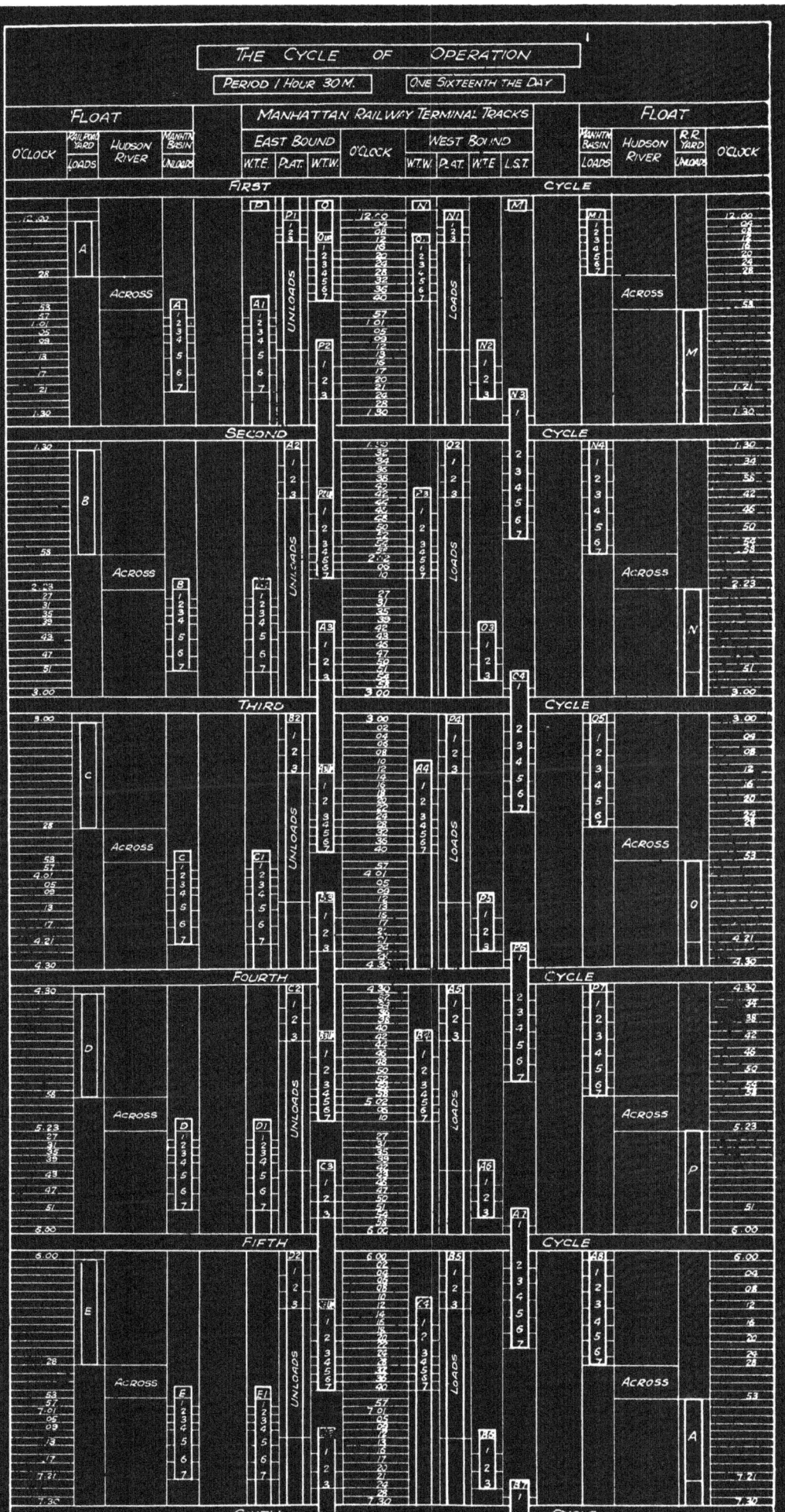

THE CYCLE OF OPERATION

In the analysis of movements within the warehouse and on the water—and the time required for each such movement—it is demonstrated that the periods allotted the several functions under the illustrative Cycle of operation—(*two hours*)—and the margins of time allowed are greater than are necessary and that shorter Cycles—one of *one-sixteenth* the day—*1 hour 30 min.* and another of *one-twentieth* the day—*1 hour 12 min.* are both operative *within* the time ascertained to be necessary for all the separate functions.

On the other hand the capacity of the Terminal System being far in excess of present needs the Cycle may if traffic require be extended to *one-tenth* the day *2 hours 24 min.* or *one-eighth* the day—*3 hours.*

Cycle Tables for these different periods have been developed—the blue prints of which accompany these sheets. The elasticity of the Cycle plan permits either contraction or extension.

The *essential* thing is the practically *operative character* of the System—whether the Cycle be extended or contracted—and after a period of practical experience under the hands of expert traffic men—and advantageous adjustments of the Schedule to traffic needs—the System will easily establish itself by practical demonstration as the *ideal method* of handling the great volume of the traffic of the *West Side* Railroads between the shores of New Jersey and Manhattan.

ONE ILLUSTRATIVE CYCLE—IN PRACTICAL OPERATION—IN ONE RAILROAD SECTION

In order to illustrate the practical operation of the *cycle* of *one* Railroad section—(and therefore of the system since the Cycles follow each other in succession indefinitely)—it is necessary at the beginning of operations to (theoretically)—prime the Terminals by locating—*trains of cars* both *loaded* and *empty* at the several points in the warehouses as they would have been left at the end of a preceding operating period or Cycle and the two Floats of the section—one at the Manhattan Basin the other at the Railroad yard.

Assuming then a supply of freight at proper points—suppose operations to begin at 12 o'clock simultaneously at the warehouse—in the several departments—and at the yard—and at that hour a train of 20 *loaded* Eastbound cars is ready at the yard—and on the floors of the Manhattan Terminal are located other trains of cars—(as designated on the Cycle Table—which follows) viz.:

Train	*Cars*			
M	20	*Loaded*—West bound	—on Delivery Tracks	(LST) of 4th (Westbound) floor.
N	20	*Empty*	on Waiting Tracks West(WTW)	of 4th (Westbound) floor.
O	20	*Empty*	on Waiting Tracks West(WTW)	of 3rd (Eastbound) floor.
P	20	*Loaded*—East bound	on Receiving Tracks	(WTE) of 3rd (Eastbound) floor.

From that moment of the beginning of operations the movements of the system—in every department—are clearly set out in the (blue print) Cycle Table or Schedule of Operation—and the table is explained as follows:

THE CYCLE TABLE

The Table shows the operation of the system under the *one-twelfth* period for 12 hours—six complete Cycles—far enough to illustrate its easy—regular—movement and establish the current of traffic—Eastbound trains—A, B, C—coming in *loaded*—Westbound trains—A, B, C—going out *reloaded*—in a continuous orderly stream—and thereafter the movement goes on in successive rhythmic Cycles—during the period of operation—whether that be limited to 8 hours, 12, 18, or 24 hours as traffic conditions may require.

The table is separated into 3 sections—those at the right and left showing the movements at the yard—on the River and at the Basin—that at the center those *within* the Terminal—on the Tracks and by the Elevators. The columns of the central section represent the several tracks on the respective Eastbound—Westbound floors viz.:—W.T.E.—the Waiting Tracks East—W.T.W.—the Waiting Tracks West—L.S.T.—the Delivery and Receiving Tracks—(or Landing Stage Tracks)—and *plat*—the load line or platform track. (The locations of these several tracks in the warehouse are shown on the floor blue prints.)

The Time Columns are repeated for convenience in showing such divisions of time as correspond to movements in each section of the table.

The letters M.N.O.P.—at the head of the columns represent the track locations of the priming lots—or *trains*—of cars (as explained above)—and A, B, C, etc., the initial Trains of cars—coming over from the yard—loaded with regular East bound freight and passing out loaded with regular Westbound freight. The figures enclosed in the box frames indicate the number of movements of the groups and strings of cars of the train designated—(by letter)—and the o'clock lines show the measure of time of each such movement. The figures attached to the letters—as N. 1, P. 4, A. 3—indicate the ordinal location of each train in its passage through the warehouse—thus N. 1 indicates the first movement or location of train N.—P. 4 the fourth of train P.—and so on.

That part of the box frame in solid color indicates the extent of the waiting period of—(1) the *Float*—(2)—the *Track*—or (3)—the *Train*—examples:

Train A is loaded to the boat at the yard—12.00-12.35 and (1) the *Float waits* 10 minutes—(12.35-12.45—Train O loads with Westbound freight—2.15-3.30—(0.2)—the cars are shifted out—(to 0.3)—3.30-3.45—and (2) the *Track waits*—15 minutes—(until P is shifted in—(P. 4) at the beginning of the next Cycle (4.00)—Train P unloads at the Eastbound platform—12.15 to 1.30—is shifted out to P. 2—1.30-1.45—and (3) the *Train waits*—30 minutes—(until 2.15 in the next Cycle—when it begins its movement *up* to Westbound floor.)

PASSAGE OF A TRAIN OF TWENTY CARS THROUGH MANHATTAN RAILWAY TERMINAL

AS ILLUSTRATED BY BLUE PRINT SHEET OF THE THIRD FLOOR IN CONNECTION WITH THE TABLE OF CYCLE OPERATION

The *loaded train* rises from the Float in the Basin under the warehouse—by the Landing Stage Elevators at the center of the Terminal—to the Eastbound floor—passes over that floor from the *East End*—to the *West End*—then —*unloaded*—it rises by the *Empty Car Elevators* (at the West End) to the Westbound floor above and passes over that floor in the *reverse* direction from the *West End* to the *East End*—then—*reloaded*—it is sent *down*—by the Landing Stage Elevators to the Float for transfer to the yard.

The line of march is always forward—continuous—as along the line of a circle and trains move only when tracks are clear—with time table right of way—and ample time for their movements—with proper waiting periods between.

For the purposes of this illustration *Train A* of the Cycle Table is selected. Its movements are shown on the Cycle Table from A at the yard at 12 o'clock—A. 1 to A. 8—through the Terminal—and A at the yard again at 9.45 o'clock—and illustrated from the Basin over the Eastbound floor—and Westbound floor—to the Basin again—on the Blue Print Sheet No. 3.

NOTE: The movements of any single train are of course all in one section—but for the purposes of this illustration the 8 sections of sheet 3—are used to show the successive movements in one section.

The Cycle Table shows that at 12 o'clock the Float at the yard begins to take on *Train A*—at 12.35 the loading is complete—at 12.45 the Float sails—and (by schedule) arrives at Manhattan Basin 25 minutes later—1.10—(the actual average time of crossing is 9 min.). The Float *unloads* (A) in 35 minutes—1.10-1.45—sending the train up by the Landing Stage Elevators—(and over the *Receiving Tracks* on the Eastbound floor)—to the Waiting Tracks *East*—A. 1 (on the Table).

The Third Floor Sheet shows at:

SECTION 1.—The *loaded* train passing over the *Receiving Tracks*—(in 3 strings—7.6.7—(A. 20 (cars)) to the Transfer Belt—over which it moves laterally—(in groups of 3) to the train's first position—(B20 on the sheet)—in 3 strings—on the waiting Tracks *East*—(A. 1 on the table). Here the Train waits 15 minutes—(1.45-2.00) until the beginning of the next Cycle (of the Table) to be switched *in* to platform to be *unloaded*.

SECTION 2.—At the beginning of the next Cycle (2.00 o'clock) the train begins to switch *in* to platform—string No. 1 (that next to the platform track) moves first over the crossover rails—enters the platform Track at switch K (C. 7 (cars)) continuing to clear the switch—when it is reversed and run back to position at the East end of the platform track clearing the switch L.

SECTION 3.—String 2 having meantime moved over the crossover rails—its head at switch K—is ready to enter and when string No. 1—reversed has cleared the switch—it moves *in* to D. 6—is reversed and run back to connection with C. 7—clearing switch K.

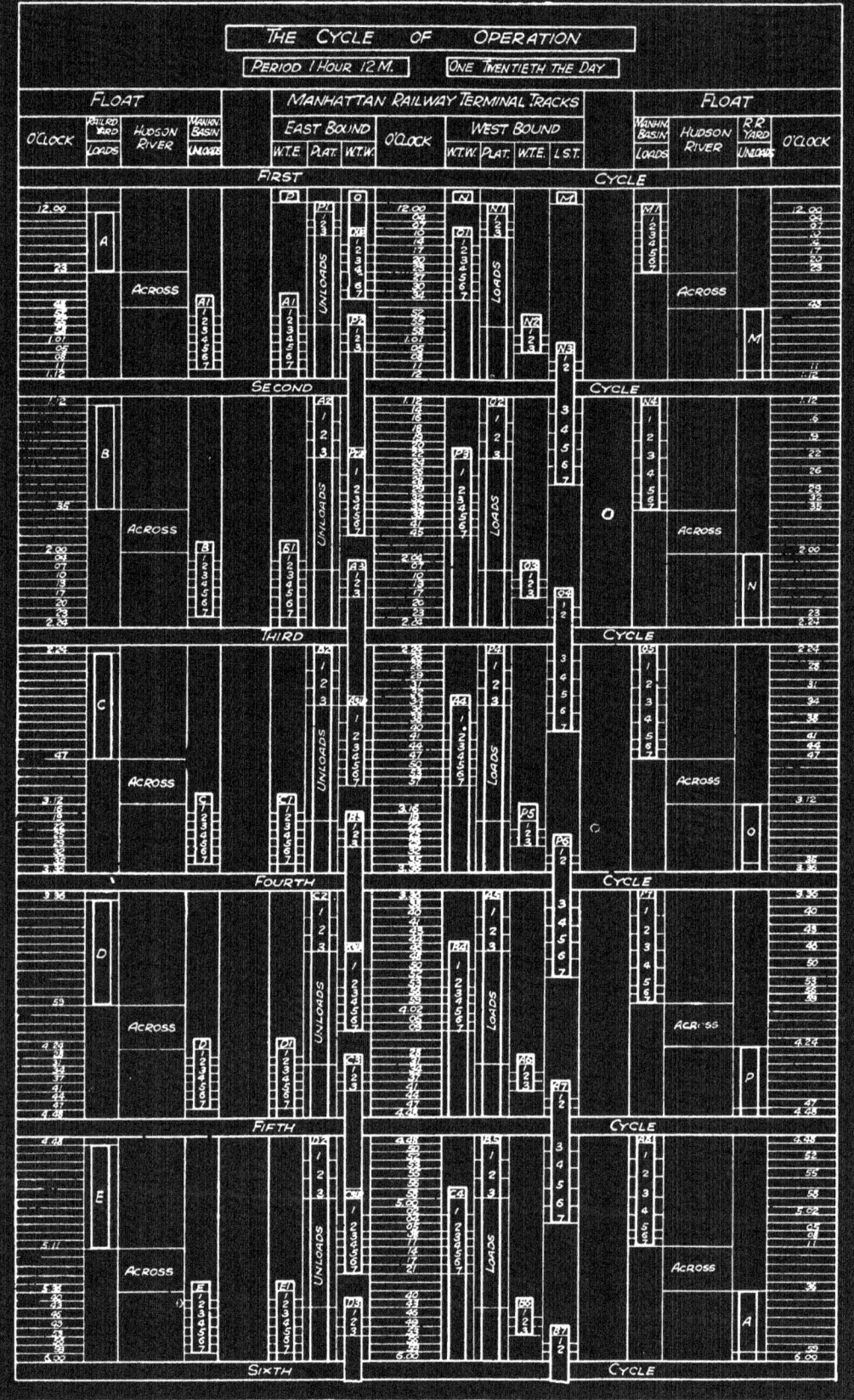

NOTE – These Tables refer to the ONE TWELFTH – 2 HOUR CYCLE

TABLE 1
THE SYNCHRONIZED OPERATIONS OF ONE CYCLE

		O'CLOCK		
AT THE YARD	A	12.00	A TRAIN of 20 LOADED East Bound cars begins to be taken on the Float	
ON 4th W.B. FLOOR	M		A TRAIN of 20 LOADED West Bound Cars – standing in 3 strings (7-5-7) on the Delivery Tracks (W1) by Landing Stage Elevators to the deck of the Float begins to go down (M) by Landing Stage Elevators to the deck of the Float	
ON 3rd E.B. FLOOR	P		A TRAIN of 20 LOADED East Bound cars standing in 3 strings on the Waiting Tracks East of the East bound floor begins to be switched in (D1) to the Platform – to be UNLOADED	
ON 4th W.B. FLOOR	N		A TRAIN of 20 EMPTY cars – standing in 3 strings on the Waiting Tracks West begins to be switched in (N1) to be LOADED	
ON 3rd FLOOR	P	2.00 35	has been switched in – to D.1 and begins to UNLOAD	
ON 4th FLOOR	N	45	has been switched in – to N.1 and begins to LOAD	
	O	2.15 3.10	A TRAIN of 20 EMPTY cars on the Waiting Tracks West begins to go up by the Empty Car Elevators to the Westbound Floor (which (N having been switched in) are now clear) – to its Q.1 position.	
AT THE YARD	A	2.35 4.00 15	Has been taken on the Float	
AT MANHATTAN	M	2.46 5.30 45	Has been taken on the Float	
AT THE YARD	A		Sails	
	M	6.15 50	Sails	
ON 4th FLOOR	O	2.50 8.00 15	Has completed its movement and is in position (Q.1) on the Waiting Tracks West – where it waits its schedule time (at the beginning of the next cycle) – to be switched in – to be LOADED (Q.2)	
AT THE YARD	M	9.30 45	Arrives and the Float begins to deliver the Cars to the yard. Arrives and the Float begins to send up the Cars by the Landing Stage Elevators to the Waiting Tracks East of the 3rd E.B.Floor (A.1)	
	A	1.10	sent over Transfer Belt laterally to Landing Stage Tracks (or DELIVERY TRACKS) on W.B. floor ready for Float	
ON 3rd FLOOR	P	1.30	Has been UNLOADED and begins to be switched out in 3 strings to the Waiting Tracks West (P.2)	
ON 4th FLOOR	N	10.00 35	sent down by the Landing Stage Elevators to the Float	
AT MANHATTAN 3rd FLR	P	1.45	Has been LOADED and begins to be switched out in 3 strings to the Waiting Tracks East (N.2)	
ON 3rd FLOOR	A		Has completed its movement up from the Float and is in position on the Waiting Tracks East (A.1)	
ON 4th W.B. FLOOR	N	2.00 11.10 to 45	Begins to be transferred (in groups of 3) from the Waiting Tracks East (N.2) to the Delivery Tracks (3,5,7)(N.3)	
	N	12.00	Has completed 3 of the stage movements over Transfer Belt and 3 cars of N are on the Delivery Tracks (N.3) on the Landing Stage ready for the Float when six begins to load (N.4) at the beginning of the next cycle (The movement N.2 to N.3 is continued and completed at 2:20 in next cycle)	

TABLE 2
THE CONTINUOUS PASSAGE OF A SINGLE TRAIN OF CARS

This Table shows the several stages and time of movement of any specific TRAIN OF CARS – LOADED – on its way from the yard – across the Hudson – through the warehouse – and across the Hudson – back to the yard RELOADED – as traced (from upper left to lower right of sheet) diagonally down and across the face of the CYCLE TABLE – for example the train of loaded Eastbound cars designated as B – TIME – NINE HOURS 45 MINUTES:-

O'CLOCK			POSITION
2.00 35	B	LOADED EAST BOUND TRAIN of 20 Cars taken on the Float at the yard – Float waits (2:35-45) 10 MINUTES.	
45		Float sails	
3.10		Float arrives at Manhattan Basin	
10 45	B	Sent up to Waiting Tracks East on Eastbound floor Train waits (3:45-4:00) 15 MINUTES	B.1
4.00 15		switched in to east bound platform to be UNLOADED	B.2
5.30 45		Switched out: UNLOADED to Waiting Tracks West on Eastbound floor – Train waits (5:45-6:15) 30 MINUTES	B.3
6.15 50		sent up EMPTY to Waiting Tracks West on Westbound floor Train waits (6:50-8:00) 1 HOUR-10 MINS.	B.4
8.00 15		switched in to Westbound platform to be RELOADED	B.5
9.30 45		switched out RELOADED to Waiting Tracks East on Westbound flr.	B.6
45		sent over Transfer Belt laterally to Landing Stage Tracks (or DELIVERY TRACKS) on W.B. floor ready for Float	B.7
10.00 35		sent down by the Landing Stage Elevators to the Float Float waits (10:35-45) 10 MINUTES	B.8
45		Float sails	
11.10		Float arrives at the Yard	
to 45		Float puts off the LOADED WESTBOUND TRAIN with CLASSIFICATION DESTINATION complete and ready for the ROAD	B
12.00		Float waits (11:45-12:00) 15 MINS.	

TABLE 3

This Table shows the Co-Operation of the Floats – 2 – in each Railroad Section – in harmony with the Cycle – the Boats leaving opposite sides of the River – Simultaneously – at cycle intervals of 2 hours. They are here designated one as THE YORK – the other THE JERSEY

O'CLOCK	THE YORK	TRAIN	O'CLOCK	THE JERSEY	TRAIN
12.00 35	At Manhattan Basin — Takes on LOADED-Westbound Train (Waits 10 mins.)	M	12.00 35	At R.R.Yard Takes on LOADED Eastbound Train (Waits 10 mins)	A
45	Sails with	M	45	Sails with	A
1.10	At R.R. Yard Arrives with	M	1.10	At Manhattan Basin Arrives with	A
10 45	Puts off LOADED Eastbd. Train (waits 15 mins.)		10 45	Puts off LOADED Eastbd Train (waits 15 mins)	
2.00 35	Takes on LOADED Westbd Train (waits 10 mins)	B	2.00 35	Takes on LOADED Westbd. Train (waits 10 mins.)	N
45	Sails with	B	45	Sails with	N
	Across			Across	
3.10	At Manhattan Basin Arrives with	B	3.10	At R.R. Yard Arrives with	N
10 45	Puts off LOADED Eastbd. Train (waits 15 mins.)		10 45	Puts off LOADED Eastbd. Train (waits 15 mins)	
4.00 35	Takes on LOADED Westbd. Train (waits 10 mins)	O	4.00 35	Takes on LOADED Eastbd Train (waits 10 mins)	C
45	Sails with	O	45	Sails with	C
	Across			Across	
5.10	At R.R. Yard Arrives with	O	5.10	At Manhattan Basin Arrives with	C
10 45	Puts off LOADED Westbd. Train (waits 15 mins)		10 45	Puts off LOADED Eastbd Train (waits 15 mins)	C
6.00 35	Takes on LOADED Eastbd Train (waits 10 mins)	D	6.00 35	Takes on LOADED Westbd. Train (waits 10 mins)	P
45	Sails with	D	45	Sails with	P
	Across			Across	
7.10	At Manhattan Basin Arrives with	D	7.10	At R.R. Yard Arrives with	P
10 45	Puts off LOADED Eastbd Train (waits 15 mins)		10 45	Puts off LOADED Westbd Train (waits 15 mins)	
8.00 35	Takes on LOADED Westbd Train (waits 10 mins)	A	8.00 35	Takes on LOADED Eastbd Train (waits 10 mins)	E
45	Sails with	A	45	Sails with	E
	Across			Across	

SECTION 4.—String No. 3 having meantime moved over the cross over its head is at switch K—and when string 2 reversed has cleared the switch—it moves to permanent position at the west end of the platform track—E. 7.

SECTION 5.—String D. 6 is now moved to connection with E. 7 and the train of 20 cars—C. 7, D. 6, E. 7—is now in *unloading* position at the platform—with—switch L open for the movement of the *empty* cars from the platform line to the waiting Tracks *West*—on their way up to the Westbound floor to be *reloaded*.

The switching *in* movements—shown at sections 2, 3, 4, 5—(of the sheet) correspond with the 1, 2, 3 movements—A. 1 to A. 2—(2.00 to 2.15 o'clock) of the Cycle Table—and the train is *unloaded* in the time corresponding to that shown on the Cycle Table—(*unloads*—2.15-3.45—1 H. 30 M.).

SECTION 6.—String C. 7 *empty* is first sent out at switch L to position on the Waiting Tracks *West*.

SECTION 7.—D. 6 is next run back East to clear switch L then out.

SECTION 8.—E. 7 having meantime moved East—its head is at switch L and when D. 6 has passed out—it moves East—(its length)—to clear the switch—then out to the waiting Tracks *West*.

The train of 20 cars *empty* is now in position in 3 strings on the Waiting Tracks *West* at the Empty Car Elevators—ready at schedule time to be sent up to the waiting Tracks *West*—(directly overhead) on the Westbound floor—to be *reloaded*.

(The switching *out* movements shown at section 6, 7, 8 correspond with the 1, 2, 3 movements A. 2 to A. 3—(3.30-3.45 o'clock) of the Cycle Table.)

Here the train waits—(on the Cycle Table) 30 minutes—from 3.45 in the 2nd Cycle to 4.15 in the 3rd—when—the *empty* train P. 3 on the 4th (Westbound) floor—having been switched *in* from the waiting Tracks *West*—to platform—P. 4—in 1, 2, 3 movements—(4-4.15)—to be *loaded* and the waiting Tracks being clear—it begins to go up—(A. 3 *up*—4.15-4.50) in groups of 3—by the Empty Car Elevators to the 4th floor.

ON THE 4TH OR WEST BOUND FLOOR

Operations are similar—on the 4th floor—except that the movements are *reversed* in order being from the *West End* to the *East End* of the floor.

The *empty* Train reaches the waiting Tracks *West* A. 4—(4.15-4.50)—where it waits—*one hour 10 minutes*—(4.50 to 6.00) when at the beginning of the next Cycle—it is switched *in* at switch L—A. 5—(6-6.15)—*loaded*—6.15-7.30—switched *out* at switch K to the waiting Tracks *East*—A. 6—7.30-7.45—moved laterally in groups of 3—over the Transfer Belt—to the Landing Stage Track—(*Delivery Tracks*)—A. 7 (7.45 o'clock in 4th Cycle to 8.20 in the 5th)—and sent down by the Landing Stage Elevators (at center) to the Float A. 8—in groups of 3—(8.00-8.35).

The Float waits 10 minutes—8.35-8.45—crosses in 25 minutes 8.45-9.10 and *Train A*—which left the rails of the yard *loaded*—at 12-12.35 o'clock—now *reloaded*—with Westbound freight is delivered again to the rails of the yard at 9.10-9.45 o'clock ready to depart for the *West*.

PASSAGE OF A LOADED TRAIN—IN PROCESSION—FROM YARD—THROUGH TERMINAL AND BACK TO YARD—RELOADED

This operation is shown in detail on (blue print) *Table No. 2* and graphically shown and described on (blue print) sheet with the heading *Processional Movement* of the system.

The time of passage from yard to yard again is:

Under the *one-twelfth* Cycle	9 *hours* 45 *minutes*
Under the *one-sixteenth* Cycle	7 *hours* 21 *minutes*
Under the *one-twentieth* Cycle	5 *hours* 59 *minutes*
Under the *average* Cycle	7 *hours* 42 *minutes*

The time required from the break-up-yard—to the break-up-yard again—by the present system—as ascertained by the recent Commission is 3½ days—(84 hours).

SYNCHRONIZED TRAFFIC MOVEMENTS

Tables Nos. 1 and 3 (blue print) show the synchronized movements of the current of traffic within *one Cycle*—from 12 o'clock to 2 o'clock and illustrate how *similar* operations are *simultaneously* going forward in all *departments* of activity *on all floors* and *on the water*.

ONE-SIXTEENTH CYCLE—AS COMPARED WITH ONE-TWELFTH CYCLE

Under the operation of this Cycle—(1 H. 30 M.)—the crossing time (25 M.) remains the same as under the One-Twelfth Cycle—the loading or unloading of the Float is reduced 5 M. (from 35 to 30)—actual time required (as shown in detail on other pages)—19 M. 29 S.—(still unused margin of 10 M. 31 S.—or 54%); the switching in and out at the crossover rails is reduced 3 Min.—(from 15 to 12)—actual time required 7 M. 43 S.—(still unused margin 4 M. 17 S. or 55%);—the loading or unloading of a car—reduced 13 M. (from 1 H. 15 M.)—to 1 H. 2 M.—and the movements over the transfer belt—7 M. (from 35) to 28 M. actual time required 17 M. 51 S. (still unused margin—10 M. 9 S.—or 56%).

ONE-TWENTIETH CYCLE—AS COMPARED WITH ONE-SIXTEENTH CYCLE

Under the operation of this Cycle (1 H. 12 M.) the crossing time remains the same as under the one-sixteenth Cycle (25 M.);—the loading or unloading of the Float is reduced 7 M. (from 30 to 23)—actual time required 19 M. 29 S. (leaving still a margin of 3 M. 31 S. or 18%);—the switching in and out at the cross over rails 2 M. (from 12 to 10) actual time required—7 M. 43 S. (still unused margin 2 M. 17 S. or 30%);—the loading or unloading of a car reduced 17 M.—(from 1 H. 2 M.) to 45 M.;—and the movements over the transfer belt 5 M. (from 28) to 23 M.—actual time required 17 M. 51 S. (still unused margin 5 M. 9 S. or 28%).

NOTE: The transfer time over the Belt—as already explained is included in other functions.

THE CYCLE METHOD CONSIDERED

The utility and effectiveness of the Cycle method will be appreciated—when it is understood that *without it*—functions would be in process without relation to each other—some operating too slowly—others too rapidly—treading upon the heels of each other—and this unevenness cumulatively intensified in successive operations—would ultimately bring events to clash with each other—creating first a tangle—then stagnation. By the *correlation* of movements and the establishment of *waiting periods* as elastic interstitial cushions or margins of time between functions—and bringing them all within a fixed period called—*the Cycle of Operation*—all unevenness is brought under control of the Schedule which absorbing the irregularities of the old Cycle begins a *new one* at the end of every *two hours*. Under this rule of order—confusion—collision—congestion are no longer possible the system moves with rhythmic precision—Cycle after Cycle—doing its work *perfectly*.

VARIATION OF SCHEDULE AND OF THE DAY PERIOD—ELASTICITY OF THE SYSTEM

While for the purposes of exposition of the principle and practical operation of the system a definite Cycle of operation has been used it will be at once apparent to the practical Railroad expert that variations of the Schedule may be made which would be of traffic advantage. For example:

Roads—as B. and O.—whose Manhattan traffic is notas great as that of others—could be advantageously operated on a special schedule of longer Cycle periods—say *one-eighth*—(3 hours) adapted to the needs of the traffic—while those of greater Manhattan traffic as the Pennsylvania—could be operated on another say the *one-twentieth*—or the *one-sixteenth* Cycle (one and a half hours)—others still on the *one-twelfth*—(2 hours)—schedule—as might be found advantageous in each case—so that a different Cycle might be in use in every section.

Similarly the *day period* of operation may be fixed as the volume of traffic in any section may demand—in each section variously—so that the day may be 8 hours in one section 12 in another—16 in another—24 in another—or operations may cease altogether in any section—or proceed at half speed in one—at full speed—in another as conditions may demand.

These or any other variations that may be deemed advantageous—may be made—the essential system being maintained—without affecting the operation of the Terminal as a whole—*a single traffic machine*.

The traffic system therefore though governed by an *operative formula* which is *determinate* is nevertheless *within* that formula *elastic*—easily adaptable and equal to any conditions that may arise of *time—distance—traffic —or operation.*

NEW YORK CENTRAL—AT SPUYTEN DUYVIL

Under the *one-twelfth* Cycle—as adapted to the New York Central at Spuyten Duyvil—(see blue print New York Central schedule—the crossing time is fixed at 60 minutes—(about ¾ speed)—which leaves a margin of 15.6 minutes;—the time of loading and unloading the Float at the Basin (or the yard) in 7 movements and of trains on the floors is reduced by one minute for each movement (from 5 to 4 minutes)—still leaving a margin over required time—at the Float—(19 M. 29 S.) for the 7 movements—of 8 M. 31 S. or 43%; and the waiting periods of the Float (of 10 minutes) after loading at either dock are eliminated. Otherwise the schedule for New York Central at Spuyten Duyvil 11.7 miles is practically the same as that for Delaware Lackawanna $^{86}/_{100}$ of *one* mile away—and all other New Jersey Roads.

BALTIMORE AND OHIO—AT STATEN ISLAND

Under the *one-twelfth* cycle—as adapted to the Baltimore and Ohio at Staten Island (see blue print Baltimore and Ohio schedule)—the crossing time is fixed at 33 minutes (about ¾ speed)—which leaves a margin of 8.2 minutes; and as in the case of New York Central the several functions are reduced by one minute and the waiting periods eliminated. Otherwise the schedule for Baltimore and Ohio at Staten Island is the same as that for New York Central and the New Jersey Roads—and the freight train makes the passage from the yard through the warehouse and back again to the yard reloaded—in practically the same time.

It will be noted that (on the B. and O. schedule) the unloading of the Float at the Manhattan Basin is completed—and the train of Cars—A—in position—A. 1—on the waiting Tracks East—of the Eastbound floor—at 1.29 and waits there 31 minutes to be switched in to platform—A. 2—at the beginning of the next cycle (2 o'clock) and similarly the Float completes delivery at the yard of Train M at 1.29 and waits 31 minutes—until the beginning of the next cycle (2 o'clock) before it begins to take on Eastbound train B.

And part of these waiting periods may be added—either to the crossing or the loading time of the Float—or both—as conditions may demand—without affecting the other functions of the Cycle within the Warehouse—and if added—for example—to the crossing time—would nearly *double* it.

There will inevitably occur delays and hindrances in the operation of the system and these are more likely to happen on the water than in the house—and these wide margins and the consequent elasticity of Schedule make it possible to adapt the passage across the water to almost any unusual conditions that may arise.

UNIFORMITY OF SERVICE

Under the operation of any given Cycle the loaded Eastbound train whether from Spuyten Duyvil—from Staten Island—or from Hoboken—passes through the Terminal—is unloaded—reloaded—and is again on the rails of these respective yards—at precisely the same time. Under the *one-twelfth* Cycle for example—the transaction is completed in each case in 9 H. 45 M.

This system of regulated Cycle movement is *the effective key* to the *new current of Railroad traffic.*

ELASTIC POWER OF THE SERVICE—NEW YORK CENTRAL'S DOUBLE SERVICE—ITS GREAT ADVANTAGE

As New York Central operates in its Eastern Dept. *two* Trunk lines—New York Central and West Shore—it will have *two sections*—(7 and 8 at the north end)—of the Terminal—and these areas may be operated as one—and at Spuyten Duyvil—a *double basin*. With these facilities at command the West Shore Float service for the smaller volume of traffic may be devoted to the uses of that Road (and Ontario Western)—for the necessary part of the day and diverted as may be required to Spuyten Duyvil for other parts—in the service of New York Central. This double service will in effect—for its period—reduce the distance by one-half—or double the transfer capacity of the Cycle itself.

With these facilities at command New York Central will be able to divert its *incoming-outgoing* traffic—in part—to that terminal yard yielding the greater advantage—Weehawken or Spuyten Duyvil—or send it all to Weehawken.

REASSIGNMENT OF TERMINAL AREAS

Similarly the Float service—under general Terminal administration—may through arrangement with the Roads—be diverted for certain periods—from the service of one Road to that of another. For example—Central of New Jersey is a large Coal carrier—but rates low in percentage of food stuffs—while Lehigh Valley low in percentage of perishable foods—rates high in Coal and higher in Grain—and B. and O. rates low in food stuffs—but high in Coal. As neither Coal nor Grain is to be delivered through the new Terminal—the Float service of these roads—for such periods as they are not needed by them—may be diverted—for example—to Pennsylvania—Erie—or Lackawanna—large handlers of food-stuffs and Metropolitan freights.

If these considerations shall make it desirable to reassign the sections—varying somewhat the order of the tentative arrangement as set out in these pages—so that the highest utility may be attained for all Roads—that can be effected—as judgment may advise. The operating formula and the general plan being fundamental—its adaptation to the detail of traffic with the maximum of advantage—for all roads—will follow naturally as the result of coöperative consideration and practical operation.

TRANSFER CAPACITY—CARS AND TONNAGE

		Cars	Tons	
Under the operation of the *one-twelfth cycle*				
Daily Transfer Capacity—*one section*		480		
Daily Transfer Capacity—*terminal*		3,840		
Tons				
Loaded—30 *in*—20 *out*—*annual capacity*			28,800,000	
One-half—15 *in*—10 *out*—*annual capacity*			14,400,000	
One-third—10 *in*—6.66 *out*—*annual capacity*			9,600,000	
Under the operation of *one-sixteenth cycle*				
Daily Transfer Capacity—*one section*		640		
Daily Transfer Capacity—*terminal*		5,120		
Tons				
Loaded—30 *in*—20 *out*—*annual capacity*			38,400,000	
One-half—15 *in*—10 *out*—*annual capacity*			19,200,000	
One-third—10 *in*—6.66 *out*—*annual capacity*			12,800,000	
Under the operation of *one-twentieth cycle*				
Daily Transfer Capacity—*one section*		800		
Daily Transfer Capacity—*terminal*		6,400		
Tons				
Loaded—30 *in*—20 *out*—*annual capacity*			48,000,000	
One-half—15 *in*—10 *out*—*annual capacity*			24,000,000	
One-third—10 *in*—6.66 *out*—*annual capacity*			16,000,000	
Annual Traffic is estimated by the				
Harbor Commission at			9,000,000	*in*—1924
and accepting the Commission's estimate of			14,500,000	*in*—1943
and its annual rate of increase at 2% the tonnage is			24,267,000	*in*—1969
			28,999,000	*in*—1978
The estimated traffic would therefore reach a volume equal to *one-half* of the *least of* the annual capacities named above in the year (fixed as *the limit*, 14,260,000 tons) of the capacity of the *automatic plan*)			48,528,000	*in*—2004
				1943
A volume equal to one-half of *the greatest*			in the year	1969
A volume equal to the least of the *full* capacities			in the year	1978
And a volume equal to the greatest of the *full* capacities			in the year	2004
Nearly *one hundred* years away.				

Note: The capacity of the Manhattan Railway Terminal in *all other* departments—Freight Platform areas—Driveways—Railroad trackage—and Motor Truck service—is in accord with the *Greatest* Float Transfer capacity here named.

THE PROCESSION

During any *one Cycle* period—*forty trains—eight hundred cars* are *in procession—within*—the Terminal—*five trains—one hundred cars*—in each Railroad section—viz.—(for example—in 5th Cycle of the Table):

Train	Cars	
1-E	20	*Loaded* East bound moving *up* from Float to Eastbound floor—to be *unloaded*.
2-D	20	*Loaded* East bound at the platform—being *unloaded*.
3-C	20	*Empty* moving from East to Westbound floor—to be *loaded*.
4-B	20	*Empty* at the Westbound platform—being *loaded*.
5-A	20	*Loaded* West bound moving *down* to the Float—for the *yard*.
	100	*Cars*.

When these cars reach and pass their successive stages in the circuit is definitely set out in the *Cycle Tables* and illustrated on the sheets—by means of which one may see—as in a moving panorama—how operations *simultaneously* in progress in all departments proceed in orderly relation—and analyze at leisure—any or all of its separate functions—in each of the *five* separate but correlated fields, viz.:

1. On the West bound floor.
2. On the East bound floor.
3. At the Float in New Jersey.
4. At the Float in New York.
5. On the water between the shores.

REMARKABLE TRAFFIC COOPERATION—A NEW TRAFFIC FACILITY

The order in which East bound cars leave the rails at the yard and are located on the Float *determines* their order in the warehouse—at the East bound platform unloading—after—at the West bound platform reloading—as well as the order of their return to the rails at the yard. This regularity of movement and precision of location of cars in their progress through the warehouse offers a strikingly novel opportunity for teamwork between the managers of traffic at the warehouse and the yard.

The location of any particular car—*inbound*—say D.L. W. 42,621 at the East bound platform being known in advance consignees will back up their teams at that point to receive the freight. Later the Westbound freight for that particular car may be collected on the Westbound platform at the point where the car will stop.

The Controller of traffic of the Railroad section of the Terminal—therefore with the coöperation of the Floor managers—the manager of the Truck system and the manager of the Float system will be able in his Manhattan Terminal office to map out in advance on his *traffic chart* the operations of the day—the location of freights east bound—westbound—on the platforms—with their character—quantities—weights—measures—classification—destination—and of cars—by their numbers—and to locate their return freights.

West bound freight will be delivered by incoming trucks opposite the car for which it is intended—sent across the platform by the down grade moving platform to the proper point on the car load line—and when the line of empty cars is switched in to be loaded—and takes its determined position—each car will stop opposite its intended Westbound freight and car loading time will be reduced to its lowest limit.

Similarly—on the Eastbound floors Trucks and Cars will be relatively located, and freights for the trucks will be at the tail board ready.

Every movement of Car and of freight being thus *known*—and charted—*in advance*—there will be no lost motion—no delay—no confusion—no digging out of freight—and a system of traffic including effective classification may be elaborated and practically operated on the broad platform areas—*never before possible* at Railroad Terminals *anywhere*—and made to attain *the ideal* of traffic facility.

ACCIDENT—INTERRUPTIONS

In the movement of so great a volume of freight as that of the West Side Railroads by a system which is essentially based upon continuous operation by fixed schedule interruptions may naturally be expected.

The Float may be blocked in the stream or held at the Basin or disabled; there may be unreadiness of freight or of cars in the warehouse or at the yard; the landing stage elevator or the empty car elevator may be disabled by accident.

THE TWO VITAL POINTS GUARDED

Of these contingencies the two vital happenings in the operation of the system to be guarded against are accidents to the Float or the Elevators—and both are so protected that delays in either case could be only fractional.

1. THE FLOAT.—The System provides in addition to the operating quota of Terminal Floats—a sufficient number of lay or extra Floats—always ready—and in case of disabling accident to any operating Float—another will immediately take its place.

2. THE ELEVATOR.—The capacity of the elevator is $3\frac{1}{2}$ times greater than the strain of any work it will be called on to do—and this margin of excess power is itself an insurance against mechanical accident.

The Elevator constructors—consulted—see no reason to anticipate delay through accident pointing to elevator systems they have established in Western Pennsylvania in the steel areas where much heavier work is successfully and continuously handled without serious accidents or important delays.

To reduce to a minimum the consequences of accident to the elevator system—the original design of an elevator of capacity to handle three cars at a time was changed to three elevators side by side each of one car capacity. The system therefore presents in this feature an added security, for while the elevators are in sets of 3 to take 3 cars at a time—they are nevertheless of independent construction and action—an accident to one in any set having no effect upon the other two and since there are 48 car elevators in the system—24 for loaded cars, 24 for empty cars —the temporary disability of one in any set in any section would affect only that section—expressed by the fraction $\frac{1}{3}$ of $\frac{1}{8}$ or $\frac{1}{24}$ of the system.

Another mishap which may be reckoned as of importance is accident to the Electric Cable Switching System. The example, however, of continuous operation of electric and cable systems in private and public undertakings indicate that interruptions are of infrequent occurrence—the delays brief—and the service is usually promptly resumed.

With these vital points covered—other accidents about the warehouse—on the tracks—on the platforms—would be only such as might occur—promptly remediable—at any large industrial plant—and are of comparatively minor importance.

SUSPENSION OR VARIATION OF OPERATIONS

In the case of none of the accidents above referred to would it be necessary to suspend operations in any Railroad section other than that in which the accident occurred—and in that—only of the machinery affected.

But in any case of general suspension—whatever the cause—the machine as a whole may be stayed—simultaneously at all points—at the yard—in the warehouse—at the Basin—(the Float if in the stream—continuing or returning to her nearest dock).

The delay ended whether after one hour or many it is only necessary in starting up again to catch step with the schedule by beginning at the point and at the time in the new period corresponding to those at which it stopped in a former and the traffic machine goes on by schedule as before.

In the same way whenever deemed advisable the schedule of any or all functions of the Cycle may be increased or decreased—the speed of operation of the system changed—at the end of any (the beginning of the next) cycle—the cycle period extended or reduced—the flow of traffic accelerated or retarded—the volume of freight increased or decreased.

At any such time of general suspension—however occasioned—whether by accident or by other conditions such as strikes—riots—fires—snowbound streets—or on the water by storms or other conditions—the excess of areas and trackage will provide room for any necessary accumulation of either freight or cars and with the restoration of normal conditions and the resumption of traffic—the system operating at capacity—in excess of normal requirements will soon recover any lost ground and reëstablish the movement of the current under the regular schedule.

THE HUDSON RIVER HIGHWAY

Inevitably there will be delays in the stream—the Hudson is a crowded thoroughfare.

First, the Motor Float driven by the Diesel (fuel oil) Marine Engine of high power—with Pilot House and Bridge raised above the car taps—affording a wide horizon—and special equipment for control (elsewhere described) is able to change direction or come to a stop more promptly to avoid collision than the North River Ferry Boat—or any other steam vessel on the River.

Second, the substitution of *sixteen* motor floats for more than *two hundred* car Floats and Tugs now necessary for the transfer of the Trunk line freights will sensibly clear the fairway.

Third, the methods provided at the Basin to meet tidal-storm and winter forces—the attacks of drift ice and débris—(detailed on other sheets)—are considered so effective as to fairly control these conditions.

Fourth, the North River Ferries are now meeting these River conditions successfully—maintaining a fairly regular schedule. At times the Boat is held up—but seldom for long periods—and the operation of their 7 lines of direct and 4 up stream crossings—is a fair demonstration of the successful operation of the New Motor Float system with somewhat similar crossings—5 direct and 3 up and down stream.

Fifth, it is precisely with River conditions in view that the system has provided wide margins of areas and of trackage in the terminal—expanded the daily transfer capacity far beyond the needs of the present—and given the motor Float its speed and power—so that if need arise—operations of the day may be accomplished in *half a day*—12 hours—*or one-third a day*—8 *hours*—or *less*.

With these broad margins of capacity *delays* from whatever cause will be *absorbed*—and may not be expected to prevent the transfer over the water on any day of all the Eastbound tonnage *in*—all the Westbound tonnage *out*—for *that day*.

MEMORANDA

CONCENTRATION

A. *One Terminal* vs. *Many*

The capacity—hence the area—of a Manhattan Terminal operated in connection with a tunnel is determined by the facilities of approach and departure for Trucks over the contiguous street areas—and the space at the platform line for their operation—together with the facilities for the movement of trains in and out—and through the streets either on the surface—over—or under it. On the other hand terminal areas are also limited by availability of site and the relative location of the longitudinal city streets and avenues. With these factors of the problem considered the recent Commission definitely ascertained by its studies that *one* joint terminal for all the West side Railroads and their traffic was not practicable either physically or financially and that the largest practicable *single* Manhattan Terminal for any system whatever operated through a tunnel, whether in connection with an Elevated—surface or subsurface—Railway would have a capacity sufficient only for a *fraction*—less than *one tenth*—of the whole volume of traffic.

It therefore became a *necessity* to have a *number* of Terminals—and it was estimated *twelve* would be required by *any* tunnel plan whatever to meet traffic demands.

That is the *fundamental* reason for *multiplied* terminals of the Automatic Tunnel plan and of *all* plans operated through a *tunnel*. They represent neither advantage nor purpose—but *necessity*.

So far from representing advantage it is shown (on other pages) that the same burdens that afflict railroad traffic to-day created by the system of scattering freights incoming—outgoing—at many stations—are not only continued but intensified by the system of *multiplied terminals*.

The higher purpose of all plans was to establish *one* joint terminal finding that impossible *multiplied* terminals followed.

MANY RAILROAD PIER STATIONS

The many Manhattan Railroad pier stations (of to-day)—as a part of present methods—are also the result not of design but of *necessity*—they have developed with the system. Physically the traffic of a single road required more terminal area than that of *one* pier—it was necessary to call into service others and competition determined their location.

Like the multiplied terminals of the Tunnel plans—the pier stations *scatter* the freights to be handled *incoming—outgoing*—at many stations—a method that is responsible for the enormous burdens of expense and delay involved in the *underloading* of cars; the excessive movement to and from Manhattan Terminals of *empty* cars; the extra tax imposed by *car detention;* and as a very *corollary* of such a system—the great expense of the maintenance and operation—of the *transfer station* on the New Jersey side largely if not mainly for the consequent consolidation service—where the *partial* loads of *two* or more cars—gathered at *two* or more stations are *reloaded* into *one* car—outbound—and the *full* load of the inbound car—is transferred to *two* or more cars—in *partial* loads for delivery at the *multiplied* Manhattan Terminals.

These evils which now bear heavily upon traffic at New York—(how heavily is indicated on other pages)—tending to stagnate the current of freight cars through the yards and to affect adversely the traffic of the Railroad back to the remotest station on its line—all belong to the system of *multiplied Manhattan Terminals*.

THE IDEAL TERMINAL

The *ideal* terminal therefore is the *single Manhattan Terminal*—where the rails and trains and the now *scattered* freights of *all* the West side Railroads may be *concentrated*—thus abolishing the *multiplied* terminal and with it the evils it imposes. At such a Terminal *all* the Westbound freight of the day—of the Erie Railroad for example—its platform location charted in advance—is assembled on the *West bound floor* of that road—and *all* the Eastbound freight (its platform location similarly charted in advance) is brought to its *Eastbound floor*—for organized delivery to consignee.

This *ideal single terminal* is the *central feature* of the *Sibley System* over the *water*—and—as the competent Engineering Staff of the Commission through scientific critical analysis has now definitely demonstrated—by *no other* system whatever—is such a consummation *possible*.

B. *Concentration at the Market Area.*

The market place—whether for money—for merchandise or for foodstuffs—is a creation of time, and means not only the physical area of the Exchange where the transactions are made but the established business areas of the Bankers and Financiers in the case of money;—of the merchant operators in the case of merchandise of the wholesale handlers in the case of foodstuffs. These establishments have grown up about and fixed—unalterably—the location of the market. For these reasons Wall St. found it impossible to move the Exchange up town—and—equally it is impossible to shift the market place for merchandise and foodstuffs to new locations. It centers at the West side of Manhattan—where it is in touch with the Railroad systems of the continent—the steamship service of the world.

Concentration of the Railroads at the market place is therefore the *ideal* consummation to be sought.

In the matter of Food—the recent Commission wisely concluded—

> The bringing together of food receivers and distributors at one point has great advantages and to attempt a violent disruption of the system would cause great confusion and loss to the food distributors—if indeed it could be accomplished. The *problem is to retain* the advantages of the present *concentration* but eliminate the great *congestion* and repeated *re-handling* that seem to be part of the (present) system.

Concentration under the new system accomplishes precisely these things—and solves the hitherto unsolvable *problem*.

C. *Congestion*

It is natural to think that concentration of the Railroad traffic at *one point* on the water front would tend to relieve but to intensify present traffic congestion. This apprehension is a reasonable one concerning concentration under present traffic systems or under methods and at structures essentially similar to those now in use. But concerning concentration under the new system and its radically different methods and structures—wholly transforming the present traffic situation—it will be readily understood from a study of these pages—it is without foundation.

Under the caption *general arrangement of floors*—it is shown that in establishing the Elevated *entrances* and *exits* for truck service at the New Terminal—not only is present congestion—caused in major part by the Railroad traffic itself—entirely eliminated by taking that traffic *out* of West St.—*altogether*—and setting it down 500 feet in shore to move unhindered in and out through uncrowded one way cross streets—but traffic in overburdened West St. now stagnant and in confusion will—with this relief—become for the first time—*liquid* and *current*—from the Battery to 60th St.

Instead therefore of intensifying present congestion it tends to abolish it altogether and not only at the front of the Railway Terminal but up and down the Hudson River front.

D. *The Railroads*

Concentration at one Terminal of all the West side Railroads such as has been planned for them by many transportation schemes has been consistently opposed by the roads mainly because each had to surrender control of its own traffic to be operated over *rails common to all;* on *platforms common to all;* and under a centralized system of operation where freights would *inevitably* be thrown together; where advantage of one road over another in the handling of freight or the prompt movement of cars was considered probable; and even the diverting of shipments possible—the General Manager exercising a certain degree of discretionary control over cars and consignments.

These have been the principal objections of the Roads and they are very sound objections and in view of this attitude of the roads it cannot be too positively stated—and emphasized that the concentration here proposed has none of these objectionable features—for whether the new single pier—now devised for the service of *one* railroad be separated by a mile from any other similar pier structure or located adjoining it—its *independence* is equally complete—while its location as *one section* of the General Terminal secures to it all the *advantages* of association, with none of its disadvantages.

This concentration therefore creates an entirely new traffic situation. It is *not* a Joint Terminal where rails and platforms are in common—but precisely the opposite—where they are *individual*. It is a collection of several such individual terminals at *one location*—each of *independent* operation—in which the *road controls* its own operations—its consignments—*unmixed* with others—its cars and their movements—over its own rails—which are in connection with the rails of its own yard—having also its own freight offices at the bulkhead front of the Terminal on 3 operating floors—for the use of its officers and operatives—in touch—at once—with its activities in Manhattan—on the platforms—in the yards across the water—yet in association with the other roads it reaps the advantage of the general service of the Motor Float fleet on the water—the organized Motor Truck service on land—and the general administration at the center of the Terminal and is in close rail connection *within the terminal*—with all Railroads for advantageous car and traffic exchange.

E. *The Effect of Lack of Concentration*

UNDERLOADING—EMPTY CAR MOVEMENT—CAR DETENTION—CAR INTERCHANGE—STAGNATION OF CAR MOVEMENT
    TERMINAL DELAYS

Every Railroad man will at once recognize this group of traffic evils as together constituting a *principal* handicap on the handling of the Railroad traffic at the port of New York—and these are *all* the effect of *lack of concentration,* and any new traffic system designed for the handling of that great volume of freight would be ineffective that did not greatly modify or wholly abolish these now fundamentally defective methods. Yet while all of the many plans—(to be operated through the tunnel)—which were examined by the Commission were rejected because *physically* impracticable—and incapable

"it was assumed"—(the Commission says)—"that (in each case) *the same average loading of cars would prevail as at present."*

That is to say the freight car of 30 tons capacity was to be loaded with but 6.31 tons—a method that uses *five cars* to do the work of one.

If, therefore, such *underloading*—the father of all the evils catalogued above—was to be continued—no traffic advantage could have been gained—and had not the plans been rejected as being impractical physically and financially the *single* consideration that these old methods and their train of evils—were to remain a permanent burden upon traffic—would have condemned them *all* utterly.

In contrast with these rejected and all other systems—as these pages will show—the new system over the water eliminates these defects—*altogether*—and with wonderful traffic results.

1. *Underloading*

If the freight for *one car* outbound is at *three* Manhattan stations it must *of necessity*—under the present system—be loaded into *three cars* and if the freight of *one car* inbound is to be delivered at *three* Manhattan stations it must *of necessity* be unloaded and reloaded into *three cars*. That necessity *creates* the New Jersey *Transfer Station* and the ills that now burden the Railroad traffic follow as natural consequences.

The analysis of tonnage made by the Commission—"for the test year 1914"—shows that at the Manhattan stations—

The average load per *loaded* car of the New Jersey Roads *inbound* was 10.93 tons and *outbound* 7.06 tons—and with the *empty* cars considered (as a part of the traffic in and out)—the average load for *all* cars in was 7.89 tons—*out* 4.72 tons.

With New York Central's traffic added the average load per *loaded* car fell to 10.64 *in*—6.82 *out*—while the averages for *all* cars became 8.24 *in*—4.38 *out*—an average for *all* cars in and *out*—of—6.31 tons.

Under present methods the Erie may load a car at Duane St.—another at pier 39—and still another at pier 7 East River all for the same destination. There may be no more freight at the three points in a day than would go into *one* car but to meet the competition with other roads Erie—must provide the *three* cars and dispatch each when a certain *very small minimum* load has been obtained.

So with *inbound* freight—one shipper (from a distant point)—may consign his goods to Duane St.—another to pier 39—another to pier 7 East River—the same train bringing in these *three* partly loaded cars one for *each station*.

Similarly Pennsylvania if at *one* Manhattan station there is not a full load for Scranton—must either dispatch the car partly loaded—or load the Scranton freight into a car with other freights—to be again unloaded and reloaded at the Waverly *transfer station*.

In contrast—under the Sibley system—(as adapted to these examples) *all* the freight of *Erie*—*inbound* and *outbound* is at *one* Terminal duplication and triplication of cars is avoided—*one* car is loaded with the freight now scattered at *three* Terminals and the other *two* cars are released for other service—and as *all* the Scranton freight of the Pennsylvania is similarly at *one* terminal—there is *no use* for the Waverly Transfer Station.

2. *Empty Car Movement*

The report of the Commission shows that—

There is a large movement of empty cars to and from Manhattan pier stations—as an integral and necessary part of the whole volume of traffic,

and in particular the Commission cites the following case of the Lackawanna—

Although the preponderance of *all* Railroad traffic is *inbound* the greater part of the traffic pier 41 (DLW) is *outbound*—hence there must be a large movement of *empty* cars *inbound* to this point to receive this freight. But even where the tonnage *in* and *out* is almost balanced there is still a movement and in *each* direction of approximately *one* empty car to every *two loaded* cars.

3. *Car Detention*

The underloading of cars and the consequent empty car movement makes it necessary to *detain* and use a great number of cars—beyond the number necessary at approximately full loads—for the handling of the whole traffic—and the methods now in use require also so much time for the delayed passage of the car through the terminals—that the sum of such car delays rises to large proportions.

The number of cars employed in handling the traffic at Manhattan stations—below 60 St.—(as ascertained by the Commission for the test year 1914)—was 530,639—for a traffic of 6,734,671 tons—proportionately the number necessary for the 10,000,000 tonnage—(the basis of the Commissions' estimate)—is 787,921—while if by better methods cars can be loaded—with 24 tons *inbound*—16 *outbound*—(the tonnage divided as now 60% *in*—40% *out*)—returned the same day—within a few hours and the excessive *empty car* movement—*eliminated*—the number of cars necessary for the movement of the same tonnage would be but 250,000—*releasing* from the Manhattan service the annual usage of 537,921 cars.

THE VALUE OF SUCH HIGHER LOADING AVERAGE

F. J. Lisman—an authority in matters of Railway Economics—in an article recently published—says:—

> To raise the minimum weight—(of freight)—per car by 10%—(on commodities other than mineral traffic (50%) would not only be equivalent to the *construction* of 125,000 additional freight cars—which at present prices of about $1,800 per car would represent an investment of $225,000,000, but it would mean a reduction of substantially 5% in operating expenses all around because it would effect a reduction of 5% in the freight train miles on the main lines.

This statement, of course, covers *all* cars—and *all* freights—(minerals excepted)—but it indicates enormous results as applied to the Manhattan freights of *all* the great Trunk Lines converging at New York—where instead of raising the minimum weight (of freight) per car by *ten* per cent—(as Mr. Lisman points out)—it is raised by *two hundred* per cent! And if 125,000 cars represent a value of $225,000,000—what would be the value of releasing from the Manhattan service the annual usage of 537,921 cars?

The Commission shows that—

> Under the present system it requires approximately *three and one-half days*—(84 hours) for a freight car to complete the Cycle from the break-up yard to Manhattan and return. At 10,000,000 annual tons of freight this means 2,700,000 car days. At the *per diem* rate of $1.00 as fixed by the American Railway Association—for cars of one road held by another the value of the car days is $2,700,000.

In contrast—under the Sibley system the time required for the passage of the Eastbound train from the yard *loaded* through the terminal—(*unloaded*)—and back to the yard *reloaded* is 7H., 42M.—the economy about 90%—or 2,430,000 car days—$2,430,000 per year—24.30 cents per ton.

4. *Car Interchange*

The Commission explains—

> Foreign cars arriving with loads at a Terminal—because of the high *per diem* charge per car established by the American Railway Association—not held but returned—empty—promptly to the owner road—the Railroads finding it cheaper to bring in their own empties for the outbound freight—(and the time—labor—expense—and method of effecting such interchange is clearly set out by the Commission—thus)—

> Suppose Erie brings in a loaded Lackawanna car destined for pier 39, Hudson River. It passes through the break-up yard at Croxton and then is drawn in a short train to Jersey City—put on a car Float—(which is towed to pier 39)—and unloaded. Then although goods are at hand at pier 39 to fill it, it belongs to the Lackawanna—and must be returned to it. Hence it is floated empty back to Jersey City—hauled back to Croxton—classified again there—delivered to the Lackawanna—classified a third time in the Lackawanna's Secaucus yard—hauled to Hoboken—and then perhaps floated to Lackawanna's Manhattan pier 41—just two doors from pier 39—to receive a load. Then it is returned to Secaucus yard and classified a fourth time—according to its outbound destination.

This—(the Commission says)—is the most prolific cause of the empty car movement—which if it could be removed would greatly reduce terminal costs at the port of New York. The cost of this wasted effort it estimates at no less than *eleven* cents per ton of freight delivered—an aggregate waste for the whole traffic of over *one million* dollars *annually*.

In contrast—under the Sibley system this Lackawanna car after it is unloaded on the Erie Railway tracks in the new Terminal is at once transferred by the *transverse railway*—(within the Terminal—connecting *all* railroads—for the exchange of cars)—to the Lackawanna section ready for the uses of that road—and—(to complete the supposed transaction)—if Lackawanna has a loaded East bound Erie car—that may be similarly transferred to Erie rails—the exchange being effected in a few minutes and practically without expense.

The system therefore removes what is considered—"the most prolific cause of the empty car movement"—which the Commission says will—"greatly reduce terminal costs at the port of New York"—and save the estimated waste of *eleven cents* per ton—or *one million* annually.

5. *Stagnation of Car Movement*

Present delays in unloading cars after their arrival at the New Jersey Railroad yard—where they are often held awaiting consignees' truck or waiting on storage facilities—or under a custom of allowed delay of one or more days—all tend to create if not disabling congestion—temporary stagnation of the current of traffic over the rails of the busy yards.

All such and other delays whether of cars of of freight can have no place in *the Sibley System* whose essential feature is *fluidity*. Cars will not linger in the yards to occupy tracks that are needed for other service—the end of their trip is the Manhattan Terminal—they pass through the yard—and on to destination.

Refrigerator cars that now are detained in the yards waiting on deliveries—have frequently to be re-iced—and in making deliveries to many trucks at various times—often opened to the detriment of their contents—are sent over at once—received on the Food Floor in a proper temperature and unloaded directly to the cold rooms.

If Eastbound freight—general merchandise—is to be held either as a traffic privilege or at the order of owners the car will—nevertheless—be unloaded and *set free* and the freight lowered by the Elevator from the platform to the storage areas below, clearing the operating floor—and the yards so kept free of congestion, *all* car movement over its rails is *facilitated*.

On this subject of *stagnation* of car movement a high Railroad authority—(Col. Hine of Erie Railway) has recently epitomized the matter as follows:—

> The real traffic problem is a Terminal one; relief must come through such terminal system as will permit *quicker movement of equipment*.

and another has said:—

> There is *nothing* on a Railroad that will save more money for it than *speeding up* of the movement of cars *through the Terminal*.

The *Manhattan Railway Terminal*—and its system of rapid movement is the *ideal physical expression* of both these sentiments—and with such facilities as are provided by the new system making the rapid and methodic movement of cars through the Terminal a simple transaction—the Roads may confidently look forward to the fruition of Railroad hopes and efforts as expressed in the slogan—

FOR THE FREIGHT CAR—30 MILES—30 TONS

6. *Terminal Delays*

The average daily mileage of all freight cars is given as about 26 miles—the speed in transit from 5 to 30 miles per hour. At a low average speed of 10 miles an hour the car would make its daily average of 26 miles in 2 hours 36 minutes—and for the balance of the day—21 hours 24 minutes or about 90 per cent of the time it is at rest—and as it is semi-officially stated that on the New York Central system there are practically no delays *except at terminals*—the warranted inference is that the Freight Car—on all Roads—is for the greater part of its resting period—in the Railroad yard.

The new system will relieve this condition of congestion and delay—the lingering of the freight car in the yard—by keeping the current of traffic in motion—for in the Manhattan Railway Terminal—operated on schedule—*delays are eliminated*.

The Car arrives at the shore—crosses to Manhattan, continues on its passage through the terminal, is unloaded—reloaded—recrosses—and is on the rails again in New Jersey ready to go out West. In 7 hours, 42 minutes, at least 9 hours, 45 minutes at most. It has made no stop at New York.

METROPOLITAN FOOD SUPPLY

A. *The Food Floor—On Second Level*

No other traffic is of so essential importance as the food supply. It has been the design of these plans, therefore, to create a system as nearly *ideal* as possible.

On the enclosed floor temperatures are maintained at a proper degree—in all seasons.

The *platform area*—126 ft. wide—1,037 ft. long—(136,857 square feet)—has at *one side*—four parallel Railroad Tracks—at the *other side* the *loading area* for Trucks 34 ft. wide—1,000 ft. long and beyond that *double parallel driveways—in—out* connected at the end of the platform with *ascending—descending*—Driveways *up* to the 3rd *level* and *down* to the *street level*—(average grade 2.6%)—

On the platform—at the *West end*—near the edge—are located *eight cold rooms*—(each 30 x 40)—opposite the Refrigerator Train on the Tracks—for the immediate or temporary care of Foodstuffs—provided with metal trolley runners—(matching similar runways on the Refrigerator car)—for the transfer of dressed meats suspended from trolley wheels—from car directly into the cold rooms. At the longitudinal *center line* 4 Freight Elevators descend to the Cold Storage areas (14 ft.) below—at the East end the platform area extends across the heads of the tracks and drives creating an area enclosed—heated and electric lighted 125 x 320 (about 40,-000 square ft.)—separated by a central (E-W) corridor into two sections, one for the use of the Railroad operatives in their handling of foodstuffs is divided into 12 offices (the greatest 60 x 22—the least 12 x 22)—the other for the use of Food Merchants—buyers and sellers—has at its center the *food exchange*—(*auction* and *sales room*) 110 ft. long—53 ft. wide, provided with telegraph—telephone—messenger—post office service—with corridors on four sides, into which open 31 surrounding offices—and sample rooms—(18 x 15). The Central corridor gives—at its West end—access to the Food platform and arriving foodstuffs—at the other—two 6-passenger Elevators and Double stairways that extend to all levels, issuing at the 3rd over the Elevated (Passenger) corridor spanning marginal way to the Entrance—Exit building where descending—(by Elevator or stairs) to the hall of Entrance the Food Merchant passes out into West St. Or from the Food platform he may descend (by Elevator or stairs) to the street level and pass out of the terminal over the Marginal Way.—Or he may pass from the Food platform of any Railroad to any platform of any other Railroad. Similarly trucks leaving the Food platform may either rise by easy ramp to the 3rd level, cross over on the elevated truckway and make exit in the cross street (near Washington).—Or drive down from 2nd to 1st level and make exit from the terminal on the Marginal Way.

MARKET AREA ON MARGINAL WAY

The Marginal Way was designed *not* primarily as a roadway for the passage of the north and south current of traffic along the water front—the highway of *that current* is *West St.* the *thoroughfare*—but was rather intended as an area over which the eddies of the current might turn *in*—where trucks being *out of the current* could maneuver to position at the piers and bulkhead sheds—or line up to wait on deliveries. And that part of the marginal way opposite any pier or bulkhead shed is the area provided for the use of that particular pier or bulkhead. Therefore all that part of this broad way which lies in front of the new Railway Terminal is for the use of Manhattan Railroad traffic.

Under treatment by the new plan this area no longer necessary for the uses of lines of trucks and confused masses of delayed freight—becomes an *exclusive court*—180 ft. wide—2,830 ft. long—extending along the whole front of the building and with the Railroad traffic lifted out of it and carried across overhead—it will be *free* and *clear* for the uses of the Railroads. Adapting it to these uses—at its East line (which coincides with the line of West St.)—there is fixed a continuous line of low separating wall (or border timber) with entrance and exit openings for trucks at each Railroad section through which no trucks will pass except on Terminal service.

In front of each Railroad section, therefore, there is a clear space 340 ft. long 180 ft. wide for the use of that Railroad—(61,200 sq. ft.). This area may be covered and lighted and used as a market area supplementary to the areas on the Food floor, for the delivery of foodstuffs—fruits, etc., to market wagons and to facilitate its use there is provided a double (up and down) inclined electrically-operated *freight escalator*—18 ft. wide 125 ft. long—which extends from the Food platform on the 2nd floor (at its East end)—down to the front line of the Terminal on the 1st floor—for the direct quick delivery of foodstuffs—in platform wagons to the *market area* on the Marginal Way. Such a market area approaches the ideal. (See diagram, page 81.)

COMPARATIVE MARKET FACILITIES—AREAS—CHARACTER

To illustrate the superiority of the new Food and Market facilities—as well in areas as in character—comparison may be made with some of the higher types of Food and Freight piers at the market center on the North River front—those of the Pennsylvania system—27-28-29—at Hubert—Laight and Vestry—and Erie Railway—20-21—at Chambers—Duane streets.

			Net Sq. Ft.
Pennsylvania	East Bound	230,935	
Less Drives and Aprons		85,066	145,869
Railway Terminal	East Bound		
2d Level—Food Platform		136,857	
3d Level—Merchandise Platform		126,802	263,659
Excess—80%			117,790
Pennsylvania	West Bound		30,000
Railway Terminal	West Bound		
4th Level			126,946
Excess—323%			96,946
Erie	East Bound	182,930	
Less Drives and Aprons		54,570	128,360
Railway Terminal	East Bound		263,659
Excess—105%			135,299
Erie	West Bound		20,000
Railway Terminal	West Bound		126,946
Excess—534%			106,946

CHARACTER

Fruits and market stuffs are sold on the piers, and buyers and sellers—horses and trucks—Fruits and Foodstuffs—all more or less thrown together contribute each a share to the condition of congestion that usually prevails.

In the handling of perishables proper temperatures are essential and an effort is made to meet this necessity by a system of heating pipes, but the bleak North River pier shed with its great side doors opened and kept open for the long process of transferring the freights from the Cars on the Floats to the pier shed cannot, of course, be kept properly heated.

Per contra—On the new Food Floor—the train of cars as it arrives at the Jersey yard—its car doors unopened—is at the platform *within* an enclosed electric lighted building where proper temperatures may be always maintained. Horses and trucks have their separate driveways, Railroad operatives their separate offices—and buyers and sellers—apart from all confusion—their sample rooms and the Auction Exchange, and at the center of the platform elevators are ready to take down any goods for Cold storage and at the end of the platform the Electric Escalator sliding down to the Marginal Way.

B. *The Food*

The Refrigerator Train.—The train of Refrigerator Cars with food for Manhattan is now usually unloaded in the Jersey yard and its contents either stored in New Jersey warehouses—or if for immediate delivery carted directly from the yard over the ferries—through the streets to destination—not only at much expense but with loss in quality of the food.

Under the New system *the train itself*, its contents untouched, is transferred across the River to unload directly into cold storage areas—where the food is kept in its original condition of purity and delivered as desired in insulated motor Trucks. This has been the *ideal* of the Municipal and State Market Commission and of the experts at Washington—the delivery of the Refrigerator train to Cold Storage areas—at the market center—an ideal that it has never before been found possible to reach. It begins a *new chapter* for the *Metropolitan food supply*.

Milk.—For this commodity—an essential element of the Food supply of New York—an *entirely new arrange-*

ment is effected that will put an end to present inadequate methods—and raise the service to a high plane of modern efficiency.

The milk car now—arriving at the New Jersey yard—brings about 250—10 gal. cans of milk usually covered with ice. The cans lifted out of their cold jackets stand naked on the open shed platform in the temperature of the day which for one-half the year may range from 65 to 90 degrees—temperatures in which bacteria—the destructive principle—multiply rapidly—and wait on delivery to trucks as they may arrive at the yard. The trucks crossing the ferry drive through the streets to the milk distributing depots in Manhattan.

The delays at the yard—the transition from cold to warm temperatures and the long passage over the ferries and through the streets all affect deleteriously the wholesomeness of this important article of food—to say nothing of the aggregate annual waste of expense.

In contrast—Under the new system—the whole milk Train—with bulk unbroken—crosses the Hudson—and the cans of milk when they are lifted out of their ice packing are on the Food Floor of the new Terminal—where proper temperatures are maintained and go at once into the Cold Rooms where ample areas are set apart exclusively for *milk service*. *Milk* and *refrigerator cars* are unloaded—re-iced—and returned in *2 hours 57 minutes*—from yard to yard again.

PASTEURIZATION.—Attached to the Cold Storage milk areas is a pasteurizing plant of high efficiency and as required milk may be passed through this process—then sent to the cold rooms—for preservation and later delivery by insulated trucks.

A pasteurizing plant for Cold Storage areas is a *new* and very advantageous feature.

Pasteurizing as applied to milk means—in a word—subjecting it to a temperature of 145 degrees—holding it there for 30 minutes—then cooling it to 45 degrees and holding it there till delivered.

On the precision and effectiveness of this process depends the degree of successful preservation—and but few commercial plants therefore reach the highest results.—Where the plant operates with high efficiency as in the laboratory of the chemist—all or nearly all bacteria—(the fermenting principle)—are destroyed when by immediate cooling the low temperature prevents their remultiplication and the milk it is scientifically determined—may be held in sound wholesome condition for many hours—for two or three or four days and even longer.

The importance of having such a plant capable of perfect results as part of the vast cold storage areas where is to be handled the food supply of so great an aggregation of humanity as that overflowing the limits of the city of New York—will appear from the annexed statement of a distinguished authority—Professor Lore A. Rogers—expert in Dairy Biology—U. S. Dept. of Agriculture.

Prof. Rogers (recognizing that but few commercial pasteurizing plants are capable of reaching such results as are obtainable in the scientific laboratory) says:

> If milk could be pasteurized commercially so that bacteria would be reduced to a few hundred per cubic centimeter and held at a low temperature until used it would be *perfectly safe* for 48 hours or even *72 hours*, and under these circumstances it would probably be in *better condition* after the long period than *ordinary* city milk *at the time it is delivered*.

With such facilities destructive conditions are under control—the city need never again face a *milk famine*, the *milk problem* of New York is *solved*.

FOGS AND THE FOOD SUPPLY

New York City's food supplies are now brought to the water's edge on the Jersey shore—and there—in large part—either temporarily stored in New Jersey cold storage warehouses or loaded to trucks and carted over the ferries to Manhattan.

Practically all the milk of the Jersey Roads is so delivered. Dressed meats are sent over to Manhattan delivery piers by Float or over the ferries by truck. But great quantities of the foodstuffs of brought to the yards are put into New Jersey cold storage warehouses—for later delivery over the Ferries by truck to Manhattan consumption—one warehouse company alone—having on the New Jersey shore 3½ million cubic feet of areas in this service—for the storage of eggs—butter—cheese—lard—breadstuffs — poultry — game — meats — fruits — canned goods—condensed milk—food of all kinds except the daily fluid milk—and market green stuffs.

There then is the Food supply that would ensure the metropolis against any menace of hunger—piled up in precisely *the wrong place* on the *New Jersey* shore—with the broad Hudson and all its possible vicissitudes separating the food from those who are dependent upon it—a situation that invites disaster!

The fog bank intervenes—traffic across the water ceases and over an Island City of 5,000,000 of people—but *one mile* away from stores of abundance—rises the menace of hunger.

The logic of this situation suggests that New York's Food supply should not be stored on the *other side* but on *this side* of the fog bank!—But as it has heretofore *never* been possible to bring the train with its load of food stuffs to Manhattan—it was necessary to unload it in the New Jersey yard—and as cold storage goods—deteriorate rapidly in open temperatures it was necessary to establish cold storage warehouses in the Railroad yard itself for quick service. That is why New York's Food supply is now stored on the *other side* of the fog bank. But under the new system—*the train* is brought over—*not* after standing on sidings waiting on unloading—but *at once* and the goods still in refrigeration transferred in proper temperatures directly from the car to the cold storage areas of the new Terminal—on the *New York side* of the *fog bank*—where an emergent supply of essentials like meats—milk, poultry game—with dairy products—butter, cheese—eggs together constituting 67% of the whole Manhattan Food supply may always remain in the cold storage areas ready to meet any conditions that may arise. Under such a system *fogs* are no longer a factor in the Food problem of New York City.

STORAGE AREAS

The *cold* and *dry storage* areas of the Manhattan Railway Terminal are *unique* among all such storage warehouses—in Manhattan—distinguished in 3 respects:

1. *In Character*

All other Food storage warehouses are scattered here and there about Manhattan Island—and with few exceptions—without either rail or water connection—depending on cartage over the ferries—and through the streets—not only at great expense—but at loss and damage of product—while the Storage areas of the new Terminal are located in the same building with—directly under—and in immediate connection by freight Elevators with—the freight platforms of *all* the Trunk line Railroads—for the transfer of freights—directly from Cars to storage—and through these Trunk lines with—the entire continental system of Railroads.

2. *In Capacity*

The immensity of the storage areas may be more readily comprehended by comparison with other areas. With more than 20,000,000 cubic feet of areas—cold and dry—(for Food)—the *food storage areas* of the Terminal are greater than the aggregate areas of *all* the food storage warehouses *now on Manhattan Island*. There are now just *fifty* such warehouses in Manhattan—18 of them Cold—32 Dry (Food) storage.

3. *In Economy—and—Convenience*

No cartage—no extra handling—no *loss* or *damage* of products by the elements—no delays—and the economies in *loss and damage* on the Metropolitan Food Supply *alone* is estimated by the U. S. Commissioner of foods at *millions*.

As for convenience it represents the acme of *convenience*.

EXPRESS SERVICE

Of this service the Commission says:

The Express Companies are poorly equipped in the way of terminal facilities to satisfactorily serve the public.

The Express business of the New Jersey trunk lines is now centered on the New Jersey shore—where transfer of packages is made to and from Express wagons—and these must cross the ferries to and fro.

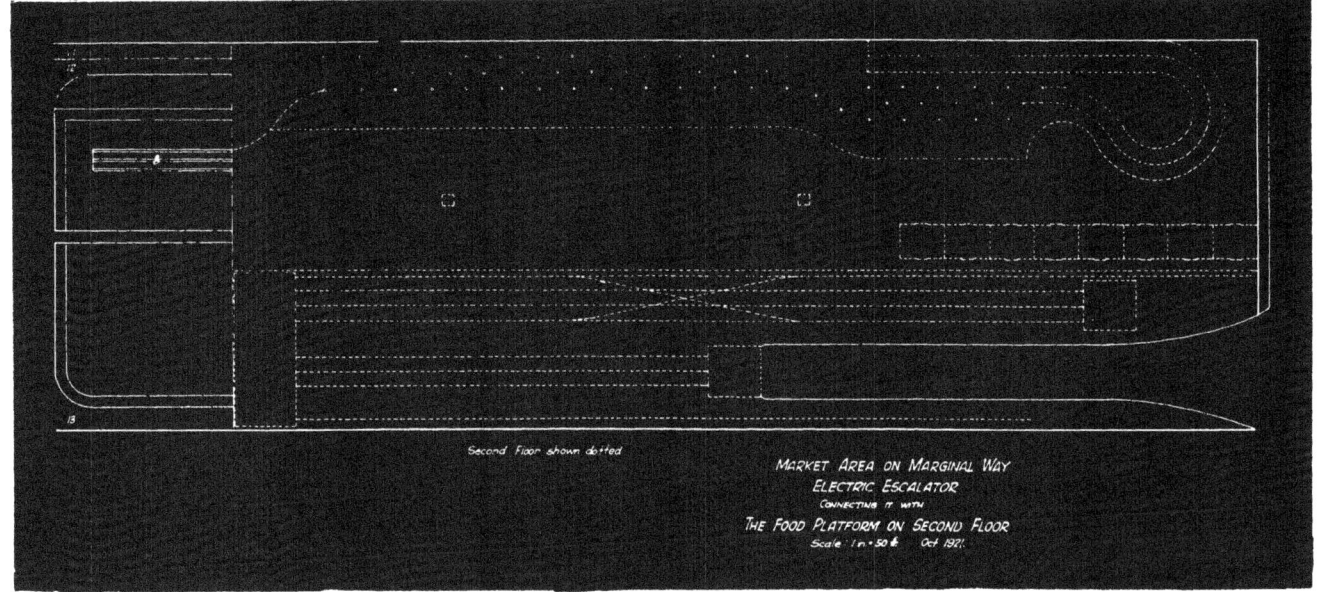

Under the New System the crossing of ferries eliminated Express service will begin and end in New York. The Express Car will cross the River to the Manhattan Railway Terminal and be delivered on tracks opposite areas set apart in each Railroad section—on Eastbound and Westbound floors and at the Central Division of the Terminal the service may have its offices of General Administration—the American Railway Express.

THE MANY PLANS REVIEWED

In view of the fact that the recent Harbor Commission with such able professional aids as General Goethals—Mr. Cresson—Chief Engineer (familiar with North River front conditions through long service in the Department of Docks)—and a large corps of experts skilled in every department of transportation—has scientifically analyzed and set aside as incapable all plans that have been proposed for the solution of the great traffic problem at the Hudson River front—it is interesting to pass them in review—and consider their fundamental features and character.

There were *twenty-three* in all—and as the *solution* they all sought was at last reached by the *twenty-fourth*—the *Sibley System*—a plan that is *simplicity* itself—it is remarkable to note the ponderous—gigantic—expensive and complex methods proposed to accomplish what was finally accomplished with comparatively so little outlay—and so *simply*.

In their chronological order from 1866—down to date—a period of over *half a century*—this is the official catalogue:

1. 1866—Mr. O. Vanderburgh, Civil Engineer—Elevated Freight line along the Hudson River front.
2. 1875—Special Committee Am. Soc. Civil Engrs.—"created for the purpose." Double track—belt line—along the water front—with fireproof warehouses having side track facilities—storage space on the farms along the newly laid out West Street.
3. 1897—Board of 3 Consulting Engineers retained by the Dept. of Docks and Ferries. A surface water front Railroad freight line connecting at Christopher St. with New York Central—and the establishment of inland terminals and Elevated passenger line on Marginal Way. Float bridges at Battery Park for New Jersey Railroad connection.
4. 1908—Merchants' Association of New York. Double track freight viaduct flanked with warehouses (or a four track freight and passenger viaduct)—along the westerly edge of the Marginal Way. Method of connection with New Jersey Railroads not indicated.
5. 1908—W. J. Wilgus—former Vice President and Chief Engineer New York Central Railroad System (as representing the Amsterdam Corporation) presented a plan—Belt line and classification yard in New Jersey—Standard cars to break bulk at transfer station there—freight put into small special cars—

(10 tons)—sent through a tunnel under the Hudson to a subway in Manhattan—running—"not only under the Marginal Way but under the sidewalks of every important street in the business section—on both sides of the street."

6. 1910—Mr. Calvin Tomkins (then) Commissioner of Docks of New York City representing the minority of a Board of Four—appointed by the Board of Estimate to study the situation—Four track elevated marginal railway—connecting with New York Central, at 60 St.—Five Union Terminals—25 to 30th St.—10th to 12th Ave.—a sixth terminal at Canal St. Float bridge connection for all the New Jersey roads at the water line between 37th and 40th St. with car storage yard on the upland opposite. Cars drawn up first from the Float to the street—then up an incline to the Elevated road.

   1911—Mr. Tomkins presented a modification of this plan increasing the number of float bridges to extend from 30th to 40th Sts.

   1912—Mr. Tomkins presented a second modification of his plan, substituting for the Float bridge connection a tunnel under the North River with a belt line and classification yard on the New Jersey meadows.

7. 1910—Messrs. Wm. A. Prendergast, Comptroller of the City of New York—John Purroy Mitchel, President Board of Aldermen, and George McAneny, President of the Borough of Manhattan, representing the majority of the Board of Four (appointed by the Board of Estimate) of which Mr. Tomkins represented the minority. Creation of Unit Terminals—located inshore opposite pier terminals—where Float bridge connection was made for the New Jersey Railroads. Cars were to be drawn up to street level—then switched back out onto the pier—then reversed and taken up an incline to an elevated railway that made connection with the second level of the intra-block terminals.

8. 1911—The New York Chamber of Commerce presented a report on the problem. Endorsing the principle of the Tomkins plan for an elevated railway on the Marginal Way—("To be built and owned by the City") and also the general features of the New York Central plans for new rail structures and elaborating on the Merchants' Association plan (of 1908)—of warehouses on the Marginal Way.

9. 1918—Mr. Amos L. Schaeffer (then) Consulting Engineer to the Bronx. Recommended the construction of an upper level over the Marginal Way—with ramps to the side streets—a surface railway to be built on the Marginal Way—with Float connection at the Battery and ultimately tunnel connection for the New Jersey Railroads.

10. 1913—Mr. D. C. Willoughby submitted to the Board of Estimate a Plan for a subway along the water front—with tunnel connection for the New Jersey Railroads—subsidiary subways with small (10 ton) cars for the distribution of freights—and warehouses on the Marginal Way. The main subway would have 6 tracks and double track subway connection with New York Central. There would be 17 warehouses—9 stories high. Elevators would raise standard freight cars.

11. 1916—Mr. Duncan D. McLean—presented to the Mayor of New York City a Plan for a 16 track subway under West St. and Marginal Way with 4 double track tunnels under the Hudson—and at intervals along the Marginal Subway 1,000 ft. inland platforms—one for each of the railroads—elevators will connect the platform with the street level.

12. 1916—Mr. Jno. Purroy Mitchel (then) Mayor of New York presented a plan prepared under his direction which contemplated a four track elevated railway on the Marginal Way down to 30th St.—then a double track elevated over private right of way (near the line of 9th Ave.) and down to Canal St. New York Central yards at 30th and 60th Sts. to be reconstructed—tracks along Riverside Park to be covered and the yard at Manhattanville much expanded with storage tracks well out into the River. The plan was endorsed by most of New York's newspapers—by the Chamber of Commerce—the Merchants' Association and other organizations and by the then Commissioner of Docks. The plan was swept aside by legislation at Albany.

13. 1917—A Joint Conference Committee of the Board of Estimate and the Public Service Commission—issued New plans and proposals—the main physical departure from the Mitchel plan being to continue the elevated railway along the Marginal Way—instead of over a private way below 30th St. New York Central refused the new conditions and the plan lapsed.

14. 1917—(Nov.)—A Special Commission created by legislature, Mr. Wm. H. Van Benschoten, Chairman—to study the situation proposed a West Side Railway—(whether elevated or subway was not determined) with tunnel connection to bring over the New Jersey roads—the yard at Manhattanville to extend to the East of the main tracks of New York Central—the tracks along Riverside Park to be depressed and covered. The plan contemplated a unified joint terminal system on the West Side of Manhattan.

15. 1918—Mr. Geo. L. Record of Jersey City and Mr. Will H. Lyford a Chicago Engineer presented to the New York and New Jersey Port and Harbor Commission a Plan (prepared by Mr. Lyford)—for handling all Manhattan freight of the New Jersey Railroads through a Union Terminal in Jersey City —the cars being turned back at that point—and Motor Trucks used to carry the freight—over the ferries—to and from inland stations in Manhattan.

16. 1918—Col. Joseph C. Bonner presented to the Commission a Rail wagon plan—Four wheeled rail wagons to be hauled either by horses or motor tractors with wheels at wide gage to straddle low flat cars running on an electric railway—moving through the Hudson-Manhattan tubes—to and from Manhattan.

17. 1918—Hon. Chas. L. Craig, Comptroller of the City of New York presented a report, recommending the construction of a Six track subway from 59th St. south with union terminals and union transfer float bridges for the New Jersey railroads—between 25th and 30th Sts. and at Leroy and Morton Sts. the connections between the bridges and the subway to cross the Marginal Way at grade. The subway route was 11th Ave. to 27th St.—10th Ave. to 15th St., Hudson St., to North Moore St.

18. 1918—Hon. Murray Hulbert, Commissioner of Docks of the City of New York reported he had given consideration to a Plan which contemplated the removal of the New York Central railroad from Riverside Park. New York Central freight would follow the main tracks from Spuyten Duyvil to Mott Haven —thence over a new rail line to a new yard on the East River—thence through a subway under First Ave. Manhattan to 34th St. thence through subways crossing Manhattan to the 60th and 30th St. yards and a subway under the West Side would extend south from 59th St. "The entire West side surface system from Spuyten Duyvil south would then be removed except the yards at 30th and 60th St."

19. 1919—Dr. Gustav Lindenthal—Consulting Engineer, advocated the Building of a bridge spanning the Hudson at 57th St. with two levels—for the transfer of freight and passengers, passenger trains to reach a Union Station near Pennsylvania Station. Elevated railway along the West side for freight trains with return tunnel at the Battery. A belt line and classification yard in New Jersey with facilities for loading and unloading motor trucks.

20. 1919—Mr. T. Kennard Thomson presented a Plan (which had before been advocated)—to extend Manhattan Island 4 miles at its south end by filling in the Upper Bay—encircle the new island with a 6 track surface railway over which the marginal way would be carried as in the Schaffer plan of 1912 (No. 9) Tunnels under the Hudson to bring the New Jersey roads over classification yard on the new ground—far south of Governors Island.

21. 1919—Mr. W. J. Bartnett presented to the Commission a comprehensive plan—Terminal on the Hackensack Meadows—motor truck service to Manhattan over the ferries at first—ultimately through 3 vehicular tunnels and over a bridge—subway under the West side Marginal Way in Manhattan from Battery Place to 79th St. with warehouses above it—and two tunnel connections with New Jersey.

22. 1919—Mr. Jno. H. Ward (the latest) submitted to the Commission, Sept. 25, 1919, a plan that contemplated a Union Terminal at Jamaica Bay—with which the New Jersey Roads would connect by car float to Bay Ridge—ultimately by tunnel under the upper Bay across to New Jersey. From the Union Terminal a system of zone deliveries to consignees by motor trucks and flat cars.

23. 1921—*Finally*—The New York and New Jersey Port and Harbor Commission—the most scientific and ablest body which had ever considered the subject—after three years of analytic engineering study of the problem and of *all preceding plans* that had been formulated for its solution—officially declared them all *incapable* and presented as the *true solution* its own creation—the *automatic electric* tunnel

plan. The *automatic electric* plan—its fundamental features—the breaking of bulk in New Jersey—the transfer of the freight in automatically operated special cars through tunnels under the river and subways under the streets—to twelve distributed Manhattan terminals located at the street level.

This 23rd and only surviving plan was itself—immediately upon publication—declared by Engineering and Transportation authority—*incapable*—and under the hand of the new Port Board (successor to the Expired Commission)—efforts were made to remedy its defects and render it capable. Its defects—however—were *fundamental* beyond the reach of change of detail, moreover, the great investment required rendered it also financially impossible.

24. 1921—*The twenty-fourth* and last plan after *all others had failed*—the *perfect solution* of the great *dual problem*—the Railroad Traffic Problem and the equally important West side problem—is *The Sibley System—over the water.*

THE AUTOMATIC ELECTRIC TUNNEL PLAN *AND* THE SIBLEY SYSTEM OVER THE WATER *COMPARED*

Three fundamental differences between the two systems stand out prominently:
1. In the *breaking of bulk* in New Jersey.
2. In the *highway* and *its equipment*.
3. In the *one* Manhattan Terminal vs. *twelve*

and these *radical* differences create a wide and deep gulf between the two systems (as presented in the parallel columns which follow)—at places fathomless—at other places very deep—but everywhere deep and wide.

THE BREAKING OF BULK

The breaking of bulk is an expensive operation estimated to cost for the double operation of unloading—reloading not less than *one dollar* per ton—and on the Railroad traffic tonnage to amount to *nine million* dollars per annum. It is—however—a *necessity* expense of the Automatic Electric plan—and this necessity entails:

A. The *transfer system* in the New Jersey yards 5 miles away from the Hudson River water front—where the freight taken out of standard cars is put into trailers which drawn along the platform by electric tractors or otherwise—are placed into specially constructed tunnel cars of the *necessarily* limited freight capacity of but *seven and a half* tons each (although the floor area of the tunnel car is greater than that of the standard car)—for a 14-mile haul underground to the Manhattan Terminal and return.

B. The Belt Line connections and the Interchange yard.

C. *Fourteen miles* of *tunnel* and *equipment* as a *highway*.

The result of this *breaking of bulk* is strikingly shown by the comparative expense of the two systems—for the construction and equipment of the necessary *highway*—between the yard and the Manhattan Terminal—for the transfer of the freight from the standard car to special car and the delivery of that special car to the Manhattan Terminal—in one case—and in the other—to deliver the standard car—itself—to Manhattan Terminal with *bulk unbroken*.

The Highway and Yard
(Alone Considered)

Automatic System		*Sibley System*	
CONSTRUCTION	$166,423,066	CONSTRUCTION	$ *Nothing*
EQUIPMENT	11,815,250	EQUIPMENT (*Motor Floats*)	6,000,000
TOTAL	178,238,316	TOTAL	6,000,000
FIXED CHARGES	%		
Int.	6.		
Ins.	.5		
Taxes	2.0		
Sinking Fund	1.68		
	10.18		
FIXED CHARGES		FIXED CHARGES	
178,238,316 @ 10.18	18,144,660	6,000,000 @ 10.18	610,800

PRESENT TRAFFIC
8,500,000 Tons
FOR HIGHWAY—*Per Ton*.............. $2.13–46/100

PRESENT TRAFFIC
FOR HIGHWAY—*Per Ton*............. EIGHT CENTS
8,500,000 Tons

NOTE: The authority for Automatic figures as here used is the Report of N. Y. & N. J. Port & Harbor Commission (1921) as follows:

COST OF CONSTRUCTION AND EQUIPMENT
Total (P. 273) at 1918 Prices... $187,906,330
Less Item G—(12 Terminals in Manhattan)................................ 56,308,760 $131,597,570
Plus 25% (P. 274) at 1920 Prices...   32,899,392

TOTAL at 1920 Prices—*for Construction* (including *Equipment*—$11,815,250) ... $164,496,962
INTEREST—During Construction at 6% Rate (less interest on on Equipment).....   13,741,354

TOTAL FOR CONSTRUCTION AND EQUIPMENT of the *Tunnel Highway* and *The Yard*
    (as above) $178,238,316

These *radical* differences extend into every department of activity and are in the aggregate so great as to be *overwhelming*.

Character

Automatic System

For Package Freight—*Only*
"Will have nothing to do with the bulky freight of the inland float bridge terminals—on the West side above 23rd St.—which it is estimated constitutes 40 per cent of their tonnage and which must be handled by Car Float."

Contemplates retention of
1. Inland Float Bridge Terminals on the West side above 23rd St.
2. 30th St. and 60th St. yards.
3. Old Cartage System.

Sibley System

For *all* Freights.

Contemplates removal of entire West side freight system and the operation of an organized motor truck system.

CHARACTER OF FREIGHTS TO BE HANDLED

The recent New York and New Jersey Port and Harbor Commission in presenting its Automatic Electric plan—said of it:

> The team track and heavy freight of the Float bridge termins—(on the North River front from 25th to 60th St.)—cannot be accommodated and these terminals *should be retained*. This would also include the 33rd St. yard of the New York Central which has float bridge connections.

and the Vice President of the Erie Railway—before the New York Railway Club—in commenting on the Automatic Electric plan—said of it:

> It would be confined only to certain kinds of domestic freight—or in other words—*small package freight* and would not be able to take care of the heavy pieces of structural steel—building materials of various kinds—machinery and other heavy articles which are so essential in our city. It would simply be a *small package railway* to release water front piers—and the overhead expense would be so *prohibitive* that with the revenues that could be earned a project of this kind could not be capitalized.
> The whole thing is a *costly dream*.

At the new Railway Terminal of the water system *all* kinds of freight are handled. The freight train just as it arrives at the yard will cross the river to Manhattan and all freight that a car will contain will be delivered either over the platforms to trucks in the regular driveways—or in the case of heavy—bulky structural material too long or too heavy to pass around the curves (of 40 ft. radius)—in the Driveway—by cranes through floor openings to trucks in the *subway circle* below the tracks—on street level—as explained on other pages. This class of freight constitutes 30 to 40 per cent of all freight coming over to Manhattan—and any system incapable of handling it even though in other respects capable would fail to fulfill the general purpose of the Railway Terminal.

If the Float Bridge Terminals 25th to 60th Sts. are to be retained and the 30th and 60th St. yards continued as the Commission's plan contemplates—the streets of the City cannot be cleared of Railroad cars and tracks.

Under the New System where *all* freights are handled and to far greater advantage than is possible under any existing or proposed Terminal System—there will be nonecessity for the uptown Float Bridge Terminals—the streets will be cleared of trains and of tracks.

Construction

Automatic System		Sibley System	
Site areas—sq. ft.	1,630,800	Site areas—sq. ft.	3,017,400
Floor areas (x 5)	8,154,000	Floor areas (x 4)	12,069,600
Cubic areas (x 75)	122,310,000	Cubic areas (x 72)	217,252,800
Operating areas (x 3)	4,898,400	Operating areas (x 3)	9,532,200
Frt. plat. areas	1,260,000	Frt. plat. areas	3,124,840
Storage areas	NONE	Storage areas, CUBIC	21,310,272
Office areas	139,200	Office areas (Railroad)	343,340
GARAGE	NONE	GARAGE	408,000
Railroad Tracks		Railroad Tracks	
MILES	3.8	MILES	29.2
		CARS	3,760
Driveways (@ 14 avg.)		Driveways (@ 14 avg.)	
MILES	9.8	MILES	37
Grades		Grades	
ASCENDING—per cent	3.9	ASCENDING—per cent	2.7
DESCENDING—per cent	4.3	DESCENDING—per cent	2.6
Total width at platform—ft.	40	Total width at platform—ft.	76
Truck spaces at platform	1,008	Truck spaces at platform	1,768
PLATFORMS in N. J.—sq. ft.	1,152,000	PLATFORMS in N. Y.—sq. ft.	3,124,840
ELEVATORS		ELEVATORS	
For cars … 48		For cars … 48	
For freight … NONE		For freight … 22	
For passengers … NONE		For passengers … 48	
Total	48	Total	128
OPERATION		OPERATION	
Elevator—foot tons	842,000,000	Elevator—foot tons	405,000,000
Haul—ton miles	65,000,000	Haul—ton miles	34,800,000
CAPACITY		CAPACITY	
LIMIT yr. 1929—*Tons*	10,000,000	LIMIT yr. 2,004—*Tons*	48,000,000
CONSTRUCTION	255,992,684	CONSTRUCTION	85,456,390
Period of construction—yrs.	3	Period of construction—yrs.	2
Int. during construction (@ 6%)	20,076,089	Int. during construction (@ 6%)	8,699,460
Fixed Chgs. @ 10%	25,599,268	Fixed Chgs. @ 10%	8,545,639
PER TON (9,000,000) …… DOLLARS	2.84	PER TON (9,000,000) …… CENTS	.95

NOTE: 1. With additional investment of $32,000,000 by Automatic for *five* more Manhattan Terminals the Limit is extended to the year 1943 and the tonnage to 14,260,000 tons.

2. New York Central yard reconstruction not included in the above total of construction of $255,992,634.

NEW YORK CENTRAL UNDER THE SIBLEY SYSTEM

FREIGHT AND PASSENGERS DIVORCED

EAST BANK OF THE HUDSON—FOR PASSENGERS

WEST BANK OF THE HUDSON—FOR FREIGHT

THE LOGICAL *route for New York Central freight traffic is via the West Shore Railroad.*
                                                                    N. Y. & N. J. PORT & HARBOR COMMISSION.

UNLESS *passenger traffic can be separated from freight traffic with added facilities for both—future calamity is inevitable.*
                                                                    A. H. SMITH   (late) PRESIDENT—NEW YORK CENTRAL

NEW YORK CENTRAL GAINS
    RECONSTRUCTION . . . $120,000,000
    CAPITAL STOCK VALUES . . 300,000,000
    ANNUAL ECONOMY . . . 15,000,000

NEW YORK CENTRAL AT SPUYTEN DUYVIL—AT WEEHAWKEN

It is very natural that New York Central should resist all effort at depriving it of the use of its rail system through the streets for the delivery of its Manhattan freights because its Float Methods and pier facilities on the water are not capable of meeting its traffic necessities nor can these be improved in the one case or expanded in the other. Its city rails—therefore—though maintained and operated at great expense and in the face of crippling conditions—constitute an essential part of its whole Metropolitan service—and until other facilities operable and acceptable are provided for that Road it is unreasonable to expect it to abandon its franchises—and yield to the demand that its rails be taken out of the streets.

As none of the many plans which have been formulated has proven capable of effecting this relief for the Road the situation remains to-day unchanged—after more than 30 years of continued effort—and the Road must of necessity continue to stand on its rights to operate its rail system—and all Metropolitan plans for the development of the West side parks—the improvement of the City highways and avenues—and the expansion and readjustment of its commercial water front—must consequently wait on the key to the situation—which is—the provision of other traffic facilities for New York Central which shall equal or surpass in efficiency—those which the Road now finds *essential* to its operation.

It is this situation—where an impassé between the city and the Road has been reached that the new Water System comes now to relieve and after *all other plans have failed.*

While none of the plans that have been proposed has proven operable—many of them involved such violent physical changes—not only in operation—but in construction and direction—that even though they had been practicable could not possibly have been acceptable to New York Central.

Such, for example—as sending its great flow of Metropolitan freight—(greater than that of any other road—approximating one-third of the whole volume)—from the North River over to the East River—and through tunnels under the City's streets from one side of the town to the other—or along the length of the Island and under the River—on a jaunt over to New Jersey through an underground circuit of 14 miles through the Jersey yards and back again through other tunnels and subways to the point of departure in Manhattan.

New York Central must have direct connection with West-Side market and business areas such as it has enjoyed for all the years of its existence. It would never consent to such roundabout difficult routes for its great stream of traffic even if they were operable, and the wonder of the situation is that in the Engineering studies of more than 40 years—in the preparation of no less than 23 different plans for the solution of the North River traffic problem involving methods for the bringing of New York Central freights from the main line at Spuyten Duyvil down to the market and business areas on the West side of town—not one of them considered the marvelous facility presented by the so convenient water surface—or visioned any method of availing of this great natural highway—sweeping along at the very edge of the Railroad yard—flowing directly to the very center of the market areas—but all of them—without exception—undertook to burrow a way for ten or fifteen miles through the solid earth.

In presenting the new water system therefore as the *perfect* system for the relief of New York Central and in view of the failure of all other known plans—the *only* plan capable of that relief—it is important to make clear the marked distinction between it and all these preceding plans that it may be understood that whereas they represented at very best nothing less than formidable traffic *experiment* the new water system proposes no such radical changes but simply *expands* a system which is in use to-day by New York Central and all the Roads —one with which they have grown entirely familiar through many years of daily service—the use of the natural facilities of *the water.* The Car Float and its service are hallowed by time.

It is also important to emphasize that none of the features of the new water system involve experiment. The raising of cars at the Terminal by Elevator and the movement of cars on the floors and the float by Electric Cable are both in practice already and both are sanctioned by high engineering authority—that of the recent commission not only but of general Engineering science;—the unloading—reloading of cars at the new terminal are features of the traffic of to-day;—while the operation of the Float by Motor Marine Engine—and on schedule—though it is a new feature is by no means an experiment—since the operative speed and regularity of the North river ferry boat are a daily demonstration of the operative speed and capacity of the new Motor Float;—and the new Cycle of operation is nothing more than a systematic method of control and coördination of the several parts of the Terminal machine on the water—in the warehouse—at the yard—operating as a whole—which under critical analysis presents—as New York Central will be able to see—its own sufficient warrant of efficiency.

If then this physical examination shall prove satisfactory to New York Central—and its further examination into the system shall reveal that under its operation the great burden of expense under which the road now maintains and operates its present rail and water system will be reduced by more than *one-half*—there would be no reason for the continuance of its City Rail System and the only remaining question would be whether the new system should meet the rail-head of New York Central at Spuyten Duyvil or at Weehawken.

The cost of bringing the freights of New York Central by rail down to 60th St.—and the maintenance of the rail system to that point aggregates a sum many times greater than that involved in their transfer for the same distance over the water while the advantages of the latter are too obvious to need emphasis.

The Schedule or Cycle of Operation for New York Central as definitely elaborated is described under the caption *The Operation of the System*—and tabulated in blueprint entitled *New York Central at Spuyten Duyvil—Its Cycle of Operation.*

This schedule shows with precision every movement of float of freight—of car—from yard to terminal—

from terminal to yard—and the time of every such separate function. The traffic officers of that Road will be able to analyze and examine it in all its parts and they will come to understand that the new service is capable of reaching New York Central—effectively—easily—very easily—at *Spuyten Duyvil* or at *Weehawken*.

Assuming then that these new facilities shall prove acceptable to New York Central the consequent change in the present methods of the Road would *solve* the vexed West side problem and—since all other plans have now officially failed—in the *only* way it can ever be solved;—lift from the shoulders of the Road the great expense it is now under for the maintenance of an antique rail freight system and its expensive operation under restraint through the streets;—enable it to convert its valuable Metropolitan areas—(now a part of that system and representing millions of investment)—to cash for its Treasury; and forever release the Road from further consideration of plans of depressed and covered trackways through the parks;—of Elevated Railways over privately acquired rights of way involving outlays of other millions;—and the Road would find itself for the first time in its history in accord with the Government of the Metropolis whose commercial interests it serves.

While for the City of New York there would result from these radical but wholly beneficent changes benefits of incalculable value!

The City streets would be forever freed of the rails and freight trains that have been a subject of bitter contention since cars first began to roll and the City Government—untrammeled—could then proceed to develop Riverside Drive and create marginal Park areas of great beauty along the scenic banks of the incomparable Hudson from 72nd St. to Spuyten Duyvil—while the Commercial water front would be opened for Marine service from the Battery to the bluffs at 72nd St.—a transformation which has been the *dream* of the *idealist*.

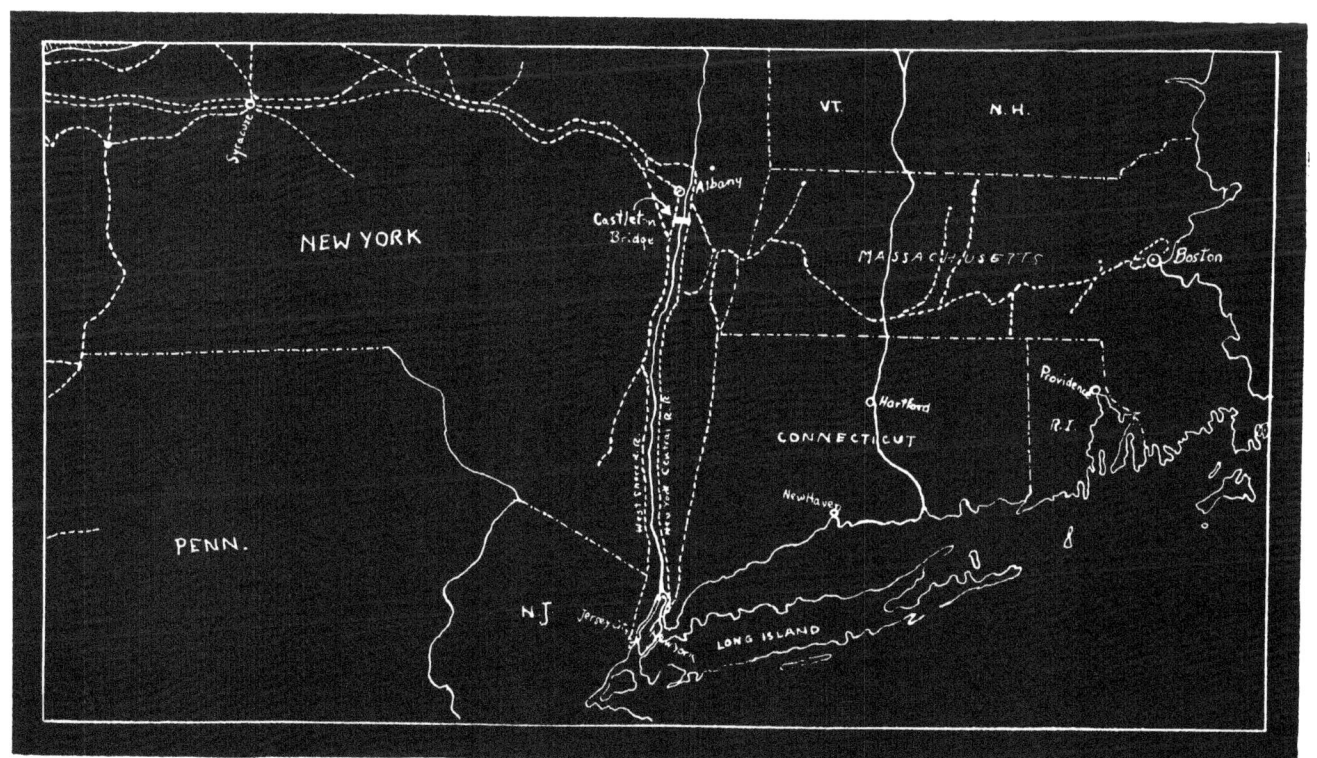

NEW YORK CENTRAL—THE NEW AREAS

The gross areas (including driveways) and the net areas (excluding driveways) of all the Railroad pier stations and bulkhead platforms—below 60th St.—on the North River and the East River—and at the Wallabout in Brooklyn—now in New York Central service (including West shore)—for Eastbound and Westbound freights aggregate and compare with corresponding areas of the two sections of the New Terminal set apart for the New York Central (West Shore) system—as follows:

Gross Areas	East Bound	Excess Per Cent	West Bound	Excess Per Cent	Total	Excess Per Cent
NEW YORK CENTRAL	416,966		73,050		490,016	
NEW TERMINAL	849,216		405,956		1,255,172	
EXCESS—GROSS AREAS	432,250	103	332,906	455	765,156	156
Net Areas						
NEW YORK CENTRAL	246,357		73,050		319,407	
NEW TERMINAL	548,460		253,892		802,352	
EXCESS—NET AREAS	302,103	122	180,842	247	482,945	151

It is thus seen that the new areas for New York Central's Eastbound traffic are more than *twice*—and for the Westbound—*four times*—as great as the present water front areas. Moreover while the present areas are in effect *reduced* by unavoidable delay in the movement of freight—creating temporary congestion—intensified by the necessary longitudinal driveways at the middle line of the pier and the consequent mingling of horses—trucks—operatives and freight—Terminal areas—where Driveways with platform areas elevated above them—each have their separate uncrowded areas—are on the contrary—in effect—*multiplied* by the freedom and facility of movement of car—of truck—of freight—so that the apparent *excess of areas*—as shown—already very great—is so again more than *doubled*.

Besides all these excessive areas—there is a new *market area* at the front of New York Central's 2 sections of the Terminal—680 ft. long, 180 ft. wide—122,400 square feet.

NEW YORK CENTRAL AT WEEHAWKEN—WEST SHORE RAILROAD

This road built to compete with New York Central from New York City to Buffalo parallels it all the way. The two roads are separated at no point by more than 10 or 15 miles and for the greater part of the way they are in sight of each other. New York Central's feeder lines east and west of Buffalo all make natural and easy connections with West Shore rails.

The recent N. Y. and N. J. Port and Harbor Commission, after an expert analysis of the freight traffic of New York Central, recorded as its judgment—(p. 286—Official Report 1921):

> "The logical route for the New York Central freight traffic is via the *West Shore Railroad* facilities being provided east of the Hudson—presumably on the upper East River—mainly for that originating east and south of Albany."

THE HUDSON RIVER BRIDGE

Since the date of the Commission's report New York Central's new railroad bridge spanning the Hudson at Castleton, 12 miles below Albany, has been opened (1925) for freight train traffic and now freights "Originating East and South of Albany"—referred to above by the Commission—may cross to connection with West Shore rails—assembling all freights of the New York Central System at the recently constructed great Selkirk yard of New York Central on the west bank of the Hudson. (See map on page 89.)

FREIGHT AND PASSENGER SERVICE DIVORCED

The late A. H. Smith, President of New York Central in a published interview, declared that:

> Unless passenger traffic can be separated from freight traffic with added facilities for both, future calamity is inevitable.

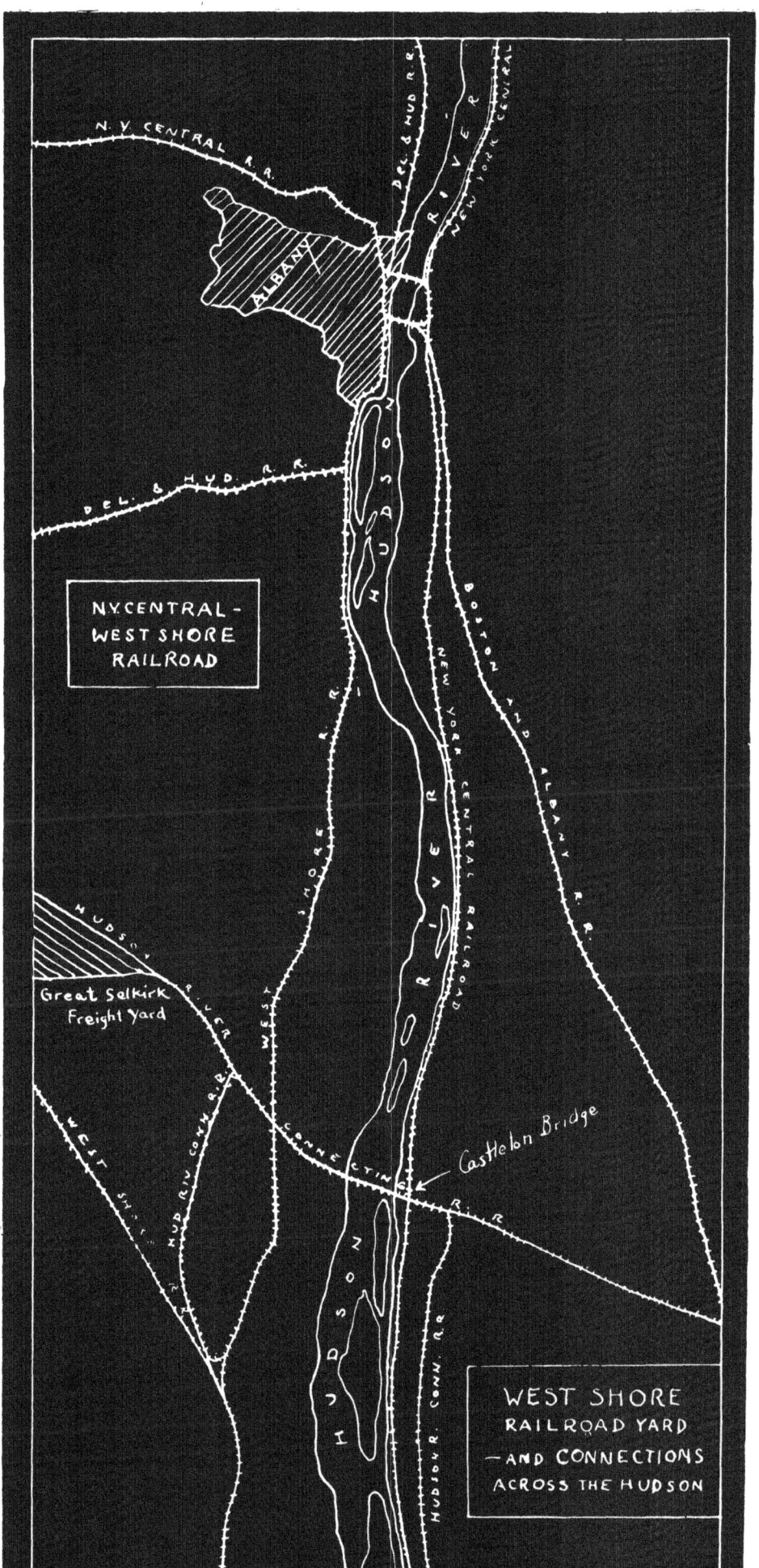

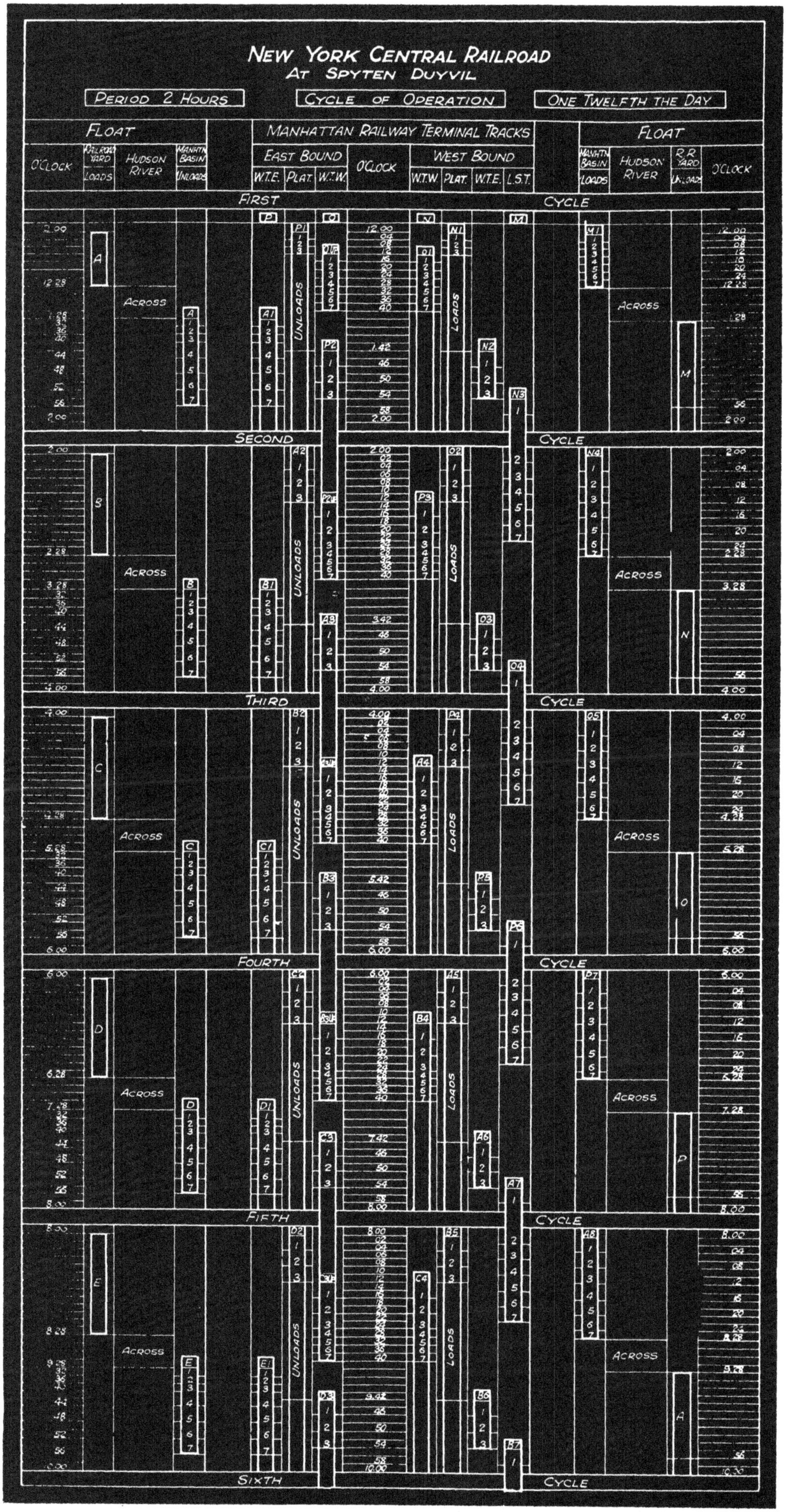
New York Central Railroad
At Spyten Duyvil
Period 2 Hours
Cycle of Operation
One Twelfth the Day
Float
Manhattan Railway Terminal Tracks
Float
O'Clock
Railroad Yard
Loads
Hudson River
Manhtn Basin
Unloads
East Bound
W.T.E.
Plat.
W.T.W.
O'Clock
West Bound
W.T.W.
Plat.
W.T.E.
L.S.T.
Manhtn Basin
Loads
Hudson River
R.R. Yard
Unloads
O'Clock
First Cycle
Second Cycle
Third Cycle
Fourth Cycle
Fifth Cycle
Sixth Cycle
Across
Unloads
Loads

Precisely in line with this sage admonition of one of the most esteemed Railroad authorities in the country, the freight traffic of New York Central is here divorced from the passenger service with immeasurable advantage for both.

Under the Sibley System all *freights* of the New York Central Lines may now go down the *west* bank of the Hudson, leaving the *east* bank a free fairway for the uninterrupted run of the *passenger train*.

With freight and passenger service thus *divorced* movement of *both* is facilitated and expedited. The side tracking of long heavy freight trains along the line to let the 20th Century Limited and other flyers pass—a railway transaction involving delays—always expensive and never without danger—becomes no longer necessary.

WEEHAWKEN THE FREIGHT TERMINUS

The Sibley System meets the *freight train* at Weehawken, transfers it *bulk unbroken* to the new Railway Terminal *on Manhattan Island* at *Canal St.*—The destination of the train remains the same—*New York City*—and New York Central *without outlay* reaches the point—*over the water*—now intended to be reached *overland* by the expenditure of $100,000,000.

THE CHANGE

The change of the freight train from Manhattan Island tracks to West Shore rails is not so radical as at first blush it may seem. It affects only the West Side rail system from Spuyten Duyvil down and leaves intact the road's rail system above the Harlem River. These subsidiary freight rails—the Putnam Division—the Harlem Division—are in connection with the new freight bridge over the Hudson at Castleton and therefore with West Shore rails for such freight train deliveries to Bronx, Westchester and other points as may be desirable.

It has been said New York Central's tracks are the Life Line for New York City. If that be so—with the connections noted (above the Harlem River)—the "Life Line" remains intact.

N. Y. CENTRAL'S GREAT GAIN

While all the roads will profit greatly under the Sibley System none will profit so much as New York Central, whose Manhattan freight system is operated under disadvantages greater than those of any other road, and this notwithstanding the supposed advantage of being able to serve certain local districts of the city, as for example the delivery of milk and other merchandise at its 30th and 130th St. stations—and the delivery of carload merchandise to warehouse sidings on Manhattan Island. An analysis of these transactions will show that they represent no net advantage to the treasury of the road.

This may be better understood from the following analysis of New York Central expense of operation:

ANALYSIS OF NEW YORK CENTRAL EXPENSE—ON THE BASIS OF CONTEMPLATED CONSTRUCTION

NOTE: The figures of assessed values of franchises and of real property now in the service of the Road on the West Side of Manhattan are from official City records. The estimates of reconstruction are those of New York Central Engineers as published—*N. Y. Times*, Dec. 18, 1923. The estimates of tonnage handled on the West Side rail System are those officially reported by the N. Y. & N. J. Port & Harbor Commission (pp. 152-164) that made an analytic study of the West Side System and the cost of service is exact as taken by the Commission from the records of the Railroads. City taxes are taken at 80% of (rate) 2.77—2.216. City, State and Road are here assumed to bear each one-third of the expense of grade crossing, and N. Y. Central is here credited with the other two thirds.

PRESENT VALUES IN WEST SIDE RAIL SERVICE

			%		
REALTY	26,167,500				
FRANCHISES	6,702,345	32,869,845	2.216	TAX	
			4.50	INT.	
		26,167,500	1.50	DPN.	
			.50	MAIN.	2,429,282

CONTEMPLATED
NEW CONSTRUCTION
ELEVATED STRUC. 100,000,000
ELEC. EQUIPMENT 20,675,000   120,675,000   2.216 TAX
                                                    4.50 INT.
                                                    1.50 DPN.
                                                     .50 MAIN.   10,518,033   12,947,315
LESS GRADE CROSSING CREDIT...... 13,334,000   4.50 INT.   600,030
TOTAL ANNUAL WEST SIDE OVERHEAD EXPENSE—NEW CONSTRUCTION   12,347,285

	Tons	At Piers	At Inland Sta.	Total
New York Central Manhattan Tonnage				
PIER STATIONS				
HUDSON RIVER	1,010,048			
EAST RIVER	335,652	1,345,700		
INLAND STATIONS				
ST. JOHNS PARK	400,962			
33RD STREET STATION	1,199,472		1,600,434	
TOTAL PIER AND INLAND.................				2,946,134

NOTE: The tonnage on Manhattan above 60th St. and at Wallabout not included—nor that of interchange or siding.

Cost of Operation Per Ton—Under New Construction Successive Operations Breakup Yard to Delivery	Direct Cost	Fixed Charges	For Pier Frts. Total	For Inland Sta.
1. Classification at breakup yard................	$0.1364	.0335	.1699	.1699
2. Breaking bulk at transfer station..............	.6667	.0078		
3. Line haul between yards and terminals	.1024	.0490	.1514	.1514
4. Switching and bridging at waterfront...........	.2528	.1537	.2528	
5. Car float operations...........................	.3280	.0500	.3780	
6. Handling freight at terminal stations...........	.9416	.3690	.9416	.9416
Rail movement below 60th St.				.1024
TOTAL CHARGES—*Pier Freights*—Per Ton.......			1.8937	
TOTAL CHARGES—*Inland Freights*—Per Ton.....				1.3653

NOTE: Item 2—Breaking bulk at Transfer Stations (.6667) omitted in favor N. Y. Central (proportion unknown). On *pier* freights (items 4.6) *overhead* omitted in favor N. Y. Central being included in overhead of new construction. On *inland* freights rail movement below 60th Street added but (in favor N. Y. Central) only at low rate—of direct cost—as (item 3) —overhead omitted.

Summary
N. Y. Central Tonnage and Costs

	Total	Per Ton	Amount	Total	Per Ton
PIER FREIGHTS	1,345,700	1.8937	2,548,352		
INLAND FREIGHTS	1,600,434	1.3653	2,185,072		
TOTAL	2,964,134			4,733,424	1.6066
NEW OVERHEAD				12,347,285	4.1910
TOTAL COST				17,080,709	
PER TON					5.7976

POSSIBLE GAINS FOR NEW YORK CENTRAL—UNDER THE NEW WATER SYSTEM

The estimated cost of delivery by the Water System from *Weehawken* to the *Manhattan Railway Terminal* at Canal St. is shown in comparison as follows:

NEW YORK CENTRAL—*Over the Land*	5.7976
SIBLEY SYSTEM—*Over the Water*	1.2426

N. Y. Central Annual Tonnage....................				2,946,134 @ 4.5550 — 13,419,640				
Additional Gain—*Present Realty Values Released*.......								
Amount as Assessed.........................				26,167,500				
Reinvested @ 6% Annual Income					1,570,050			
Total Estimated Gains by the Water Route for N. Y. Central Treasury—*Annually*.....................								14,989,690

Common Capital Stock
Effect of Sibley System Applied to N. Y. Central

Amount of Present Issue	Par	Rate Divi.	Sat. Close	Sept. 25, '26 Mkt. Val.	Extra Div.	New Div.	New Values New Mkt. Val.	Gain
304,800,000	100	7%	143	435,864,000	4.9	11.9	740,968,800	305,104,800

THE WEST SIDE REDEEMED—RIVERSIDE PARK AND THE CITY'S AVENUES RELEASED—THE VEXATIOUS GRADE CROSSING PROBLEM SOLVED

With this solution of the West Side problem that has been a grievous burden to the City of New York for more than 40 years and for which it has not been possible to find a solution—West Side streets and avenues freed of freight trains and freight stations would take on new life—take up new enterprises—realty values rebounding would take on new values and *Riverside Park* released from the destructive bondage of iron rails the incongruous burden of noxious freight trains could be developed as an area of natural beauty and recreation.

CONSTRUCTION — ORGANIZATION — OPERATION

METROPOLITAN RAILWAY TRANSFER, INC.
THE LINK BETWEEN THE YARD AND THE STORE

The service operated as a UNIT is of 3 elements.

1. MARINE—SCHEDULE MOTOR FLOAT Service for the transfer across the Hudson of the FREIGHT TRAIN—bulk unbroken—to be UNLOADED in NEW YORK CITY.
2. TERMINAL Operation and STORAGE.
3. LAND—SCHEDULE MOTOR TRUCK Service for delivery and collection.

THE TERMINAL

The terminal building located at the bulk head line of the Manhattan water front, Desbrosses to Christopher St., 2,820 ft. long N-S., 1,080 ft. wide (out to pier head line), 4 stories high, is ONE structure yet a composite of 9 independent buildings. It includes 8 juxtaposed railroad terminals or SECTIONS each 340 ft. wide, 1,080 ft. long (bulk head to pier head line), 4 stories high—distinctly separate from adjoining structures. Each railroad independent in structure is also independent in operation with its own platforms, tracks, basin and float service, directing the flow of its own freights unmixed with those of any other road. It is in effect the extension of its own rails across the Hudson to terminate in its own terminal in NEW YORK CITY.

The GARAGE and ADMINISTRATION building interposed at center, 100 ft. wide, 1,080 ft. long, 4 stories, separates the terminal structure into 2 WINGS of 4 sections each, and under the general administration of the railway terminal as a UNIT each road, while preserving its individual entity, avails of the advantage of the general facilities operated for the benefit of all roads.

THE BASIN

At each railroad section there is the distinctive feature of the System, the INSET BASIN, which admits the MOTOR FLOAT to position 500 ft. into and under the structure and to connection at the center of the section with the CAR ELEVATOR which, operating down to the level of the deck of the CAR FLOAT, elevates cars to any of the 3 operating floors above to be "spotted" at the platforms for unloading and reloading.

MOTOR FLOAT

At each railroad section there are TWO motor floats operating—the capacity of each a TRAIN OF TWENTY ONE cars. In operation each begins to take on a train—one at the yard—one at the New York Terminal—at the same time—they pass in midstream.

THE SCHEDULE OF OPERATION

The System is governed by a schedule of operation which is the same for all roads.

Baltimore & Ohio at Staten Island, 6 miles, New York Central (including West Shore) at Weehawken 3 miles, Pennsylvania, Erie, Jersey Central, Lehigh Valley, and Delaware, Lackawanna on the Jersey shore 1 mile away.

Within this general schedule there are, however, in the passage of the train through the terminal, FIVE distinct functions moving at varying speeds and times, and while the general schedule governs these movements as a whole it does not in their relation to each other. The faster movement would overtake the slower—confusion, congestion and ultimate paralysis would follow. To control this menace there came the CONCEPTION of the CYCLE OF OPERATION.

THE CYCLE OF OPERATION

The principle of the Cycle is the establishment of an arbitrary period within which the several functional movements of the train through the terminal that proceed under the general schedule shall begin and end. It may therefore be likened to "a wheel within a wheel"—the greater wheel the general schedule.

The five movements of the train from the rail to the rail again are:
1. Across the Hudson from the yard to the terminal and up to 3rd floor.
2. Unloads on 3rd floor.
3. Moves up from 3rd to 4th floor.
4. Reloads on 4th floor.
5. Descends to float and across to rail.

The Cycle is that period of time required for the longest of these five functional movements with an added marginal period for security. The time under schedule required for example to perform function No. 1—to take on the train, cross and put it off—is 1 H., 45 M.—the Cycle adds 15 minutes for rest before beginning the next movement and so establishes 2 hours as the CYCLE PERIOD.

Within this arbitrary period all movement comes to an end and waits to the beginning of the next cycle, and functions of unequal periods are so equalized and brought into harmonious coördination with the general flow of freight through the terminal.

THE CYCLE IN OPERATION

For the purposes of the cycle and to avoid fractions of time, cars, and tons, the day of 24 hours is divided into multiple parts as ONE EIGHTH, 3 hours; ONE TWELFTH, 2 hours; and these divisions give name to the cycle as EIGHTH CYCLE, TWELFTH CYCLE.

The TRAIN moves forward through the terminal as upon the single line of a circle and, under the limitations of the cycle, moves only when it has the right of way. Cars can never, therefore, overtake one another—congestion and confusion become impossible—with ample time and to spare for each functional movement the orderly procession continues with certainty and celerity—cycle following cycle indefinitely.

It is this conception supplementing others of fundamental character which makes the schedule of operation effective.

THESE METHODS UNDER SCRUTINY—OFFICIAL APPROVAL

These methods and the system have been under the critical examination of the official engineering staff of the Port Authority and declared by Maj. Genl. George W. Goethals, Chief of Staff—PERFECT. The facts of this approval are related on page 15.

It has also been under examination by the PENNSYLVANIA RAILROAD and the Engineering department of that road in its official report (copy of which was delivered to the author of the System) declared the System IDEAL in the following words:

p. 2. THE SIBLEY SYSTEM has been called the IDEAL system and it is so in that.
1. It provides for the orderly movement of freight through a modern terminal.
2. It includes store door delivery.
3. It would have a single service of delivery and collection of freight for all railroads.
4. It would use the streets for transportation at night.
5. It would unload cars in New York.

p. 5. To the writer of this report it does not seem that the Sibley System is as great a departure from accepted methods as would seem at first inspection. The terminals are similar to those recommended by the N. Y.–N. J. Port & Harbor Commission. The Car Elevators have the design of the Otis Company behind them.

(The Motor Float intended to cross the Hudson in 6 minutes is designed by the Bethlehem Ship Building Corp.)

p. 2. The writer believes that the terminal would operate successfully at the lower speed proposed by its author—the two hour cycle.

THE SYSTEM IN OPERATION

Following his approval of the System the author of the Pennsylvania report proceeds to describe the system in operation. He says:

p. 3. We will consider a particular case. Car P. R. R. 47324 was loaded at Harrisburg with miscellaneous merchandise for New York City. On that day freight was received for all of the districts in New York covered by the present five pier stations. The whole amount of freight at hand was one car load. Under the Sibley System the car would be made up with a train for New York and dispatched direct to Jersey City. It did not stop at Philadelphia Transfer for reloading with shipments from other cities into whole car loads for the several points in New York. Nor did it stop at Meadows Yard for car classification as between the 125th Street stations, 37th Street station, etc. With one delivery point only in New York it ran direct to the water front at Jersey City.

Here it was loaded on a float with eighteen other cars. The float was not convoyed by a tug but moved under its own power. It is different in other respects from the ordinary car float. It has propellors on either side to facilitate quick turning and designed to hold the float broadside against the current of the river.

As the float crosses the Hudson it approaches a great terminal station built on riparian land from Desbrosses St. northward. It is 2,830 ft. by 1,080 ft., four stories high. There are eight entrance slips for floats from the eight trunk line railroads. All freight cars now received at points south of 60th Street are to be floated into these slips.

The car from Harrisburg enters the slip reserved for the exclusive use of the Pennsylvania R. R. After the float is within the terminal a water gate is raised to form a quiet basin and the opening in the building is closed to protect the contents of the terminal from the weather.

When the float is berthed the inshore end is in contact with three car elevators. Three cars are drawn onto these elevators by means of electrically operated cables. The float is prevented from rising when the cars are moved from it by vertical jacks which depress the vessel at its four corners.

Car P. R. R. 47324 goes up with the first lift. It leaves the elevator at the third floor and is moved by a transfer table to "waiting tracks." At this floor there is a freight unloading platform, 120 ft. wide and 1,000 ft. long. Along this platform there are nineteen cars which were brought over from Jersey City by a preceding float. While P. R. R. 47324 and its companion cars are accumulating on the waiting tracks the unloading of the preceding band of cars is being completed. At a scheduled time these cars begin to move away from the platform. At a scheduled time P. R. R. 47324 and the other cars begin to move into the platform. They lie there 1 hour and 15 minutes. At a scheduled time the band of cars is empty and begins to move away from the platform. They are taken by lifts to the fourth floor where by a similar operation the westbound loading is taken on. The loaded cars are returned to the float by the same elevators which raise them from the floats.

If P. R. R. 47324 had contained produce it would have gone to the second floor. The barrels of apples would have been delivered to trucks at that floor or lowered to the first floor for storage.

If it had contained steel shapes, cranes would have taken them off at the second floor and set them down on auto drays at the first floor level.

The merchandise unloaded at the terminal is taken on by a truck of the Terminal Company (it might be a team or auto sent by the consignee). The truck traverses a bridge spanning West Street. It passes into an "entrance building" and by descending driveways arrives at the street level. It has avoided the congestion of West Street.

The merchandise being for store door delivery it will likely move at night. The down town streets are bare of travel. The trucks arrive at the trader's place of business, the driver unlocks the outside door of the "shipping room," delivers his shipment and takes on board Westbound freight. To this door only the railroad holds a key.

During the day the merchant has trucked into the shipping room outbound shipments. The clerk representing the railroad has visited the store at the close of the day, receipted bills of lading and, having accepted responsibility, has locked the inside door with his own lock. The shipping room is then accessible only to the carrier until the morning when the clerk returns to obtain a receipt for the night delivery and to remove his lock from the door.

The car floats under average conditions make a round trip in four hours. The cars complete the circuit from New Jersey and back again in nine hours and forty-five minutes.

OPERATION OF THE SYSTEM OUT ON THE ROAD

The author of the Pennsylvania report having thus approved terminal operation of the system sees also as a railroadman how it will effect radical changes in railroad operation out on the road. The words of his report on this subject are separated from other matters and here repeated.

p. 3. Car P. R. R. 47324 was loaded at Harrisburg with miscellaneous merchandise for New York City. On that day freight was received for all of the districts in New York covered by the present five stations. The whole amount of freight was one carload. Under the Sibley System the car would be made up with a train for New York and dispatched direct to Jersey City. It DID NOT STOP at Philadelphia Transfer for reloading with shipments from other cities into whole carloads for the several points in New York. NOR DID IT STOP at Meadows Yard (N. J.) for car classification as between the 125th St. Stations, 37th St. Station, etc. With one delivery point only in New York it RAN DIRECT TO THE WATER FRONT at Jersey City.

"With ONE delivery point only in New York" the whole present system of handling freight not only at the Manhattan terminal but from one end of the road to the other is changed. The car from Harrisburg P. R. R. 47324 is typical.

> It did not stop at Philadelphia Transfer for RELOADING with shipments from other cities into WHOLE carloads for the several points in New York.
>
> With ONE delivery point only in New York it ran DIRECT to the water front at Jersey City.

The Philadelphia Transfer transaction (at similar centers for all the other roads) represents practically the REHANDLING of the entire volume of Manhattan freights and a consequent vast expense estimated at beyond $25,000,000 annually for the Pier Station freights alone; for the entire volume of trunk line freights more than double that sum.

ONE MANHATTAN TERMINAL

With all freights handled at ONE New York Station instead of at 34 Pier Stations, 100 Manhattan Stations, full loaded instead of fractionally loaded cars move in and out over the roads, as the Pennsylvania report indicates, and ONE car may do the work of THREE—and 250,000 cars, the terminal work now requiring, as the recent Commission shows, the annual use of 750,000. The value of the release of half a million cars—the saving of their operation and haulage over long distances is beyond estimate.

THE OPERATION OF UNLOADING THE FREIGHT CAR

Every traffic man is familiar with the unloading of the freight car at the railroad terminals of to-day, for example, at the railroad PIER STATION terminal, and every traffic engineer knows that the process requires the use of 10 hand trucks operated by 10 longshoremen for each car besides 4 men within the car to break down the freight and load it onto the hand truck. He also knows that the freight must not only be taken out of the car but moved from the car by the hand truck over an inclined gang plank up to the pier floor, and across the floor to position and that from 50 to 100 men are operating on the pier to receive the freight from the hand truck and tier it up into position where it awaits the coming of the consignees' cart, when it has to be again broken down and hand trucked to cart tail.

Every traffic engineer knows that the period of time required to unload the Eastbound car which contains (according to the official report of the N. Y.–N. J. Port & Harbor Commission) an average of less than 12 tons is not less than from 3 to 5 hours.

Therefore no traffic engineer would be ready to concede the possibility of unloading the Eastbound car—carrying double that tonnage, 24 tons—with the use of but 6 men, without a hand truck and within ONE HOUR.

The explanation that follows will, it is believed, demonstrate for the traffic engineer that this can be accomplished.

METHOD OF OPERATION

The passage through the terminal of ONE Eastbound train of 21 cars moving under schedule from the yard—to the yard again—will illustrate that of ALL trains, and it is therefore a description of THE SYSTEM IN OPERATION.

NOTE 1.   W.T.E.—W.T.W.—indicate Waiting Tracks East—West.
     2.   90% of tonnage distance avg. 1.88 miles—time actual 8.43 m.   Detail pp. 49–70.

MOVEMENT OF ONE TRAIN THROUGH THE TERMINAL

Eastbound loaded train—from New Jersey, across the Hudson to New York.
Through the terminal, unloaded and reloaded—across the Hudson again to New Jersey.
IN 5 CYCLES OF 2 HOURS EACH. TOTAL—10 HOURS.

Number of Movement		Time				Actual	Waits	Schedule
1.		M. 12.00	FLOAT	Loads N. J.		20		35
		P.M. .20			WAITS		25	10
		.45		Sails				
		.54		N. Y. Basin		9		25
					WAITS		16	
		1.10		Up to 3d fl.				
		.45		On W.T.E.		35		35
					WAITS		15	15
	1.	2.00		TIME		64	56	120
2.		2.00	TRAIN					
		.15		Switched In		15		15
		.57		Unloaded		42		75
		3.30			WAITS		33	
		.45		Switched Out		15		15
					WAITS		15	15
	2.	4.00		TIME		72	48	120
3.		4.00						
					WAITS		15	15
		.15		Up to 4th fl.				
		50		On W.T.W.		35		35
					WAITS		70	70
	3.	6.00		TIME		35	85	120
4.		6.00						
		.15		Switched In		15		15
		.57		Loaded		42		75
		7.30			WAITS		33	
		.45		Switched Out On W.T.E.		15		15
					WAITS		15	15
	4.	8.00		TIME		72	48	120
5.		8.00						
		.35		Down by Elev.		35		35
			FLOAT		WAITS		10	10
		.45		Sails				
		54		N. J. Yard		9		25
					WAITS		16	
		9.10		Unloads				
		.45		On the Rail		35		35
					WAITS		15	15
	5.	10.00		TIME		79	41	120
				OVER AND BACK		322	278	600
				10 HOURS FROM RAIL TO RAIL				

NEW CONCEPTIONS

The unloading of the car under the Sibley System involves a new conception. It will be explained in detail below. There are many new conceptions embodied in the Sibley System all radical in character and effect:

No. 1. THE INSET BASIN admits the floating car to position into and under the warehouse 500 ft. to connection at the center with

   2. THE ELEVATOR rising to deliver the FREIGHT CAR at new heights and multiplying operating areas on one base thus permitting concentration at

   3. ONE TERMINAL for all roads and the elevator descending to the level of the deck of the float in the basin beneath the warehouse the method of

   4. DEPRESSION of the Float in the water secures—and for the first time—the LEVEL TRANSFER of the car from the Water to the Land. Then follows the conversion of the Float from a DEAD to a LIVE

   5. MOTOR FLOAT which, moving rapidly to and fro across the Hudson, substitutes 16 for a navy of more than 2,000 vessels now in this Transfer Service—so accomplishing what has never before been seen—

   6. THE FREIGHT TRAIN on Manhattan Island.

   7. THE CYCLE of operation then followed to establish the orderly movement of the train through the terminal on schedule and this elevated to a HIGHER PLANE the operation of

   8. THE FREIGHT SERVICE to move on schedule with the regularity of the PASSENGER SERVICE and

   9. THE TRANSFER OF THE CAR—which now occupies 129 hours—is accomplished in 9 hours 45 minutes.

SUPPLEMENTING these, and similarly radical and effective in character, is the method of

10. UNLOADING THE FREIGHT CAR and HANDLING FREIGHT—now to be described—

    A. The Eastbound platform 126 ft. wide is graded DOWN 1.5% from the car door to the opposite side where the truck backs up.

    B. In the movement of freight from the car to position on the platform the UNIT of transfer is ONE TON.

    C. The measure of one ton is 4 x 5 x 5 ft. high = 100 cubic ft.

    D. The means of transfer is the *new* PLATFORM WAGON, called the UNIT, 5 x 6 in basic area, provided with universal swivel ball bearing rollers 2 inches in diameter, the bottom riding but half an inch clear of the floor.

    E. The TON once loaded on that UNIT remains on it while it is in the terminal. The UNIT moves or stands — not the TON—hence there is no handling and rehandling of freight within the terminal.

    F. A TRANSFER BELT 16 ft. wide, 53 ft. long moved by gravity and controlled electrically extends from the car door to the longitudinal passage way at center. A second belt coöperating extends across this passage way 10 ft. A third completing the Transfer Belt as a whole extends 43 ft. to the Truck Loading Area—at outer edge of the platform, 20 ft. wide x 1000 ft. long. Each of these belts operates independently of the others.

    G. Within the car 4 men, 2 at each end, break down the freight and load the UNIT approximately ONE TON. Hence there are two UNITS being loaded at once.

    H. Two men move the loaded UNIT the average distance of 12.5 ft. to position on the belt at the car door.

    I. When 3 UNITS are in position on the belt, abreast, a button touched releases the belt and it moves automatically the length of the UNIT and a new belt area is thus in position for the next 3 UNITS, when the belt moves one length more, and so on.

    J. The car contains 24 tons—24 UNITS are required.

    K. When 24 UNITS are in position on the belt, they extend 8 x 6 = 48 ft., thus stopping 5 feet short of the middle belt and the CAR is UNLOADED. Time 3.5 min. (2 tons, 1 at either end) = for 24 tons 3.5 x 12 = 42 MINUTES. Time allowed under TWELFTH Cycle 1 Hour, 15 Minutes.

    L. In the interval before the next train is at platform (1 Hour 18 Min.) the belt moves the 24 UNITS over to the truck-area, and the end of the belt at the car door is ready for the next train.

    M. The major operation is loading the UNIT—every other single operation is effected within that time.

    EXAMPLE: In the movement of one ton of flour, 10 barrels, it is loaded onto the UNIT and one movement of 12.5 ft. by two men removes it from the car to the belt. And the belt moves it 106 ft. across the platform to position on the transverse edge (20 ft. wide) for truck delivery — a movement which under present methods requires the use of 10 hand trucks and 10 men besides the gang of 50 to 100 men who must tier it up in position.

ORGANIZATION

The plan of organization of the Company for practical operation is complete, officers and men designated, wages determined, time and cost of operation ascertained. For 24-hours operation (3 shifts) there are in the MARINE service 240 officers, 384 men, LAND service 727 officers, 8,226 men, including 176 officers and men in the department of security commanded by the captain of the PATROL, a total of 9,577 officers, and men.

The service is divided into 3 main departments:

    1. TERMINAL   2. MARINE   3. LAND

Under the President these are controlled by 6 VICE PRESIDENTS:

1st Vice President—Director General	4th Vice President—Land Service
2nd Vice President—Terminal Service	5th Vice President—Chief Engineer
3rd Vice President—Marine Service	6th Vice President—Legal Relations

1. TERMINAL SERVICE—2ND VICE PRESIDENT

Controls all operations WITHIN the terminal and is Director of Storage. The service is separated into Eastbound and Westbound movement with managers for each; under each of these are managers, one for movement of cars, one for movement of freights. Under each of these are managers of the Wing, under these of section, under these of floor, and under these are the freight and car handlers in every section on every floor.

2. MARINE SERVICE—3RD VICE PRESIDENT

Controls the operations of the Float service, at the basins, across and on both banks of the Hudson River.

The service is separated into Eastbound and Westbound movement with managers for each. Under these are superintendents at each of the railroad yards and in each of the railroad sections of the terminal, and under these are the basin operators on both sides of the river.

3. LAND SERVICE—4TH VICE PRESIDENT

Controls all freight movement between the terminal and the store. The service is separated into Eastbound and Westbound movement with managers for each in the terminal. Under each of these are superintendents for the Wing, the section, the floor, and under these the freight handlers under gang leaders.

He is Director of the GARAGE and controller of TRUCK MOVEMENT. The service is separated into Eastbound and Westbound movement, with managers for each for the terminal. Under each of these superintendents for the Wing, the section, and under these are the operators, the chauffeurs, helpers, and the men in the shops.

As Director of truck movement he controls also the movement of the merchant-operated truck and by his superintendents its operations are brought into coördination with scheduled terminal operation.

CHIEF ENGINEER—5TH VICE PRESIDENT

Controls LIGHT, HEAT, POWER, mechanisms of movement and skilled operators. He maintains all schedules of operation ashore and afloat, the Float, the Car, the Elevator, the Truck. The service is adapted to the 3 departments of service, Terminal, Marine, Land, with an Assistant Chief Engineer in charge of each. The Terminal service under the 1st. Asst. Chief Engineer is in charge of the operation of the Elevators and cables, with Assistant Engineers for the Wing, the section. The Marine service under the 2nd Asst. Chief Engineer is in charge of Float movement and Basin operation at all sections, and at the yards—with Asst. Engineers for the Wing, the section. The Land service under the 3rd Asst. Chief Engineer is in charge of the operation of the Garage, with Asst. Engineers for the Eastbound and Westbound movement—for the Wing and section.

THE CHART ROOM—1ST VICE PRESIDENT AND GENERAL MANAGER—CHIEF OF RECORDS

Directs the operation of the system; maps out the entire freight movement for the day of all roads Eastbound and Westbound, and operations in every department of the service under his hand are harmonized and brought into coördination.

In the Chart room are one hundred and twelve recorders and superintendents. These are separated first into railroad groups—one group for each section—then into Eastbound and Westbound recorders. They are supervised by Asst. Chief Recorders, one for Eastbound, one for Westbound traffic. Under each of these are supervisors of cars, supervisors of freights, and under these supervisors for the section.

RAILROAD COÖPERATION

To aid the Chief of Records the roads are brought into coöperation. Within the terminal there are provided 608 railroad offices for clerks and officers of the roads, 76 for each railroad. They are located in a strip of the terminal, 50 ft. wide, running the whole length of the terminal and fronting on West Street, at the heads of all platforms. The strip is divided longitudinally by a wide corridor separating the offices into two rows—those at the rear for the clerks—opening on the platforms. Here the roads are in practical touch with the daily traffic movement.

EASTBOUND—In these offices every detail of the Eastbound car is known and in cooperation with the traffic clerks. Chart operators have mapped out before its arrival at the shore the entire progress of the car through the terminal and back to the rail, reloaded and ready to start West. They have classified the car by number, owner, relative position in the arriving train; tabulated weight and character of its goods; noted name and location of consignee and getting in touch with him have learned whether his goods are to go to store or storage. They know the exact location the coming car will take on the Eastbound float that brings it over from New Jersey and therefore the spot at platform where it will unload on the Eastbound floor and the spot on the Westbound floor where sequently it will take on its Westbound reload.

Charts are ready for the terminal service and these, descending through the superior heads to the managers in every department of activity, they all know not only the movement required in their several departments but its relation to the whole. They work intelligently all to one end.

WESTBOUND—The Chart room has also learned by card, telephone, and otherwise the location character tonnage and intended railroad routing of all outgoing shipments for the day. They have adapted the Westbound reloadings to the coming Eastbound cars. The Garage service moves in accordance.

EASTBOUND-WESTBOUND—Superintendents of Truck service with charts in hand direct the incoming truck to the point at the platform where its Eastbound load is to be taken on, or the Westbound load is to be put off.

GENERAL—Movement in any part of the system is co-ordinate with that in all parts. There is no delay, no lost motion, confusion is eliminated.

COST OF OPERATION

THE DAY fixed as the standard of labor is 8 hours and as the Transfer System may operate a greater or less time, as the flow of freight may demand, and also to avoid fractions of days, it is necessary to use the universal standard of 24 hours (3 shifts of 8 hours each) as THE DAY.

The cost of operation is therefore that of operating the terminal as a whole, which includes the charges of general administration, overhead and operatives in the handling of that annual volume of tonnage the System is capable of transferring in 24 hours' daily operation.

OPERATIVES

On this basis the salaries and wages of all operatives from the President down to the freight handler on the floor within the terminal and on the water are separated into two classes. The first based on annual service (like that of the President) represents a FIXED charge. The second (like that of the freight handler) represents service which is measured by the hour or day of 8 hours and the wage is trebled for the 3 shifts in the standard day of 24 hours. This service is a VARIABLE charge.

ANNUAL CHARGES

To the sum of these fixed and variable charges of operation for the year is added the FIXED charge on construction and equipment and the aggregate represents the annual charge against the annual tonnage of capacity.

COST PER TON

With this standard of cost of operation and tonnage for the day of 24 hours established the cost PER TON for any part of the day and any part of the tonnage is readily ascertained by adding the corresponding part of the variable charge to the sum of the annual fixed charge (which remains constant), and dividing the result by the number of annual tons transferred in such period.

With this explanation the method of the tables which follow will be understood.

TABLES

A. Terminal and Land service
B. Marine
C. Construction—Equipment
D. Overhead and operating charges

E. Railroad and Land charges
  1. Terminal charges
  2. Construction charges
  3. Summary
  4. Distribution of Terminal charges
  5. Distribution of ALL charges

F. Railroad Transfer cost per ton—12th Cycle
G. Railroad Transfer cost per ton—16th Cycle
H. Railroad Transfer cost per ton—20th Cycle
I. Railroad Transfer cost per ton—24th Cycle

TABLE A
TERMINAL & LAND SERVICE : ORGANIZATION : ADMINISTRATION

					Operatives				Operating Charges	
Officers.	Men.	Salaries.	*Supt.*	*Men*	*Fl.*	*Sec.*	*Shf.*	*Men*	*Per Annum*	*Fixed*	*Variable*
ADMINISTRATION: Offices at Center											
GENERAL STAFF:											
President and Genl. Manager			1						40,000		
1 Vice Pres. Director General			1						25,000		
2 Vice Pres. Terminal			1						20,000		
3 Vice Pres. Marine			1						15,000		
4 Vice Pres. Land			1						15,000		
5 Vice Pres. Chief Engineer			1						15,000		
6 Vice Pres. Legal			1						15,000	145,000	
Controller			1						10,000		
1st Asst.			1						7,500		
2nd Asst.			1						5,000		
Secretary			1						5,000		
Asst.			1						4,000	31,500	
OFFICE STAFF:											
Clerks, Steno., Tel., Porters,								46	65,000		
Supplies									20,000	85,000	
TERMINAL DEPARTMENT											
2d Vice Pres., Manager											
1st Asst., Eastbound			1							5,000	
2nd Asst., Westbound			1							5,000	
AIDS: Supt. North Wing			1						3,000		
South Wing			1						3,000	6,000	
Section			24			8	3		2,500		
Floor			72	3		8	3		2,000		204,000
OPERATORS: ELEVATORS											
For Cars				6		8	3				
For Freight				6		8	3				
For Passengers				6		8	3	432	1,500		648,000
AMOUNT FORWARD			112					478		277,500	852,000

	Supt.	OPERATIVES				Men	OPERATING CHARGES		
		Men	Fl.	Sec.	Shf.		Per Annum	Fixed	Variable
AMOUNT FORWARD	112					478		277,500	852,000
CABLES		4	3	8	3				
TRACKS		4	3	8	3				
BELTS		2	3	8	3				
BASIN		8		8	3				
MEN						912	1,500		1,368,000
FREIGHT: EASTBOUND—21 CARS ×		6	1	8	3				
WESTBOUND—21 CARS ×		6	1	8	3				
MEN						6,048	1,250		
SUPTS.	288	4	3	8	3		1,500		7,968,000
ASST. MANAGER									
CAR INTERCHANGE	1						3,500		
AIDS:									
SUPT. NORTH WING	1						2,500		
SUPT. SOUTH WING	1						2,500	8,500	
OPERATORS:									
SWITCH MEN		4		8	3	96	1,500		144,000
DEPT. OF MARINE SERVICE.									
3rd Vice Pres., MANAGER									
FLOATS: 1ST ASST. MANAGER N. Y. SIDE	1						3,500		
AIDS: SUPT. NORTH WING	1						2,500		
SUPT. SOUTH WING	1						2,500		
2ND ASST. MANAGER N. J. SIDE	1						3,500	12,000	
SUPTS. AT YARDS	7						2,500	17,500	
DEPARTMENT OF LAND SERVICE									
4th Vice Pres., MANAGER									
1ST ASST. MANAGER: EASTBOUND	1							4,000	
AIDS: NORTH WING	1							3,000	
SUPTS. Section	12		3	3			2,500		30,000
Floor	24	2	4	3			2,000		48,000
SOUTH WING	1							3,000	
SUPTS. Section	12			4	3		2,500		30,000
Floor	24	2	4	3			2,000		48,000
2ND ASST. MANAGER: WESTBOUND	1							4,000	
AIDS: NORTH WING									
SUPTS: Section	12			4	3		2,500		30,000
Floor	24	2	4	3			2,000		48,000
SOUTH WING									
SUPTS. Section	12			4	3		2,500		30,000
Floor	24	2	4	3			2,000		48,000
3RD ASST. MANAGER: GARAGE	1						7,500		
SUPT. EASTBOUND	1						5,000		
AIDS: NORTH WING	1						4,000	16,500	
Section	12			4	3		3,000		36,000
Floor	24	2	4	3			2,500		60,000
AMOUNT FORWARD	597					7,534		346,000	10,770,000

	Supt.	Operatives Men	Fl.	Sec.	Shf.	Men	Operating Charges Per Annum	Fixed	Variable
AMOUNT FORWARD	597					7534		346,000	10,770,000
SOUTH WING	1							4,000	
Section	12			4	3		3,000		36,000
Floor	24	2		4	3		2,500		60,000
SUPT. WESTBOUND	1						4,500		
AIDS: NORTH WING	1						4,000	8,500	
Section	12			4	3		3,000		36,000
Floor	12		1	4	3		2,500		30,000
SOUTH WING	1								4,000
Section	12			4	3		3,000		36,000
Floor	12		1	4	3		2,500		30,000
UTILITY MEN:		36			3	108	1,000		108,000
SUPPLIES								20,000	
DEPARTMENT OF RECORDS									
1ST ASST. RECORDER: EASTBOUND	1						4,000		
RECORDERS		100			3	300	1,200		360,000
SUPTS. NORTH WING	1							3,000	
Section				4	3	12	1,500		18,000
SOUTH WING	1							3,000	
Section				4	3	12	1,500		18,000
2ND ASST. RECORDER: WESTBOUND	1						4,000		
SUPTS. NORTH WING	1							3,000	
Section				4	3	12	1,500		18,000
SOUTH WING	1							3,000	
Section				4	3	12	1,500		18,000
AIDS: Steno., Tel., Clerks, etc.		18			3	54	1,200		64,800
SUPPLIES								10,000	
DEPARTMENT OF SECURITY									
CAPTAIN OF PATROL	1						5,000		
LIEUTS. NORTH WING	1						4,000		
SOUTH WING	1						4,000		
SERGTS. Sections		1		8			2,500		
HOUSE PATROL Floors		4	4	8			1,500		
OUTER PATROL Trucks		20					1,500		
MEN						156		254,000	
DEPARTMENT OF ENGINEERS									
5TH VICE PRES. CHIEF ENGINEER									
1ST ASST., CHIEF ENGINEER									
TERMINAL OPERATION	1						6,000		
ENGINEERS IN CHARGE									
CABLES NORTH WING	1						4,000		
SOUTH WING	1						4,000		
Section	8						3,000		
ELEVATORS NORTH WING	1						4,000		
SOUTH WING	1						4,000		
Section	8						3,000		
2ND ASST., CHIEF ENGINEER									
MARINE SERVICE	1						5,000	75,000	
AMOUNT FORWARD	716					8200		737,500	11,606,800

	Supt.	Operatives					Operating Charges	
		Men	Fl.	Sec.	Shf.	Men	Per Annum	Fixed	Variable
ENGINEERS IN CHARGE									
AMOUNT FORWARD	716					8200		737,500	11,606,800
FLOATS North Wing	1							4,000	
South Wing	1							4,000	
BASINS N. Y.—N. J.	2							8,000	
3rd Asst. Chief Engineer									
LAND SERVICE	1							4,000	
ENGINEERS IN CHARGE									
North—South Wing	2						3,500	7,000	
LIGHT 65,936,160,000 sq. ft. hours @ .03									
Watts = 19,780,848 K. W. H. @ .02							395,617		
HEAT 10,523,000 sq. ft. @ .03							315,696		
POWER 5,100,000 K. W. H. @ .02							102,000	813,313	
Utility Men		7		3		21	1,500		31,000
DEPARTMENT OF LAW									
6th Vice Pres., Manager									
AIDS: Corporation—Real Estate	2						5,000	10,000	
Operation— Relations	2						5,000	10,000	
STAFF: Clerks, Stenographers, etc.						5	3,000	15,000	
Supplies								23,000	
GENERAL EXPENSE								100,000	
TOTALS—TERMINAL CHARGES	727					8,226		1,735,813	11,637,800

TABLE B : MARINE SERVICE : FLOATING

	Floats	Operatives					Variable	
		Officers	Men	Per Annum	Shf.	Men	Amount	Charges
OPERATION								
FLOATS	16							
CAPTAIN		48		2,400	3		115,200	
1st OFFICER		48		1,800	3		86,400	
2nd OFFICER		48		1,500	3		72,000	
CHIEF ENGINEER		48		2,400	3		115,200	
ASST. ENGINEER		48		2,100	3		100,800	
Engine Room			2	1,200	3		115,200	
On Deck			6	1,200	3		345,600	
TOTALS		240				384		950,400
FUEL OIL CONSUMPTION								
1 Bl. 45 gals. per hour								
Cost—$2.25 per barrel	Gal. Oil	Floats	Cycles	Sec.	Days			
IN MOTION 25 MIN. each cycle (Schedule)	20	2	20	8	300		96,000	
SUPPLIES							20,000	116,000
TOTAL—VARIABLE								1,066,400

TABLE C : CONSTRUCTION : EQUIPMENT

Blue prints and designs of the system with full descriptive matter have been submitted to constructors. Estimates follow.

STRUCTURE:

TURNER CONSTRUCTION CO.—Estimate includes foundation, heating, lighting, freight and passenger elevators and stairs, but not car elevators. Original estimate $65,000,000 reduced by negotiation to ... $59,000,000

ENTRANCE BUILDINGS	$1,080,052		
DRIVES	376,105	$1,456,157	
CLEARING SITE		3,805,463	
PENNSYLVANIA RAILWAY Estimate		5,261,620	
TOTAL FOR STRUCTURES			$64,261,620

EQUIPMENT

PENNSYLVANIA RAILWAY Estimate.—Includes car elevators, tracks, cable ways with electrical control, transfer belts and platform trucks ... 14,934,078

TOTAL STRUCTURE AND EQUIPMENT ... $79,195,698

FLEET

BETHLEHEM SHIP BUILDING CORPORATION Estimate.—20 Motor Floats, steel construction, 300 ft. long, 44 beam, 5 draft, Diesel Engine, speed 14 knots. ... 6,000,000

TOTAL CONSTRUCTION EQUIPMENT ... $85,195,698

TABLE D : SUMMARY OF OVERHEAD AND OPERATING CHARGES

				CHARGES	
CONSTRUCTION	Amount	%	Fixed	Variable	Total
STRUCTURE	64,261,620	10.18	6,541,833		
EQUIPMENT	14,934,078	10.18	1,520,289		
FLEET	6,000,000	10.18	610,800		
TOTAL CONSTRUCTION	85,195,698				
FIXED CHARGES			8,672,922		
OPERATION					
TERMINAL			1,735,813	11,637,800	
FLEET				1,066,400	
TOTALS					
CONSTRUCTION	85,195,698				
FIXED			10,408,735		
VARIABLE				12,704,200	
TOTAL CHARGES					23,112,935

TABLE E : RAILROAD AND LAND CHARGES

NOTE: The RAILROAD obligation ends with the deposit of the freight on a platform in New York accessible to consignee's cart. Expense of terminal operation beyond that point is for account of the LAND service. To assign to each such interest its proper part of the Terminal operating expense an analysis has been made and the respective proportions ascertained.

		SYSTEM		R. R. Transfer Percentage		
1. TERMINAL CHARGES (Table A)		*Fixed*	*Variable*	%	*Fixed*	*Variable*
ADMINISTRATION—OPERATION						
Administration		261,500		50	130,750	
Floor Officers		16,000		50	8,000	
Superintendents			204,000	50		102,000
Operatives			2,016,000	78		1,584,000
Freight handlers			7,991,000	75		5,994,000
Car Interchange		8,500	144,000	100	8,500	144,000
Marine Service						
Terminal Officers		29,500		100	29,500	
Land Service		14,000	312,000	0		
Garage		53,000	444,000	0		
Records		40,000	496,800	50	20,000	248,400
Security—(Patrol)		285,000		50	142,500	
Engineers		60,000		82	49,000	
Engine Room—Light, Heat, Power		813,313	30,000	50	406,656	15,000
Legal		55,000		50	27,500	
General Expense		100,000		50	50,000	
ADMINISTRATION—OPERATION						
SYSTEM		1,735,813	11,637,800			
RAILROAD TRANSFER					872,406	8,087,400
2. CONSTRUCTION CHARGES						
STORAGE AND GARAGE AREAS CREDITED TO RAILROAD TRANSFER						
STRUCTURE		*Sq. Feet*	%	*Amo.*	*Amo.*	*Amo.*	TOTAL
2820 × 1070 × 4 =		12,069,600					
STORAGE FLOOR		3,017,400					
LESS BASIN AREAS		475,430					
STORAGE AREA		2,541,970	21.0				
GARAGE AND ADMINISTRATION							
100 × 1070 × 4 Floors		428,000					
GARAGE	50%	214,000	1.8				
ADMIN. 50% less R. R. 25%	25%	107,000	0.9				
TOTAL STORAGE & GARAGE AREAS			23.7				
STRUCTURE TOTAL FIXED CHARGES							6,541,833
Storage			21.0	1,373,785			
Garage			1.8	117,753			
Administration			0.9	58,876			
TOTAL			23.7		1,550,414		
RAILROAD TRANSFER			76.3			4,991,419	
TOTAL			100.0				6,541,833

3. SUMMARY—CHARGES

		SYSTEM		R. R. TRANSFER		FIXED AND VARIABLE	
		Fixed	*Variable*	*Fixed*	*Variable*	*R. R. Trans.*	*System*
1. TERMINAL							
STRUCTURE	64,261,620	6,541,833		4,991,419			
EQUIPMENT	14,934,078	1,520,289		1,520,289			
ADM. OPERATION		1,735,813	11,637,800	872,406	8,087,400		
TOT. TERMINAL		9,797,935	11,637,800				
R. R. TRANS.				7,384,114	8,087,400		
2. FLOAT	6,000,000	610,800	1,066,400	610,800	1,066,400		
TOTALS							
R. R. TRANS.				7,994,914	9,153,800	17,148,714	
SYSTEM	85,195,698	10,408,735	12,704,200				23,112,935

4. DISTRIBUTION OF TERMINAL CHARGES	*Land*	*Railroad*	*%*	*Fixed*	*Fixed*	*Variable*
TOTALS					1,735,813	11,637,800
ADMINISTRATION						
Railroad		130,750	50			
Storage	65,375		25			
Garage	32,687		12.5			
Land	32,688		12.5			
TOTAL			100	261,500		
OPERATION						
Terminal	33,000	95,000				
Garage	53,000					
Patrol	142,500	142,500				
Records	20,000	20,000				
L. H. P.	406,657	406,656				
Legal	37,500	27,500				
General	50,000	50,000		1,474,313		
LAND	863,407					
RAILROAD		872,406				
TOTAL FIXED					1,735,813	
VARIABLE						
Supts.	102,000	102,000				
Operatives	432,000	1,584,000				
Frt. Handlers	1,997,000	5,994,000				
Term. Service	312,000	0				
Car Interchange		144,000				
Garage	444,000	0				
Records	248,400	248,400				
Utility Men	15,000	15,000				
TOTALS VARIABLE	3,550,400	8,087,400				11,637,800

5. DISTRIBUTION OF ALL CHARGES

FIXED		%	Amo.	Storage	Garage	Land	Total
Administration				65,375	32,687	32,688	
Operation							
L. H. P.		12.5	50,832				
Patrol		12.5	17,812				
Legal		50.	16,250	84,894	53,000	594,763	
Totals Adm. & Operation				150,269	85,687	627,451	863,407
Construction				1,373,785	117,753	58,876	1,550,414
Total Fixed				1,524,054	203,440	686,327	2,413,821
VARIABLE							
Total Variable					444,000	3,106,400	3,550,400
Totals				1,524,054	644,440	3,795,727	
LAND—	FIXED & VARIABLE						5,964,221
RAILROAD							
Structure & Equipment							
Fixed			7,384,114				
Variable			8,087,400				
Float							
Fixed			610,800				
Variable			1,066,400				
	FIXED & VARIABLE						17,148,714
SYSTEM—	FIXED & VARIABLE						23,112,935

TABLE F

RAILROAD TRANSFER COST PER TON   TWELFTH CYCLE—2 HOURS
OPERATION—24, 20, 16, 10 HOURS   TONNAGE (E 24 + 16 W)—24, 20, 16, 10 MILLION TONS

NOTE: To find cost per ton for any tonnage—at the period of operation named: Divide FIXED sums by the tons of the desired tonnage—VARIABLE sums by the multiple part of the day—and that result by the tons of the period.

				Day	Five Sixths	Two Thirds	Five Twelfths
Multiple Parts of day							
Hours of Operation				24 H.	20 H.	16 H.	10 H.
Daily cars—Eastbound				2,016	1,680	1,344	840
ANNUAL TONS				24,192,000	20,160,000	16,128,000	10,080,000
ANNUAL CHARGES							
24 HOURS OPN.	Fixed	Variable	Total	Fix. Var. Tot.	Fix. Var. Tot.	Fix. Var. Tot.	Fix. Var. Tot.
TERMINAL							
Fixed	7,384,114			31	37	46	74
Variable		8,087,400		34	34	34	34
Total			15,471,514	65	71	80	108
FLOAT							
Fixed	610,800			03	03	04	06
Variable		1,066,400		05	05	07	04
Total			1,677,200	08	08	11	10
SYSTEM							
Fixed	7,994,914			34	40	50	80
Variable		9,153,800		39	39	41	38
Total			17,148,714	73	79	91	118

TABLE G

RAILROAD TRANSFER COST PER TON — SIXTEENTH CYCLE—1 HOUR, 30 M.
OPERATION—24, 15, 12, 8 HOURS — TONNAGE (E 24 + 16 W)—32, 20, 16, 10 MILLION TONS

Multiple Parts of day				Day			Five Eighths			One Half			One Third		
Hours of Operation				24 H.			15 H.			12 H.			8 H.		
Daily cars—Eastbound				2,688			1,680			1,344			896		
ANNUAL TONS				32,256,000			20,160,000			16,128,000			10,752,000		
ANNUAL CHGS. 24 HOURS OPN.	Fixed	Variable	Total	Fix.	Var.	Tot.	Fix.	Var.	Tot.	Fix.	Var.	Tot.	Fix.	Var.	Tot.
TERMINAL															
Fixed	7,384,114			23			37			46			69		
Variable		8,087,400			25			25			25			25	
Total			15,471,514			48			62			71			94
FLOAT															
Fixed	610,800			02			03			04			06		
Variable		1,066,400			04			04			04			04	
Total			1,677,200			06			07			08			10
SYSTEM															
Fixed	7,994,914			25			40			50			75		
Variable		9,153,800			29			29			29			29	
Total			17,148,714			54			69			79			104

TABLE H

RAILROAD TRANSFER COST PER TON — TWENTIETH CYCLE—1 HOUR, 12 M.
OPERATION—24, 16, 12, 6 HOURS — TONNAGE (E 24 + 16 W)—40, 26, 20, 10 MILLION TONS

Multiple Parts of day				Day			Two Thirds			One Half			One Fourth		
Hours of Operation				24 H.			16 H.			12 H.			6 H.		
Daily cars—Eastbound				3,360			2,240			1,680			840		
ANNUAL TONS				40,320,000			26,880,000			20,160,000			10,080,000		
ANNUAL CHGS. 24 HOURS OPN.	Fixed	Variable	Total	Fix.	Var.	Tot.	Fix.	Var.	Tot.	Fix.	Var.	Tot.	Fix.	Var.	Tot.
TERMINAL															
Fixed	7,384,114			20			30			37			73		
Variable		8,087,400			20			20			20			20	
Total			15,471,514			40			50			57			93
FLOAT															
Fixed	610,800			02			03			03			06		
Variable		1,066,400			03			03			03			03	
Total			1,677,200			05			06			06			09
SYSTEM															
Fixed	7,994,914			22			33			40			79		
Variable		9,153,800			23			23			23			23	
Total			17,148,714			45			56			63			102

TABLE I

RAILROAD TRANSFER COST PER TON TWENTY FOURTH CYCLE—1 HOUR
OPERATION—24, 16, 10, 5 HOURS   TONNAGE (E 24 + 16 W)—48, 32, 20, 10 MILLION TONS

				Day			Two Thirds			Five Twelfths			Five Twenty Fourths		
Multiple Parts of day															
Hours of Operation				24 H.			16 H.			10 H.			5 H.		
Daily cars—Eastbound				4,032			2,688			1,680			840		
ANNUAL TONS				48,384,000			32,256,000			20,160,000			10,080,000		
ANNUAL CHGS. 24 HOURS OPN.	*Fixed*	*Variable*	*Total*	Fix.	Var.	Tot.	Fix.	Var.	Tot.	Fix.	Var.	Tot.	Fix.	Var.	Tot.
TERMINAL															
Fixed	7,384,114			15			23			36			73		
Variable		8,087,400			16			17			17			17	
TOTAL			15,471,514			31			40			53			90
FLOAT															
Fixed	610,800			01			02			03			06		
Variable		1,066,400			02			02			02			02	
TOTAL			1,677,200			03			04			05			08
TERMINAL															
Fixed	7,994,914			16			25			39			79		
Variable		9,153,800			18			19			19			19	
TOTAL			17,148,714			34			44			58			98

SUMMARY : RAILROAD TRANSFER COST PER TON

Table	Cycle	Hours of Operation	Annual Tons		Per Ton	
F	12	10	10,000,000		$1.18	
		20		20,000,000		$0.79
G	16	8	10,000,000		1.04	
		15		20,000,000		0.69
H	20	6	10,000,000		1.02	
		12		20,000,000		0.63
I	24	5	10,000,000		0.98	
		10		20,000,000		0.58

CAPACITY

The capacity of the System may be considered under two heads:
 1. Transfer Capacity—(movement from shore to shore).
 2. Terminal Capacity—(movement through the terminal).

1. TRANSFER CAPACITY

The measure of transfer capacity is the CAR, not the TON. The ton is the measure of the car. The System transfers CARS regardless of the TONS they contain. The number of EASTBOUND cars that can be transferred within the 24 hour period over and back marks the capacity of the System. That number under the 24th cycle is

 (*formula*) FLOAT TRAIN—21 Cars × 24 Cycles × 8 Sections =   DAILY CARS   4032

A. TONNAGE CAPACITY of the Car is 30 tons INBOUND—20 tons OUTBOUND.
On this basis the capacity of the System is

 (*formula*) 4032 Cars × 30 + 20 tons × 300 days =   ANNUAL TONS   60,480,000

B. Analysis of one entire year of Metropolitan carload freights of all the trunk lines as presented in the American Railway Association's report for the year 1923 shows the movement East and West bound of 2,420,000 cars with the average load of 22.2 tons (both ways) equivalent to 26.64 East bound (60%), 17.76 West bound (40%). On this basis the capacity of the System is

 (*formula*) 4032 × 26.64 + 17.76 × 300 days =   ANNUAL TONS   53,706,240

C. The average car tonnage used in the operating tables of the System is less than either of these, namely 24 tons East bound, 16 West bound. On this basis the capacity of the System is (*formula*) 4032 × 24 + 16 × 300 days =   ANNUAL TONS   48,384,000

2. TERMINAL CAPACITY

A. PLATFORM FACILITIES

Under present methods the Pier Station areas insufficient at most are blocked with masses of freight lingering under the 48 hour allowance. Freights of Monday are still on the floor when the freights of Tuesday arrive. So that the areas are never cleared—a condition of confusion and congestion always prevails.

Under the Sibley System, facility and celerity of movement and the convenience of storage areas below permit the use of the same areas many times during the day's operation and so in effect they are multiplied far beyond any possible requirement.

An illustration will make this clear. The area of the 3rd floor platform is capable of taking on 4.575 cubic tons, yet but 21 cars (24 tons each), 504 tons, are to be unloaded on it in the schedule period of one cycle (say 2 hours) and during that same period the platform may be cleared by delivery to the Motor Truck System which is moving in correspondence or to the storage areas below. So that if it were possible to use the area to its capacity, all departments of operation brought into effective cooperation, 12 times during the 24 hours, 54.900 Eastbound tons could pass in over this single platform in one day while the total daily Eastbound tonnage of a 20,000,000 annual tonnage is 40,000 daily tons, and for one section but 5,000 tons. The utmost capacity of the single Eastbound platform (there are 2 in each section) is therefore 10 times as great as the volume of freight to be transferred.

B. TRUCKING FACILITIES AT PLATFORM

There are 2 Eastbound platforms in each section. That on the 3rd floor is 992 ft. long. At this one platform 76 8- to 10-ton trucks may stand (13 ft. between centers) and with but 2 tons at a load and allowing 20 minutes for locating and loading time 5,472 trucks could be loaded during the 24 hour day with 10,944 Eastbound tons, at one platform of 8 sections, 87,552 Eastbound tons, while the total Eastbound tonnage of an annual tonnage of 20,000,000 tons for all roads is but 40,000 daily. With 10-ton loads for Eastbound deliveries as designed, the excess is much greater.

C. RAILROAD TRACKAGE

There are 29 miles of railroad tracks with the capacity of 3,760 cars, more than double the operating trackage required for the 20,000,000 annual tonnage. The transfer of an annual tonnage of 50,400,000 expected in the next century would require the use of but 3360 cars.

The capacity of the System on LAND is in excess of that on the WATER.

3. PRESENT AND FUTURE CAPACITY

The N. Y. – N. J. Port & Harbor Commission reports the annual rate of increase of the Metropolitan tonnage at 2.5% per annum. At that rate the capacity of the Sibley System will not be reached until some time beyond the year 2000. The System is so designed that at such far away period its capacity may be increased by the addition of section after section at either end indefinitely—the organized administration at center continues unchanged.

The TRANSFER and TERMINAL CAPACITY of the System is therefore practically UNLIMITED.

RAILROAD TONNAGE OF PORT OF NEW YORK FOR THE YEAR 1926

NOTE:—Estimate based upon the records of the railroads as reported by the recent N.Y.–N.J. Port and Harbor Commission with prescribed annual increase since the date of such records.

	%			
TOTAL TONNAGE			95,065,000	
Interchange	17	16,171,250		
Fuel Ore Grain	52	49,181,250		
N. Y., N. H., L. I. (East Side)	1	1,108,820		
New Jersey & Staten Island	3	2,820,500	69,281,820	
REMAINDER—METROPOLITAN FREIGHTS	27			25,783,180
PRESENT METHODS	100			
CAR FLOAT			7,500,000	
LIGHTERAGE			12,500,000	
MISCELLANEOUS			5,783,180	25,783,180

CHARACTER AND EFFECT OF THE SIBLEY SYSTEM

1. TRANSFER OF THE TRAIN

All engineers and students of the railroad traffic problem at New York, called by the Engineering Press "The greatest traffic problem before the world" have recognized that the only possible solution of the problem was the transfer of THE TRAIN—bulk unbroken—and the universal effort and especially the intensive studies through a period of 3 years of the Engineering Staff of the recent N. Y. – N. J. Port & Harbor Commission, an aggregation of exceptional ability, have been directed primarily to that end.

With all known plans under its analysis that Commission reached and declared the scientific conclusion:

The New Jersey FREIGHT TRAIN cannot be brought to Manhattan through a TUNNEL, over a BRIDGE or otherwise. Bulk MUST be broken in New Jersey.

The Sibley System achieves this "scientific impossibility."

It transfers THE TRAIN bulk unbroken to be unloaded and reloaded on Manhattan, changing the DESTINATION OF A CENTURY from the Jersey Shore to NEW YORK CITY, and so SOLVES THE PROBLEM that for more than 30 years has defeated all other effort.

2. ONE UNIVERSAL TERMINAL

All engineers and students of the railroad traffic problem have recognized that the ideal consummation to be sought in the effort at its solution was the transfer and delivery of the freights at ONE universal Manhattan terminal. They have all failed in this effort and the efficient staff of Engineering experts of N. Y. – N. J. Port & Harbor Commission, after intense studies of several years reached and declared the scientific conclusion:

> ONE universal terminal structure for the trunk line freights is physically IMPOSSIBLE. To handle such a volume of freight (10,000,000 annual tons) — would require the use of no less than TEN Manhattan terminals and to find location for these they would have to be distributed in a line extending from the Battery to 47th Street (about 4 miles) and would even then be too close together for commercial advantage.

The Sibley System achieves this "scientific impossibility."

It concentrates the freights of ALL the trunk lines at ONE TERMINAL — 10 million tons — 20 million tons.

3. NEW YORK CENTRAL—WEST SIDE PROBLEM

Engineers and expert students of the traffic problem have for many years given intense study to this problem, an integral part of the greater traffic problem. The N. Y. – N. J. Port & Harbor Commission said of it:

> The so called West side problem has been pressing for a generation and conditions have become such that a solution for the disposition of the N. Y. Central tracks at grade must be found even if none could be found for the accommodation of the New Jersey railroads.

These efforts have all failed.

The Sibley System separating the freight and passenger service at Albany brings the New York Central freight train down over West shore rails to Weehawken and the Motor Float service transfers it from that point 3 miles from the terminal as easily as the train of the Pennsylvania and the Erie one mile away.

The System thus provides the SOLUTION of this long standing West side problem hitherto found impossible of solution by a service that is at once practical and for New York Central highly profitable.

RIVERSIDE PARK RELEASED—WATER FRONT OPENED

It liberates Riverside Park and the streets of New York, from St. John's Station at Canal Street to Spuyten Duyvil; releases many City blocks on the West side, an area extending from 10th to 12th Avenue in width and from 33rd St. to 60th St. used wholly or in part for railroad purposes and reclaims the valuable water front, 60th to 72nd Sts., now occupied as a railroad yard, and opens it for Ocean Steamship service.

MILLIONS SAVED FOR THE CITY, THE STATE, THE ROAD

It saves to the City and State of New York and New York Central $150,000,000 contemplated expenditure for new structures, besides sparing the City of New York the calamitous blocking of its highways and water front with such structures and the operation of freight trains through its streets and for New York Central provides a service that will effect for the road ANNUAL ECONOMIES OF $15,000,000.

4. LIMITATION OF PREVIOUS EFFORTS AT SOLUTION

A. PIER STATION FREIGHTS

The trunk line freights for transfer are estimated at 25,000,000 annual tons, 7,500,000 (30%) are moved to and from Manhattan Pier Stations by CAR FLOAT.

It is the transfer of this fraction of the whole volume of freights which has been under study by the engineers and experts and no plan heretofore devised has had any greater object. They have all failed.

B. LIGHTERAGE FREIGHTS

The remainder of the freights now transferred across the water by LIGHTER to and from many and distant points on the shore line of New York within Metropolitan limits is by far the greater part—70%— of the whole volume. In view of the failure to effect the transfer of the minor part of the freights—30%— the transfer of the major—70%— has long ago been abandoned by science as an impossibility and the N. Y.–N. J. Port & Harbor Commission has declared that for the service by lighters there is no possible substitute, it must always remain.

The Sibley System achieves both these "impossibilities" and transfers ALL the freights: Pier Station freights, lighterage freights, a total of 25,000,000 annual tons.

5. THE PIER STATION STRUCTURE *DISAPPEARS*

Transferring all the Pier Station freights these structures now in railroad use, 34 Manhattan Piers, 27 on the Hudson River front, are released. The expense of maintenance is ended, the thousands of employees, officers and men, now necessary to their operation are dismissed and 2 miles of this valuable water front are opened for the Ocean Steamship Service where now not a pier can be had.

6. THE LIGHTERAGE STRUCTURE *DISAPPEARS*

Transferring all merchandise freights now delivered by the LIGHTERAGE SERVICE the lighterage piers, float bridges (except 8), float bridge terminals at points of delivery and receipt in New Jersey and New York, aggregating more than 100 structures, are released and with these the thousands of railroad employees and the great number of yard engines now necessary to operate these facilities.

7. THE LIGHTERAGE LIMIT *DISAPPEARS*

For more than 50 years it has been the custom of the roads to deliver freight by lighter to ship side and to distant points within a so called "lighterage limit" area about 10 miles in several directions from the end of the rail. With the passing of lighterage service, the lighterage limit DISAPPEARS.

8. THE CAR AT SIDING *DISAPPEARS*

All cars being unloaded at once their freights delivered directly to consignee or to Terminal storage areas there are no cars to be switched to the merchant shippers' side tracks—there to be detained as storage vans. The goods are delivered by the organized Motor Truck System as desired in half the time at half the cost and the ancient and expensive custom of cars at sidings EAST of the Hudson DISAPPEARS.

9. THE RAILROAD NAVY *DISAPPEARS*

Operating on the WATER with 16 scheduled MOTOR FLOATS the System releases a railroad navy of car floats, lighters, barges, tugboats, more than 2,000 vessels, now in the service of transferring the same volume of freight—the Hudson River fairway is cleared, THE FLEET DISAPPEARS.

10. THE STREET TRUCK FLEET *DISAPPEARS*

Operating on the LAND and AT NIGHT with 848 Motor Trucks and trailers delivering all the freights to all points within the Metropolitan district or beyond 10, 20, 50 miles away in less than one half the time, at less than one half the expense of present methods the fleet of 5,000 trucks and 7,000 horses no longer useful for this service DISAPPEARS.

11. STREET CONGESTION *DISAPPEARS*

All the congestion of today is caused by the TRUCK in the street on its way to and at the PIER. With the passing of both TRUCK and PIER street congestion DISAPPEARS.

12. DELAY AT TERMINAL *DISAPPEARS*

Railroad operation out on the road is of high efficiency. Delays are at the terminal where cars must wait on terminal methods.

A recent official analysis by the Port Authority of the actual average movement of THE CAR from the yard across the Hudson to ship side, the delivery of the freight and return to the yard EMPTY, shows that the passage over and back required 129 hours. It was then switched aside to wait on further delays indefinitely.

The passage of THE SAME CAR under the Sibley System from the yard across the Hudson, through the terminal unloaded, RELOADED and back to the yard is 9 hours 45 minutes and leaving the other car in the yard empty, in the 119 hours, 15 minutes of difference between the movement of the two typical cars across the Hudson that of the Sibley System moving out over the road LOADED at the average rate of 20 miles an hour would be 2385 miles away approaching the Pacific Coast, while the other car would still be on the waiting tracks on the west bank of the Hudson.

13. THE WAITING JERSEY CAR *DISAPPEARS*

32,500 waiting cars are spread out on hundreds of tracks covering hundreds of acres in the New Jersey yards. This vast pool is the DAILY residue the year round, some arriving, others departing, as reported by the American Railway Association.

Under the Sibley System no cars stop in New Jersey. THE TRAIN goes on to its destination, New York City, is unloaded, reloaded and is again on its way Westward within 10 hours. This "vast pool" of waiting cars DISAPPEARS.

14. THE HARBOR BELT LINE *DISAPPEARS*

As all freights of the trunk lines are delivered across the Hudson by the Sibley System, the roads have no interest in their movement beyond that point and as railroad use is the only possible source of revenue to serve as the basis of construction of such rail lines on the New Jersey shore, and within terminal limits, the HARBOR BELT LINE DISAPPEARS.

15. ONE DELIVERY POINT

One delivery point on Manhattan and that the nearest to the rail head meets the carriers' obligation.

The Sibley System provides that one delivery point, and one hundred delivery points of the present service are abandoned.

The location of that ONE delivery point is not only at the shortest distance from the end of the rail, it is also at the center of that condensed West side business area where within a radius of ONE MILE 60%, TWO MILES, 90%, of all railroad freights originate and are delivered.

16. THE CAR RELEASED

The transfer of THE CAR immediately upon its arrival at the shore line, its unloading (freight delivered to consignee or to storage) releases it for its proper function LONG DISTANCE service.

17. HALF A MILLION CARS RELEASED

As all the freights, Eastbound and Westbound, of all roads are at ONE TERMINAL, cars are well loaded and at the estimated average car tonnage, 250,000 cars will do the terminal service that with the fractional loads reported by the N. Y.–N. J. Port & Harbor Commission now require the use of 750,000.

18. EFFECT BEYOND THE TERMINAL AREA

The System with its full loading of cars, facility, celerity and regularity of movement, will necessarily affect the operation of the freight service out to the remotest station and if the figures of the recent N. Y. & N. J. Port & Harbor Commission fairly reflect the facts of present methods, the economies effected may reach many millions OUT ON THE ROAD.

19. THE SCIENTIFIC FREIGHT TRAIN

The arrival of the car at New York, its unloading, reloading and departure on schedule time, practically making no stop at this Eastern terminal of the trunk lines, elevates the freight service to the plane of the passenger service and the FREIGHT TRAIN may arrive and depart with the regularity of the PASSENGER TRAIN.

COMPLETE TRANSFORMATION

The streets of New York will present a new and strange aspect. With the disappearance of the west side rail system and thousands of horses and trucks they will be comparatively empty. On the water front where now 30–40 docks and piers are occupied as a floating railroad yard day and night and ocean commerce crowded out is driven elsewhere —the ancient pier structures are removed and two miles of the line are opened for marine service.

The stream with 2000 vessels now in railroad service substituted by 16 will be comparatively clear.

The Jersey shore now covered with acres of waiting cars will be cleared and 84 lighterage piers that now occupy the 2 miles of water front will be swept away. A CHANGE AS RADICAL AS THAT FROM THE HORSE TO THE AUTOMOBILE.

FINANCIAL

PRESENT COST OF TRANSFER

NOTE—A recent investigation of traffic conditions at New York was made May-November 1928 by the Interstate Commerce Commission. Following is an extract from its official report:

    INTERSTATE COMMERCE COMMISSION—Docket No. 19715—Sheet 60, Cost of transfer across the Hudson to Manhattan Pier Stations.

    PENNSYLVANIA RAILROAD made an estimate of its pier station costs. These costs ranged from $3.91 per ton at pier 4 to $4.90 at pier 27 and averaged $4.57 per ton.

PIER STATION FREIGHTS

    10,000,000 annual tons
    (*Pennsylvania Railway Estimate*)   per ton 4.57   45,700,000

LIGHTERAGE FREIGHTS

    10,000,000 annual tons
    (*N. Y.–N. J. Port & Harbor Com. Estimate*)   per ton 3.05   30,500,000

TOTAL— 20,000,000 annual tons   76,200,000

COST UNDER SIBLEY SYSTEM

    20,000,000 annual tons   per ton 0.98   19,600,000

ANNUAL ECONOMY FOR RAILROADS   56,600,000

DISTRIBUTION

	%	
PENNSYLVANIA	25	14,150,000
ERIE	09	5,094,000
CENTRAL OF NEW JERSEY	08	4,528,000
DELAWARE—LACKAWANNA	10	5,660,000
BALTIMORE AND OHIO	10	5,660,000
LEHIGH VALLEY	08	4,528,000
N. Y. CENTRAL—(West Shore)	30	16,980,000
TOTAL	100	56,600,000

METROPOLITAN RAILWAY TRANSFER, INC.
Executive Offices: 50 West 32 Street, New York

Printed in Dunstable, United Kingdom